T0193027

The TWO EDWARDS

How King Edward VII and Foreign Secretary Sir Edward Grey Fomented the First World War

PETER HOF

Published by:
Trine Day LLC
PO Box 577
Walterville, OR 97489
1-800-556-2012
www.TrineDay.com
TrineDay@icloud.com

Library of Congress Control Number: 2018938997

Hof, Peter.
–1st ed.
p. cm.

Epub (ISBN-13) 978-1-63424-175-5
Mobi (ISBN-13) 978-1-63424-176-2
Print (ISBN-13) 978-1-63424-174-8
1. World War, 1914-1918 -- Causes. 2. World War, 1914-1918 -- Historiography. 3. Conspiracies -- 20th century. 4. Edward -- VII, -- King of Great Britain, -- 1841-1910. 5. Great Britain -- History -- Edward VII, 1901-1910. 6. Grey of Fallodon, Edward Grey, -- Viscount, -- 1862-1933. I. Hof, Peter. II. Title

First Edition
10 9 8 7 6 5 4 3 2 1

Printed in the USA
Distribution to the Trade by:
Independent Publishers Group (IPG)
814 North Franklin Street
Chicago, Illinois 60610
312.337.0747
www.ipgbook.com

For Brigitte, without whose support and encouragement this volume could not have been written.

Author's note:

"England," "Britain," "Great Britain," "United Kingdom," have all meant different things at different times in history and represent peoples and cultures that are distinct and unique. But there is such a thing as common usage. European diplomats have used (until recently) the term "England" exclusively. On this account I will follow the example of English/British statesmen (such as Winston Churchill) and use the above terms interchangeably with all due apologies to readers from Wales, Scotland, and Ireland. References to Russia use the Gregorian calendar.

I am indebted to the Hoover Institution for the use of their superb archives and their expert and unstinting assistance, as well as to the Guardian for permission to print two of their articles in Appendix 1 & 2 respectively.

***

Table of Contents

We are not a young people with an innocent record and a scanty inheritance. We have engrossed to ourselves an altogether disproportionate share of the wealth and traffic of the world. We have got all we want in territory, and our claim to be left in the unmolested enjoyment of vast and splendid possessions, mainly acquired by violence, largely maintained by force, often seems less reasonable to others than to us."

– Winston Churchill in a comment to his British Cabinet colleagues in January 1914 (cited in John Darwin, *The Empire Project*, Cambridge 2010, p, 268)

I have come to think that Germany is our worst enemy and our greatest danger ... I believe the policy of Germany is to be that of using us without helping us: keeping us isolated, that she may have us to fall back on.

– Edward Grey (Bernstein, Liberalism and Liberal Politics, p. 182)

Grey's Germanophobia and his zeal for the Entente with France were from the outset at odds with the views of the majority of the Liberal Cabinet. This division ought to have caused trouble much sooner than it did.

– Niall Ferguson, *The Pity of War*, p. 58

Serbia has passed only through the first stage of her historic career. To reach her goal she must endure another frightful struggle, in which her very existence will be staked ... Serbia's Promised Land lies in the territory of the present Austria-Hungary, and not that for which she is now striving, with the Bulgarians blocking the way."

– Letter from Sasonov to Hartwig, May 8, 1913, cited in Deutschland Schuldig? German Foreign Office White Book, p. 99.

In my years at school, my thought, bowed before the spectre of defeat, dwelt ceaselessly upon the frontier which the Treaty of Frankfurt had imposed upon us, and when I descended from my metaphysical clouds, I could discover no other reason why my generation should go on living except for the hope of recovering our lost provinces."

– Raymond Poincaré, Revue de l'Université de Paris, October, 1920. (Cited in Dupin, M. Poincaré et la Guerre de 1914, pp. 101-2.)

Prologue

Supporters and detractors agree. The 1904 Entente Cordiale and the 1907 Anglo-Russian Convention together represent the signature achievement of the near decade-long reign of King Edward VII. Also agreed is that the initiative for this radical diplomacy came from the King himself. Still very much at issue is the King's motive. The central role played by King Edward in the creation of the Triple Entente is fully acknowledged, but did the King aim at nothing more than an innocent resolution of long-standing problems with England's traditional enemies, or did he have the more sinister motive of clearing the diplomatic decks for a future war with Germany? The purpose of this volume is two-fold: first, that King Edward VII did indeed reach an understanding with both members of the Franco-Russian Alliance for the purpose of defeating Germany, as charged by Wilhelm II and others; and second, that the evidence for this conclusion is not only obvious but an embarrassment of riches.

The very first impulse towards the First World War is found in the French determination to recover the "lost provinces" dating from 1871. The second came when the ancient Russian *drang nach Constantinople* was combined with the French lust for *revanche* in the Franco-Russian Alliance of 1894 and divided Europe into opposing camps. When Czar Alexander III died unexpectedly in 1894, Franco-Russian plans for a war against the Central Powers were put on hold. This created a precarious balance of power which lasted until 1904 when England unbalanced the scales. England's need to confront the perceived German challenge to her long-standing world hegemony produced the Entente Cordiale with France and started the transformation of the moribund Franco-Russian Alliance into the very potent Triple Entente. This upset the Continental balance of power and resulted in the First Moroccan Crisis of 1905.

The Anglo-Russian Entente of 1907 (and the 1908 Young Turk rebellion) triggered the Bosnian Crisis of 1908 and the Italo-Turkish Tripolitanian War of 1911, while in that same year Europe was again pushed to the brink by the 2nd Moroccan Crisis when Lloyd George actually threatened Germany with war. The next year, 1912, saw the rebirth of French nationalism under Raymond Poincaré even as the Balkan League grabbed a big slice of European Turkey. This succession of crises in the wake of King Edward's Ententes with France and Russia served to prime the fuse until "some damned foolish thing in the Balkans" on June 28, 1914, unleashed the First World War.

The Franco-Prussian War of 1870 was *the* water-shed event in the pre-war history of Europe. This brief but bloody contest between Prussia and France had ended with an unprecedented, unexpected, humiliating defeat for Imperial France. While the historical facts of the war are not in serious dispute, historians have generally neglected to emphasize the full extent of the calamitous French defeat and its subsequent effect upon the course of European politics. As past is prologue, that *eminence grise* of American politics, George F. Kennan, tells us that

> Throughout these years (1871-1914) the revision of the humiliating Treaty of Frankfurt, by which Germany had sealed her victory over France in 1871, remained at all times the supreme and undeviating objective of French statesmanship.[1]

Professor Kennan elaborates:

> The sense of humiliation and resentment flowing from the defeat of 1870 was profound and enduring. France was not accustomed to the experience of total defeat in the modern manner. The desire for revenge permeated, in one way or another, almost the whole of French society. It would, as Bismarck believed, probably have existed, and this in scarcely smaller degree, even had the Germans not insisted on taking Alsace and Lorraine; but this loss of territory served as a convenient symbol and rallying-point for it. Equally profound was the belief that France would never be able to achieve this revenge by her own efforts alone: that to make this possible she would have to have an ally. For these reasons, the thought of an alliance with Russia was never, through the entire period from 1871 to 1894, wholly absent from the minds of French political and military leaders. There never was a time when this possibility did not appear as the greatest hope, the highest ultimate objective, of French policy.[2]

French leaders have frankly admitted culpability. Louis Napoleon acknowledged: *"I admit that we were the aggressors; I admit that we were defeated and that, therefore, we were compelled to pay the cost of the war or abandon part of our territory."*[3] Much later, Clemenceau admitted that *"In 1870, Napoleon III, in a moment of folly declared war on Germany without even having the excuse of military preparedness. No true Frenchman has ever hesitated to admit the wrongs of that day that were committed by our side. Dearly have we paid for them!"*[4] To Bismarck, he [Napoleon III] maintained that he had been *"driven into it by the pressure of public opinion."* Nevertheless, the eclipse of Imperial France by the birth of the German nation rankled, and its effects hung over the political landscape like a chill and foreboding fog.

The French desire for *revanche* - kept alive in French hearts by Gambetta's stirring slogan: *"Speak of it never! Think of it always."* – compelled

Bismarck to create alliances for the sole purpose of denying the Powers of Europe as potential alliance partners to an implacably hostile France. But when Kaiser Wilhelm II followed the wrong advice of Baron von Holstein and allowed the Re-insurance Treaty to lapse, thereby setting Russia adrift, France saw her chance. After years of negotiations Czar Alexander III affixed the royal Russian signature to the Franco-Russian Alliance, which was intended *"to oblige Germany to fight simultaneously in both East and West."* This "Fateful Alliance" was not a counterweight to Bismarck's Triple Alliance as wrongly asserted by some historians. In fact, it was an agreement between France and Russia to attack Austria and Germany at the first opportune moment, but the untimely and unexpected death of Alexander III in 1894 and his succession by his weak and vacillating son, Nicholas II, put Franco-Russian plans on hold. French Ambassador Georges Louis described accurately, and in writing, the universally accepted objectives of the Franco-Russian Alliance:

> It is not specifically written down in any definite agreement, but it is the supreme goal of the Alliance which one takes for granted. If the Russians open the question [of the Straits] with us, we must respond: "Yes, when you aid us with respect to Alsace-Lorraine."[5]

No longer confident of victory after the death of Alexander III, France and Russia stood down, thereby creating a balance of sorts with Bismarck's Triple Alliance. This was the kernel of the alliance systems which divided Europe into opposing camps, and the balance between them – however tenuous – was maintained until the creation of the Anglo-French Entente Cordiale in 1904. The world was taken by surprise by this entirely unexpected agreement between two traditional enemies who had been at war (or close to it) for centuries. Repercussions were not long in coming. Suddenly infused with new confidence and even renewed, albeit secret, hopes for the recovery of her lost provinces, France made bold to press for the creation of a Moroccan protectorate in North Africa. It was her deliberate failure to consult with Germany as required by the 1880 Treaty of Madrid which led to the 1st Moroccan Crisis of 1905. France pulled back from the brink of war by firing her Foreign Minister (Delcassé) and agreeing to a Conference at Algeciras, but in 1911 France again threatened war with another unseemly grab for Morocco. In both Moroccan crises, Germany was on solid legal and moral ground while France was in violation, first of the 1880 Treaty of Madrid, and again of the 1906 Act of Algeciras, and yet again of the 1909 Franco-German Agreement. England's indecorous support of France, including an explicit threat of war with Germany in 1911, was not one of Albion's better moments.

Even before the ink was dry on the 1904 Entente Cordiale, King Edward planned a similar arrangement with Russia but he was obliged to wait for the end of Russia's catastrophic confrontation with Japan and the opposition of Count Witte. Meanwhile, he prepared the diplomatic ground by a meeting with Alexander Isvolsky in 1904 when the latter held a minor diplomatic post in Copenhagen. In 1907, with Isvolsky now Russian Foreign Minister as a result of the King's efforts, England and Russia officially resolved their differences as Germany and Austria began to mutter darkly about *"einkreisung"* (encirclement) by *Eduard der Einkreiser* (Edward the encircler). Just as with France in 1904, the 1907 Anglo-Russian Convention led to immediate repercussions. Emboldened by British support, Alexander Isvolsky concluded his infamous Buchlau Bargain with Austrian Foreign Minister Alois Aehrenthal, which led to the Annexation Crisis of 1908, again pushing Europe to the brink of war.

It is often alleged that Edward VII was a constitutional monarch and therefore lacked the power or the authority to institute fundamental, far-reaching policy decisions, but this is true only in the strictest technical sense. In fact, when the royal yacht, HMY *Victoria and Albert,* commissioned in 1899, exited Portsmouth harbor and headed for the open sea escorted by a flotilla of British warships, an extraordinary metamorphosis took place on board. The constitutional monarch shed his carapace of constitutional limitations and emerged transformed into a fully blossomed King of England with all the power and prestige accruing to the position, exalted and magnified by centuries of precedence. Safely out of reach of troublesome Ministers who might remind His Majesty that he was overstepping his constitutional authority, the King was free to interact and parley with the crowned heads of Eurasia to whom he was in most cases related, secure in the knowledge that his various agreements and decisions would be rubber-stamped by Sir Edward Grey (after Lansdowne) and the British Foreign Office.

> Though some have contended that at all times he (Edward VII) was the mere servant of the foreign policy of his Foreign Ministers, first of Lord Lansdowne, and after 1905 of Sir (later Lord) Edward Grey, the balance of the best contemporary evidence, both English and foreign, is to the effect that he was in the main his own Foreign Minister, initiating, commanding, and controlling all our policy towards other Powers.[6]
>
> "... and in the first number of our most popular organ, *John Bull,* beginning a series of Open Letters with one to the King, its eminent editor, Mr. Bottomley wrote: "With your Majesty on the throne a Parliament is almost a redundancy, You are our Foreign Minister, our Ambassador to all the Courts.... So long as you live, European war will be impossible." (May 12, 1906).[7]

But why would the mighty British Empire decide to confront Germany? The answer is that since unification of a bewildering patchwork of kingdoms, fiefdoms and principalities in 1871, the German economy became a powerhouse that was nothing short of spectacular. By the turn of the century, Germany had overtaken her European neighbors in virtually every conceivable economic/military category. By 1908, Germany was on schedule to surpass Great Britain in the export of finished goods and it did not take a crystal ball to see that German trade and industry would soon overshadow and eclipse Great Britain. The economic statistics to support this are overwhelming. Typical is the following from the *Encyclopedia Britannica*:

> The economy, 1890–1914
>
> The speed of Germany's advance to industrial maturity after 1890 was breathtaking. The years from 1895 to 1907 witnessed a doubling of the number of workers engaged in machine building, from slightly more than one-half million to well over a million. An immediate consequence of expanding industrial employment was a sharp drop in emigration; from an average of 130,000 people per year in the 1880s, the outflow dropped to 20,000 per year in the mid-1890s. The surplus population continued to leave Prussia's eastern provinces, but the destination was the growing and multiplying factories of Berlin and the Ruhr rather than the Americas. Earlier British fears of German competition were now fully justified. While Britain produced about twice as much steel as Germany during the early 1870s, Germany's steel production exceeded Britain's in 1893, and by 1914 Germany was producing more than twice as much steel as Britain. Moreover, only one-third of German exports in 1873 were finished goods; the portion rose to 63 percent by 1913. Germany came to dominate all the major Continental markets except France.

An English historian noted that:

> With the end of the [Boer] war, it was assumed that the reasons for the hostility between Germany and Britain would diminish and calm down. After all, the two nations still had close trading ties, many Germans and British attended the other country's universities, the British Left had closer relations with the German Social Democrats than any other European left-wing party, and of course there were the blood ties of the royal family. But in one section of the British press the antipathy did not go away. In the right-wing papers a new kind of story about Germany began to appear, suggesting that it had long-term hostile intentions against Britain, and noting with some anxiety that Germany was overtaking Britain: its population was bigger, its shipbuilding outstripping the British for the first time. The stories were true: by 1913, Germany would have a population of 65 million to Britain's 46 million; and while Britain's GDP had been 40 percent bigger than Germany's in 1870, by 1913 it would be 6 percent smaller.[8]

Other sources such as the International Monetary Fund speak of the economic "colossus" and the cultural renaissance that was Germany in the years after 1871. In fact, if there was a "place in the sun" (Bülow) anywhere in the world, it was Germany in 1914.

The fact is that "hegemony" was actually the British motive. It was Great Britain who felt her world hegemony – won and maintained by battleships, boots, and bullets – to be threatened by an ascendant Germany, just as she had once felt threatened by the rise of various European Powers, especially France. This traditional British policy - euphemistically termed "balance of power" by British apologists – has been described many times, in many ways by Britain's own diplomats and statesmen. Colonel William Robertson of the British War Office Intelligence Department stated the case as well as any:

> For centuries past we have thwarted ... each and every power in turn which has aspired to continental predominance; and concurrently, and as a consequence, we have enlivened our own sphere of imperial ascendancy ... A new preponderance is now growing, of which the centre of gravity is Berlin. Anything ... which would assist us in opposing this new and most formidable danger would be of value to us."[9]

Thus, the fateful British decision was made just as it was made earlier in the case of Portugal, Spain, Denmark, Holland, and France. It was not taken suddenly, nor was it shouted from the rooftops or trumpeted in banner headlines. Driven by the burgeoning German economy and navy, it crystalized slowly over the years as Great Britain came once more to the decision to apply her traditional solution to the problem of rising challengers.

It is possible – even probable – that England would have accepted the "new preponderance" even as she had little choice but to later accept the new preponderance from America, when this was grandly announced by the 1909 circumnavigation of the globe by Theodore Roosevelt's Great White Fleet. But the Franco-Russian Alliance was handy and available. Russia was in the process of recovering from her calamitous confrontation with Japan and was completing a thorough modernization of her armed forces – the largest in the world by far. The French army was larger per capita than that of Germany and was poised on the Lorraine border itching for action and bursting with élan. Encouraged by the prospect of being aided by this impressive Franco-Russian land Armada, England decided yet again upon another of her balance-of-power schemes.

By the summer of 1914, Anglo-German relations could be described as cordial and even the naval race had receded. Churchill recalled that

> naval rivalry had ... ceased to be a cause of friction.... We were proceeding inflexibly ... it was certain we could not be overtaken.[10]

In a January 1914 interview with the *Daily News,* Lloyd George put the matter even more succinctly:

> Relations with Germany are infinitely more friendly than they have been for years ... Germany has nothing which approximates to a two-power standard.... That is why I feel convinced that even if Germany ever had any idea of challenging our supremacy at sea, the exigencies of the present situation have put it completely out of her head.[11]

Such pacific sentiments were fully reflected in the traditional Anglo-German Kiel Week celebrations in the summer of 1914. Festivities included formal banquets, balls, dinner parties, toasts, tennis and soccer matches. The sunlit shores were black with happy, flag waving spectators all of which contributed to an atmosphere of real camaraderie between German and English sailors. Alas, at two-thirty in the afternoon of Sunday, June 28, a German launch drew alongside the Kaiser's yacht, *Hohenzollern,* and threw a message onboard which brought the electrifying news of the Sarajevo murders. Robert Massie described what happened next:

> The character of Kiel Week changed. Flags were lowered to half-mast, and receptions, dinners, and a ball at the Royal Castle were cancelled. Early the next morning, the Kaiser departed, intending to go to Vienna and the Archduke's funeral. Warrender (the British commander) struggled to preserve the spirit of the week. Speaking to a hall filled with sailors from both fleets, he spoke of the friendship between the two countries and called for three cheers for the German Navy. A German admiral called for three cheers for the British Navy. The two admirals shook hands. On the morning of June 30, the British squadron weighed anchor and left the harbor. The signal masts of German warships flew the signal "Pleasant journey." Warrender sent a wireless message back to the German fleet: "Friends in past and friends forever."[12]

It seemed fantastic that these two nations would be involved in fratricidal war barely a month later, but the Triple Entente, fashioned by Edward VII and Edward Grey, had stood ready for action since 1907. Now thoroughly primed by the two Moroccan crises, the Annexation Crisis, the election of Poincaré, and the Balkan Wars, the long fuse was ready to be detonated by "some damned foolish thing in the Balkans..." as Bismarck had prophesied.

The radical policy of the two Edwards in aligning the British ship of state with both members of an explicitly anti-German alliance, while refusing any similar accommodation with Germany, is sufficient in and of itself in proving a hostile motive, but the political predilections of the King and his Foreign Secretary lend strong corroboration.

King Edward came to the throne at age 60 after he learned the fine art of being discrete (at the cost of considerable scandal and the stern disapproval of his mother, Queen Victoria) and to limit his public utterances to diplomatic boilerplate about the blessings of peace, but his startling association with Léon Gambetta and Théophile Delcassé while still Prince of Wales lit up the political landscape – as we'll see in the next chapter.

Was England justified in confronting Germany? Was it reasonable for England to expect other nations to blithely accept the prospect of a British naval blockade? At the Paris Peace Conference in 1919, Lloyd George informed Colonel House that *"Great Britain would spend her last guinea to keep her navy superior to that of the United States or that of any other power. No Cabinet could officially continue in the Government in England that took a different position."* To this House responded drily: *"We do not intend to have our commerce regulated by Great Britain whenever she is at war."*[13] This was a reasonable response from House and it was no less reasonable coming from Kaiser Wilhelm or Tirpitz.

Certainly, nations have gone to war for far less. For Great Britain, there were the traditional reasons such as that cited by Colonel Robertson (above) and others, and there were larger historical precedents as well. Some two thousand years earlier, Rome's leaders decided that Carthage was getting too big for her britches. This resulted in the Punic Wars, Hannibal's revenge, and the disappearance of Carthage from the world map. Centuries before this, Persia decided that Greece should be taken down a notch or two. This resulted in the revenge of Alexander the Great and the demise of the Persian Empire. There were also the more relevant precedents of William the Conqueror in 1066 and William of Orange in 1688. Now, in the 20th century, the conservative Tory Press played on fears about the growing strength of the German Hercules. They raised the spectre of the German navy landing an army somewhere on the English coast, and the alarming prospect of being governed by *nummer 10, Downinge Strasse.*

But however history judges her actions, it is time for England and the world to acknowledge the radical diplomacy with (mainly) France and Russia carried on by King Edward VII, and the secret Anglo-French, Anglo-Russian, Anglo-Belgian military planning conducted by Edward Grey, which led directly to the outbreak of the Great War of 1914-1918, a war in which Great Britain did indeed play the decisive, dominant role; which was fully commensurate with her 1914 status as the largest, most powerful Empire in the history of the world.

***

Endnotes

1. Kennan, George F., *The Fateful Alliance*, 30.
2. Kennan, George F., *The Decline of Bismarck's European Order.*
3. Cohen Mels, *Conversations*, quoted in Wellesley/Sencourt.
4. Clemenceau, *Saturday Evening Post*, October 24, 1914.
5. Judet, Ernest, *Georges Louis*, 143.
6. Farrer, James Anson, *England Under Edward VII*, 5.
7. Ibid., 88.
8. Carter, Miranda, George, Nicholas, and Wilhelm II (Kindle Locations 5365-5372).
9. RPO FO 800/102, *Robertson Memorandum on Entente with Russia*, 29 March, 1906.
10. Churchill, *The World Crisis*, Vol. 1, 178.
11. Rowland, *Last Liberal Governments*, Vol. 2, 278.
12. Massie, *Dreadnought*, 852,3.
13. Viereck, *The strangest Friendship in History*, 231.

Chapter One

BERTIE

In the fourth year of her reign at the tender age of 22, Queen Victoria gave birth to her second child, the future King of England. Frets and worries about the Queen's "difficult" pregnancy were happily resolved when the birth of a healthy Albert Edward was announced on 9 November 1841 to a relieved nation. For the first time in almost eighty years, England had a suitable male heir. Long live the King!

Bertie, as he was nicknamed by family members, was said to lack the intelligence of his older sister and showed a marked preference for the outdoors to the study of algebra. But he ploughed on doggedly, albeit it without enthusiasm, and mastered his lessons well enough to escape a light corporal punishment sometimes contemplated by his demanding parents. In the summer of 1855, Bertie, now the fourteen year-old Prince of Wales, and his older sister, Vicky, accompanied their parents on a state visit to Napoleon III and his wife Eugenie. The combined effects of Paris and the first welcome cessation of rigorous daily study had a lasting effect on the young Prince. A Frenchman writing more than a century after the event captured the essence of Berties's first trip abroad:

> In the Tuileries, he breathed for the first time that *odore di femmina* whose trail he was to follow for the rest of his life. The scented, alluring women not only kissed him (was he not a child?) but also curtsied to him, and as they bent forward, their décolletage revealed delights that were veiled at Windsor.[1]

In November of 1858, when Prince Edward came of age at seventeen, he was given a £500 yearly allowance and his first taste of independence. During the course of the next few years he attended the universities of Edinburgh, Oxford, and Cambridge, traveled abroad, while developing his taste for cigars, shooting, cards, and women. At age 20 and a boy no longer, he was sent to Ireland to serve with the 2nd Battalion, Grenadier Guards to broaden his experience. No doubt believing that they were only carrying out the spirit of the mission, his young fellow officers smuggled the fetching Dublin actress, Nellie Clifden, into his bed. Of course the delicious gossip soon reached the ears of his father who delivered himself of a stern lecture to his errant son. Unfortunately, the doting but strict Prince Albert was infected with the typhus germ and died some months later on December 14, 1861.

This brought front and center the next milestone: marriage. During the course of some years of mixing and matching political considerations, religious affiliations, and physical characteristics – not necessarily in that order – the final choice fell on the attractive Danish princess Alexandra, the daughter of Prince Christian of Schleswig-Holstein-Sonderburg-Glucksberg. Things seemed to go well and the two were married in St. George's Chapel at Windsor, on March 10, 1863, with all the grand pomp and circumstance befitting the future King and Queen of England. Alexandra's father, whose private life was a public scandal, duly inherited the throne of Denmark in November of 1863. But as Queen Victoria had feared, the newly-crowned King Christian IX supported unilateral changes in the status of the duchy of Schleswig in violation of the London Protocol of 1852. This brought Denmark into conflict with Prussia and Austria and resulted (after a further brief war between Prussia and Austria in 1866) in the annexation of Schleswig and Holstein by Prussia. Alexandra was livid. Denying that her father had incurred any blame for the loss of the duchies by his unquestionably illegal action, she developed a fanatical hatred for all things German that stayed with her to the end of her days:

> For the rest of the nineteenth century and, more important, for the first decade of the twentieth, when Edward was on the throne himself, the anti-Prussian lobby of England found a permanent focusing point around Alexandra. Though she was never a significant figure politically, the intensity and consistency of her feelings acted as a catalyst for many of her English sympathizers. At the most they disliked, distrusted and perhaps feared the Prussians. Alexandra, whether as Princess or Queen, positively hated them. Her husband could not have remained entirely unaffected by this domestic pressure, especially after his own infidelity put him so heavily in his wife's private debt.[2]

After returning from a seven-day honeymoon at Osborne House on the Isle of Wight, the bridal pair set up housekeeping in London. There was Marlborough House for frequent and elaborate social functions and hunting parties, and there was Sandringham for private marital bliss. But Prince Edward had always been a hedonist to the core and marital vows could not hope to contain his relentless pursuit of pleasure. It was hardly surprising therefore that Alexandra soon became "*the most courteously but most implacably deceived royal lady of her time.*"[3]

Neither marriage nor children nor royal decorum could divert the future King from pursuing his favorite pastime at the Paris brothel of Le Chabanais. There did come a point when the aging Prince's ever-expanding girth threatened to put an end to such pursuits, but as necessity is the mother of invention, an ingenious French furniture designer came up with the inspired *siege d'amour*, or "love-chair." Resembling something out of a medieval torture chamber, the contraption allowed the corpulent Prince to indulge in his fantasy of having sex with two ladies while protecting them from being crushed by his weight. We may forgive the petite Mademoiselles of Le Chabanais for possibly having concerns about the sturdiness of the device while the Prince was in the throes of royal passion.

The precise function of the "chair" remains a matter of conjecture but any mental imagery of the rotund Prince/King in action on his love-chair may not be for the faint of heart. History in any case records no untoward incidents and the chair itself, now owned by the Soubrier furniture-making family who originally custom-built the chair for Bertie, has never been on public display.

Queen Victoria blamed her eldest son (wrongly) for the premature death of her beloved Albert, the Prince Consort, and complained bitterly to family relations about the Prince's pleasure forays in London and Paris, sexual and otherwise, and grew increasingly disillusioned. The Prince's philandering and his fixation on trivial pursuits such as horse-racing and baccarat confirmed the image of an irresponsible playboy in his mother's eyes. Of course, it was not uncommon for crowned heads to have doubts and fears about the ability of their offspring to carry out their weighty responsibilities, but a decadent lifestyle alone does not explain the extreme strictures imposed on the Prince by his mother and we must look elsewhere for an explanation.

The deep political divide between mother and son was first revealed in January of 1864 when Prussian and Austrian armies invaded Denmark. Aside from the relative merits of the opposing sides, the Prince joined his Danish wife in passionate condemnation of Prussia, while Queen Victoria was just as adamant in support. The Prince, increasingly frustrated by his mother's steadfast refusal to allow his participation in the affairs of State, now demanded that he be accorded access to Foreign Office despatches. The Queen refused, citing his lack of discretion. When informed of the refusal, the Prince wrote a letter of protest to which the Queen replied that *"you could not well have a Government key which only Ministers, and those immediately connected with them, or with me, have."*[4] While the Prussian-Danish war was causing his wife sleepless nights, the Prince again defied his mother's explicit wishes and triggered another exchange of letters when he met (on April 22, 1864) with the Italian revolutionary leader, Giuseppe Garibaldi.

In June of 1866, when a dispute about the status of Holstein led to war between Prussia and Austria, anti-Prussian sentiment of the Prince and Princess of Wales rose to a fever-pitch. In fact, *"the Prince of Wales's abuse of Prussia was robust and indiscreet, while the hatred for everything Prussian felt thereafter by the Princess of Wales became personal and, for that reason, embar-*

rassing."[5] Already on 6 June, ten days before the war had broken out, Bertie told the French Ambassador in London, Prince de la Tour d'Auvergne, that he was praying for an Austrian victory and that the best way to contain Prussian militarism was for France and England to join hands in an alliance. A seven-week campaign resulted in the annexation of Schleswig-Holstein by Prussia to the undisguised consternation of the Prince and Princess, but much worse was to come. On July 19, 1870, the French Emperor, Napoleon III, declared war on Prussia. The much-disputed cause was accurately summarized by the Oxford historian, Michael Howard:

> There can be no doubt that France was the immediate aggressor, and none that the immediate provocation to her aggression was contrived by Bismarck; but the explanation that the conflict was planned by Bismarck as the necessary climax to a long-matured scheme for the unification of Germany – an explanation to which Bismarck's own boasting in old age was to give wide currency – is one which does not today command general assent. The truth is more complex. War between France and Prussia was widely foreseen when, after Austria's defeat in 1866, the North German Federation was formed. The resulting change in the European balance of power could be made acceptable to France only if her own position was guaranteed by those compensations on the left bank of the Rhine and in Belgium which Napoleon instantly demanded and which Bismarck point-blank refused. After 1866 the French were in that most dangerous of all moods; that of a great power which sees itself declining to the second rank. In all ranks of French society war with Prussia was considered inevitable."[6]

World sympathy was almost unanimous in favor of Prussia, Queen Victoria wrote *"We must be neutral as long as we can, but no one here conceals their opinion as to the extreme iniquity of the war and the unjustifiable conduct of the French!"*[7] Poincaré, Clemenceau, and even Napoleon III himself admitted culpability, but Princess Alexandra had a different opinion. She hoped from the bottom of her heart that Prussia would be annihilated and the Prince of Wales shared that opinion. Having expressed to the Austrian Ambassador, Count Apponyi, his fervent hope that Prussia would be taught a lesson at last, the Prince was vexed and dismayed to learn of the calamitous French defeat at Sedan on 2 September and the astonishing surrender of the French Emperor and the proclamation of a Republic in Paris. This bad news was crowned by the official proclamation of the 2nd German Reich on 18 December at France's venerable Hall of Mirrors at Versailles. To reassure his mother, the Prince was obliged to concede that *"Of course I consider the French quite in the wrong, and, as all our relations are in Germany, it is not likely that I should go against them ... I am afraid that Alix's feelings are strongly against Prussia. They have always been so since that unfortunate Danish war."*[8]

In 1894, France broke out of the diplomatic ring which had been constructed by Bismarck with the purpose of isolating a resolutely hostile France when Russia, after four years of intensive negotiations, agreed to affix the royal Russian signature to the Franco-Russian Alliance. On that momentous occasion, the following conversation took place between Czar Alexander III and his Foreign Minister, N. K. Giers, which revealed the purpose of the new alliance:

> "We really do have to come to an agreement with the French," he said. "We must be prepared to attack the Germans at once, in order not to give them time to defeat France first and then to turn upon us ... We must correct the mistakes of the past and destroy Germany at the first possible moment."

With Germany broken up, he argued, Austria would not dare move. Giers, gathering his courage in the face of this unexpected statement, put the obvious question to his sovereign:

> "But what would we gain by helping the French to destroy Germany?" "Why, what indeed?" replied the Czar. "What we would gain would be that Germany as such would disappear. It would break up into a number of small, weak states, the way it used to be."[9]

Franco-Russian plans were put on hold indefinitely by the untimely death of Alexander III at forty-nine years of age on November 2, 1894. Meanwhile, the Prince of Wales had not been idle. His offer to deliver letters of friendly advice from the British Government to the Emperor Napoleon III and to King William of Prussia were ignored, while his views about methods of effecting a settlement between Prussia and France were dismissed as "royal twaddle." On November 18, Lord Granville reported to Gladstone that the Prince had been *"more than usually unwise in his talk."*[10]After the war, the Prince again angered his mother when he offered the beautiful Empress Eugenie (and later the Emperor Napoleon III) the Chadwick House in which to live in comfortable exile without consulting her or the Cabinet.

A truly alarming sign of the Prince's evolving anti-German political predilections came with his first meeting with Léon Gambetta. If there was one man in France who symbolized the eventual return of Alsace-Lorraine after a successful war with Germany, it was the squat, disheveled firebrand Léon Gambetta – the French war hero who in 1870 inspired the nation with his spectacular escape from besieged Paris in a hot-air balloon and combined the Interior and War Departments to organize the Government of National Defence. With his fiery oratory, he roused the nation to an all-out *guerre à outrance* with these stirring words:

> We must set all our resources to work – and they are immense. We must shake the countryside from its torpor, guard against stupid panic, increase partisan warfare and, against an enemy so skilled in ambush and surprise, ourselves employ ruses, harass his flanks, surprise his rear – in short inaugurate a national war.... Tied down and contained by the capital, the Prussians, far from home, anxious, harassed, hunted down by our awakened people, will gradually be decimated by our arms, by hunger, by natural causes.[11]

In the post-war years Gambetta had kept the flame of the lost provinces burning in French hearts with his famous slogan: *"Speak of it never! Think of it always!"* This oddest of odd couples, *"Two men, whom birth and social context could hardly have been set further apart, the one destined to a crown, the other the apostle of republicanism,"*[12] were in fact well matched by a common goal. Gambetta himself put it this way: *"It is no waste of time to talk with him even over a merry supper at the Café Anglais. He loves France both in a gay and a serious sense, and his dream of the future is an entente with us."*[13]

Many of the top-secret meetings between the Prince and Gambetta were arranged by the Marquis Henri-Charles Breteuil, who described Gambetta at one such meeting (12 March, 1881), in his memoirs: *"One had to admit that this short, fat man, with his red shining face, his Cyclops eye, his long hair and his heavy, vulgar walk, seemed to spread himself across the elegant floor of our drawing-room like an oil-stain on a piece of silk."*[14]

When Gambetta died unexpectedly (on 31 December, 1882) the Prince resumed his quest for an *entente* with a one-time journalist and life-long French patriot, Théophile Delcassé, who was even more impassioned about Alsace-Lorraine and who would become Foreign Minister in 1898. As with Gambetta, and for the same reason – *Le Prussianisme, voilà l'ennemi* – the political marriage of minds with Delcassé was instantaneous. For the rest of his long apprenticeship, these were the influences that shaped and strengthened the political aims that the Prince of Wales would later pursue as King:

> The empathy which grew up over the years between the Prince of Wales and France was a total one, enveloping his body, mind and spirit. It was to have a strong influence on his political thinking as, in the opposite sense, did all that gradually accumulated distaste for the Prussia of his German relatives, with its puritanical, military pipe-clay capital.... The country to which he was most devoted and where he felt most at home happened to be the mortal enemy of Prussia,

> the country he came most to dislike and where, despite all the blood links, he felt least at ease. The equation had lethal balance about it."[15]

Lethal indeed! These were the attitudes that later hardened and coalesced into the font of King Edward's anti-German *weltanschauung* and later found expression in the radical diplomacy which exploited Franco-Russian ambitions for Alsace-Lorraine and the Straits, respectively. These were the attitudes that hitched the British horse to the Franco-Russian cart, thereby creating the Triple Entente. It could well be said that King Edward VII discovered the moribund spear of the Franco-Russian Alliance. Sir Edward Grey felt its heft, polished and sharpened it, and used the Sarajevo crisis to hurl it at Germany.

***

Endnotes

1. (Jullian, Philippe, *Edward VII*, 72.
2. Brook-Shepard, Gordon, *Uncle of Europe*, 38-9.
3. Ibid., 38.
4. Royal Archives, F. 44 8/17.
5. Magus, Philip, *King Edward the Seventh*, 94).
6. Howard, Michael, *The Franco-Prussian War*, 40.
7. Queen Victoria to the Crown Princess of Prussia, Osborne, 20 July, 1870.
8. R.A., F.449/112.
9. *Lamsdorf Diary*, March 8, 1892. Cited by Kennan, *The Fateful Alliance*, 153-4.
10. *The Political Correspondence of Mr. Gladstone and Lord Granville, 1878-1876.*
11. Reinach, Joseph, *Depeches, Circulars, Decrets, Proclamations et Discours de Léon Gambetta*, 1, 41-5.
12. Dunlop, *Edward VII and the Entente Cordiale*, 57-8.
13. Lee, *King Edward VII, a Biography*, 1, 451.
14. Dunlop, 58.
15. Brook-Shepherd, Gordon, *Uncle of Europe*, 67.

HARPER'S WEEKLY
A JOURNAL OF CIVILIZATION

Vol. XLIX. New York, Saturday, July 1, 1905 No. 2

AN INTERRUPTED TÊTE-À-TÊTE

Chapter Two

The Entente Cordiale and The 1st Moroccan Crisis

After a record-setting reign of 63 years, Queen Victoria passed away on January 22, 1901, and her eldest son, Bertie, having served the longest apprenticeship in history as Prince of Wales, was officially crowned King Edward VII on August 9, 1902. He was a womanizer, a glutton, fat, balding, obsessed with uniforms and decorations, and sixty years old. Both occasions were duly commemorated with the colorful pomp and ceremony for which England is justly famous.

The new King let it be known early on and in no uncertain terms that he was not to be regarded as a mere figurehead and automatic rubber stamp for Cabinet decisions, but intended to be a full and active participant in the nation's affairs – especially foreign affairs. Certainly, the King had opinions on domestic affairs. He was opposed to Irish home rule; opposed to women's suffrage; opposed to reform of the House of Lords; opposed to ending the Boer war; opposed to ending Kitchener's scorched-earth tactics against the Boers, but it was in the realm of foreign affairs and the creation of the Triple Entente – his signature achievement – by which the King reserved top honors for himself in the annals of royal posterity.

It all began at the turn of the century when tentative, unofficial feelers for an Anglo-German alliance foundered on a childish dispute between the German Chancellor Bernard von Bülow and British Colonial Secretary Joseph Chamberlain, when the latter compared the behavior of Prussian soldiers during the Franco-Prussian War to Kitchener's scorched earth tactics in the Boer war. Bülow demanded an apology; Chamberlain refused. This resulted in a report (January 30, 1902) to Berlin by the German Ambassador, Metternich: *"I hear in the strictest confidence that negotiations have been going on for the last ten days between Chamberlain and the French Ambassador [Cambon] for the settlement of all colonial differences between the two powers."*[1]

A week later (February 8), King Edward invited ministers of the Crown and foreign ambassadors to Marlborough House for dinner during the course of which Chamberlain confronted Baron Hermann von Eckhardstein, who represented Germany, and complained about the Chancellor's speech in the Reichstag and the German press: *"It is not the first time that Count Bülow has thrown me over in the Reichstag. Now I have enough of such treatment and there can be no more question of an association between Great*

Britain and Germany."[2] At the same meeting Chamberlain's tantrum was given the royal imprimatur by the King who offered Eckhardstein an aged 1888 cigar and a whiskey-and-soda and informed him: *"For a long time at least, there can be no more of any question of Great Britain and Germany working together in any conceivable matter. We are being urged more strongly than ever by France to come to an agreement with her in all colonial disputes and it will probably be best in the end to make such a settlement."*[3] Eckhardstein was not informed that the initiative for such a settlement had come, not from France, but from the King himself; beginning with his secret meetings with Léon Gambetta decades earlier and (later) Théophile Delcassé, while still Prince of Wales.

With the blessed end of the Boer war on May 31, 1902, which had cost England so dearly in blood and treasure and almost as much in pride and prestige, the glittering coronation of Edward VII could finally take place under conditions of peace. With the end of "splendid isolation" and Germany safely out of the picture, the road to Paris could finally be cleared of longstanding diplomatic obstacles and the new King wasted no time in beginning his self-appointed task of laying the foundation for the construction of the Triple Entente.

When King Edward suggested adding France to the itinerary of his first official visit to Europe, Prime Minister Arthur Balfour and the Cabinet immediately vetoed the idea and for good reason. England and France had been traditional enemies for centuries. Trafalgar and Waterloo were not forgotten; while more recent memories of the Boer war and the disputed acquisition of Malta kept passions at a fever pitch. As recently as 1898, England and France had stood eye-to-eye at Fashoda and narrowly averted yet another war when France blinked and swallowed a bitter diplomatic defeat. Given such French hostility, the King's personal safety could not be guaranteed.

But King Edward insisted and thus it was that after visits to King Carlos of Portugal, Gibraltar, Malta, Rome, and (after some considerable awkwardness), the Vatican, the royal British party stepped off the train at the Bois de Boulogne station in Paris on May 1, 1903.

They were met by a sullen, mostly silent crowd, except for some booing and occasional cries of "Vivent les Boers!," "Vive Marchand!," "Vive Fashoda!," and even "Vive Jeanne d'Arc!" This was much to the discomfiture of Foreign Minister M. Delcassé who was riding with Sir Charles Hardinge, the King's ever-present foreign policy advisor, in the carriage following the King's. But King Edward, who was no intellectual or reader of books, now gave a convincing display of the character trait for which he would be most remembered. He had a gift for combining the prestige and gravitas of a British King with an endearing attitude of easy-going, good-natured, hail-fellow-well-met *bonhomie,* which proved irresistible. In a dozen speeches he fully recognized the wars and hostilities of the past but said that this was all the more reason for new and friendly relations. It worked like magic. In the space of three days, King Edward changed the attitude of a nation and, despite some continued disrespect shown by extreme nationalists, departed Paris to cries of "*Vive Notre Roi!*" The Belgian Minister in Paris in 1903 reported: *"It is said there that Edward VII has won the hearts of all the French. Seldom has such a complete change of attitude been seen as that which has taken place in this country ... towards England and her Sovereign."*[4] Negotiation between the King, Cambon, Delcassé, and Lansdowne, on a world-wide array of conflicts now moved onto a fast track and agreement was soon reached on long-standing disputes about Newfoundland, the New Hebrides, the Pacific, Asia, Madagascar, Gambia, Siam, and a host of lesser issues.

By far the biggest and most consequential issue was that France would henceforth recognize English predominance in Egypt, in return for English recognition of French predominance in Morocco. This Anglo-French *Entente Cordiale* was officially signed on April 8, 1904, by Lord Lansdowne and M. Paul Cambon, but it should be remembered that the real author was King Edward: *"The English King was the initiator of the rapprochement. He it was who both conceived and facilitated it while many still believed that the moment was premature."*[5] Lord Cromer confirms that the Entente Cordiale was *"the work of that very eminent diplomatist, His Majesty the King and Lord Lansdowne."*[6]

British statesmen vehemently denied that the Entente Cordiale was aimed at Germany. Sir Arthur Nicolson declared that *"There was no question of 'encircling' Germany. In dealing with both France and Russia we had honestly no other object than to place our relations on a safer and more secure basis in the interests of peace."* But then he admitted frankly: *"... yet the subconscious feeling did exist that thereby we were securing some defensive guarantee against the overbearing domination of one Power ... "*[7] More directly to the point, Massie wrote that *"Great Britain had decided not to tolerate German hegemony on the Continent. From this vague but powerful instinct flowed the Entente with France, the rebuilding of the Royal Navy, and the Entente with Russia."*[8]

The unprecedented agreement was duly approved by the House of Commons and the Chamber of Deputies, but some loud voices of protest were heard, the most influential of which was Lord Rosebery who warned that *"sooner or later it must lead to war."*[9] He would soon realize how close he had come to the truth.

Grey himself commented that

> If there is a war between France and Germany it will be very difficult for us to keep out if the entente and still more the constant and emphatic demonstrations of affection ... have created in France a belief that we should help her in war.... All the French officers take this for granted.... If the expectation is disappointed France will never

> forgive us.... The more I review the situation the more it appears to me that we cannot keep out [of a war] without losing our good name and our friends and wrecking our policy and position in the world."[10]

The Oxford historian Niall Ferguson commented:[11]

> Thus, within half a year of coming into office, Grey had presided over a transformation of the Entente with France, which had begun life as an attempt to settle extra-European quarrels into a de facto defensive alliance.[12] He had conveyed to the French that Britain would be prepared to fight with them against Germany in the event of a war. And the military planners had now decided more or less exactly what form support for France should take.[13] Grey later claimed not to have known the details of the Anglo-French military discussions, but this seems highly unlikely.[14]

From the start, the Kaiser had no illusions about the intentions of his royal uncle. Despite a long list of personal shortcomings attributed to him by Anglo historians, the Kaiser was a keen and perceptive observer of the political scene. He noted on numerous social occasions as well as in his memoirs that in his opinion the *Entente Cordiale* was aimed at Germany. A Canadian historian confirmed that:

> The Anglo-French Entente was the crucial event which determined the history of the twentieth century. England's decision to ally herself with France involved her in France's aggressive designs and inevitably brought her into conflict with Germany. The immediate result was the beginning of a period of continental strife, initiated by French Foreign Minister Théophile Delcassé. He had the conviction that with British support he could challenge Germany by ignoring her interests in Morocco and proceeding with the conquest of that country.[15]

An English historian further confirmed:

> Our *entente* with France had committed us irrevocably to the French policy of reprisals for 1870, which Gambetta had advised his countrymen not to speak about but never to forget. King Edward's earlier intimacy with Gambetta, and his friendship in later years with Delcassé and Clemenceau, cannot have left him in ignorance of the feelings towards Germany which these men and other political and social leaders represented."[16]

France had long recognized that Russia's internal problems and the threatening war with Japan limited her value as an alliance partner, but the powerful British Empire was a different story altogether. With British backing, the defeat of Germany suddenly became possible and the fading dream of conquering Alsace-Lorraine was infused with renewed hope. The equilibrium between the Franco-Russian Alliance and the Triple Alliance, which had maintained a balance of power in Europe since 1894, however fragile, was now upset by the Entente Cordiale and the repercussions were not long in coming.

In 1830 the French seized Algiers, thus beginning the colonization of French North Africa. This was followed in 1881 with the establishment of a French protectorate in Tunisia. Now, fortified by England's backing and approval, French Foreign Minister Delcassé made bold to press French ambitions in Morocco to transform that independent and sovereign nation into a French protectorate, thereby more than doubling her growing colonial empire in North Africa. Accordingly, shortly after negotiating an agreement with Spain on the partition of Morocco, a French delegation headed by Saint-René Taillandier arrived at Fez to initiate the establishment of a French protectorate.

The problem was that Delcassé had failed to consult with Germany, as he was obliged to do under the terms of the Madrid Agreement of 1880 to which France, Germany, and England were signatories. It is true that Chancellor von Bülow had expressed German disinterestedness in Morocco after the conclusion of the Entente Cordiale, but as Bülow had stated in a speech to the Reichstag, this concession was contingent upon mandatory consultation with the signatories and German commercial interests in Morocco being recognized and preserved. Germany had more immediate concerns as well.

Friedrich von Holstein, the capable but secretive head of the political department at the German Foreign Office, was obliged to admit that his belief that England would never join France had been mistaken. Now, in the crisis of 1905, *"when this danger was clear before my eyes, I became convinced that, before the ring of the Great Powers enclosed us, we ought to try with all our might to break through the ring, and we must not shrink from the most extreme measures."*[17] As Holstein was then the driving force behind German foreign policy, a brief biographical note about him is in order.

Friedrich August Karl Ferdinand Julius von Holstein was born on April 4, 1837, to a minor Prussian military officer. After 1871, Holstein earned the gratitude of Otto von Bismarck by helping him to force the resignation of his political enemy, Harry von Arnim, who was then German Ambassador in Paris and Holstein's superior. Holstein's reward was to be assigned to the German Foreign Office in Berlin. He became a close personal friend of Bismarck and often joined him and his wife and sons in the family home for dinner until Bismarck's dismissal in 1890. The friendship ended suddenly and dramatically when Holstein advised that the top-secret Reinsurance

Treaty with Russia should be allowed to lapse in deference to the Dual Alliance with Austria-Hungary. Bismarck was furious. This secret treaty with Russia was the keystone in his arch of defensive treaties designed to deny the Powers of Europe as potential alliance partners to a France intent on *revanche*. He warned – prophetically as it turned out – that France and Russia would seek to end their isolation with a mutual alliance. Just as Bismarck had foreseen, the Franco-Russian Alliance was duly signed in 1894 and, with the inclusion of England in 1904 and 1907 as a result of King Edward's efforts, evolved into the Triple Entente. Holstein felt that the Reinsurance Treaty with Russia was incompatible with the terms of Germany's treaty with Austria and that if the Reinsurance Treaty were revealed, it could leave Germany open to charges of political bigamy. Bismarck vehemently disagreed and on this issue, the two good friends became bitter enemies. Robert Massie paints this picturesque portrait of the mysterious Herr von Holstein:

> Year after year, Friedrich von Holstein sat at his desk in his little room on the ground floor at No. 76 Wilhelmstrasse. He unlocked the door himself in the morning, took his seat, and began a day which would last at least twelve hours. He was disturbed only by messengers, who knocked softly, entered bowing, deposited or picked up documents, and departed noiselessly. Time passed and his routine never varied. Sitting at his desk, he watched imperial chancellors come and go, state secretaries relieve each other, ministers and ambassadors march past. He alone remained. Never seen, he became a legend. Chancellors and state secretaries were dependent on him. He did everything for them, drafting their reports to the Emperor, writing their speeches, sending their dispatches, preparing memorandum, never relinquishing his own secret correspondence authorized years before by Bismarck, sharing it with no one. His memory astonished and terrified Foreign Office clerks; he knew what every document contained, what action had been taken, where every piece of paper was filed.[18]

Thus did Holstein rule the Foreign Policy roost until his fall in 1906. The Kaiser's intimate friend and constant companion, Philip von Eulenburg, credited Holstein with the single-handed formulation of German foreign policy: *"Holstein's political judgment was, after Prince Bismarck's retirement in 1890 until his own in 1906, the prevailing one in all questions of German foreign policy. Neither Caprivi, nor Hohenlohe, nor Bülow ever promulgated an edict of even the most insignificant political matter without Holstein putting in an oar. Caprivi's and Hohenlohe's foreign policy was pure Holstein."*[19] Eulenburg explained that *"Holstein's great talents [were considered] to be indispensable. No one could replace his understanding of complex questions of international importance ... In the Emperor's and the Government's interests, he had to be humored, as one humors a bad-tempered, erratic, positively dangerous sporting dog for the sake of a good nose."*[20]

In Holstein's defense, it may be noted that he never engaged in secret policies that were in direct contravention to the policies of his Government and the Reichstag as Edward Grey did with his military "conversations" with France and Belgium. Nor did he ever resort to the sort of dangerous, inflammatory language used by Sir Eyre Crowe in the 1907 Crowe Memorandum solicited by King Edward (see below).

Grey had meanwhile been busy attuning the new Entente Cordiale to fit more closely with the intent of the King. It was Grey who expanded Lansdowne's "conversations" into full blown military planning between the British and French general Staffs. And *"it was Grey who provided the advocates of an expeditionary force with a helpful nudge."*[21]

As Delcassé had inexplicably determined to ignore Germany, and the German Consul at Fez had received the details of the proposed French program, the Wilhelmstrasse decided that some action was needed to compel Delcassé to comply with his obligations under the 1880 Madrid Agreement to consult with Germany and take her commercial interests into consideration, some aspects of which exceeded those of France. After some hints from Berlin, the Sultan of Morocco appealed to Germany for support, the result of which was that on the morning of March 31, 1905, the German liner, *Hamburg*, dropped anchor in Tangier harbor. Kaiser Wilhelm came ashore and rode majestically to the German Legation mounted on a white charger. He addressed the Sultan and his welcoming committee with the usual diplomatic boilerplate and concluded with these words:

> Commerce can only progress if all the Powers have equal rights and respect the independence of the country [Morocco]. My visit is the recognition of this independence.

This was no more than the oft-repeated German position first stated by Bülow in April, 1904, that, while Germany had no territorial ambitions in Morocco, she fully intended to maintain and protect her economic interests there.

The French charge that Germany had suddenly changed her policy with regard to Morocco, or that Germany wanted to take advantage of Russia's problem with Japan in order to attack France, was patently false. As Professor McCullough reminds us:

> It should be emphasized that the Kaiser's visit to Tangier represented no change in German policy. The frequently repeated statements of that policy never varied from the line laid down by Bülow in April, 1904, that, while Germany had no territorial ambitions in Morocco, she intended to maintain her economic interests there. These state-

> ments were made many months before the defeat of Russia by Japan was anticipated, and German documents show that the decision to take action in Morocco was made long before the battle of Mukden. There is no evidence to indicate that German policy was influenced by the Russian disasters of 1905. The decisive German action began early in January when the French intention to proceed rapidly with the 'Tunisificaction' of Morocco – bringing it under French control – became apparent, and when the Kaiser dropped his objections to opposing France.[22]

In fact:

> The first Morocco crisis was the inevitable result of the determination of Théophile Delcassé the French Foreign Minister, to demonstrate to Germany that she was powerless in the face of Anglo-French solidarity. The policy of ignoring Germany while disposing of Morocco was Delcassé's personal policy, and was opposed by the diplomatic corps, the Colonial party, the Chamber of Deputies and eventually all his Cabinet colleagues.

and:

> Delcasse's refusal to discuss Morocco with Germany continued throughout the negotiations with England, and was emphatically affirmed by his failure to give the German Government official notification of the agreement of April 8, 1904. Germany was thus given no opportunity to discuss the possible effects of the agreement on German interests in Morocco."[23]

King Edward wasted no time in expressing his royal displeasure with his German nephew. On April 15, 1905, he fired off a letter to Foreign Minister Lansdowne:

> The Tangier incident was the most mischievous and uncalled for event which the German Emperor has ever been engaged in since he came to the throne. It was also a political theatrical fiasco, and if he thinks he has done himself good in the eyes of the world he is very much mistaken. He is no more nor less than a political 'enfant terrible' and one can have no faith in any of his assurances. His own pleasure seems to wish to set every country by the ears. These annual cruises are deeply to be deplored, and mischief is their only object.

The King made no mention, then or later, of the 1880 Madrid Convention which was the legitimate basis of German claims. Also overlooked by the King was the irony that he himself was in the middle of a Mediterranean cruise of his own, or that he had set Italy "by the ears" by trying to detach her from the Triple Alliance with promises of territory. Nor was the King dissuaded from his heavy-handed intervention in Russian affairs with his strenuous promotion of Alexander Isvolsky. Meanwhile, in the face of Delcassé's continued refusal to negotiate, Bülow had few options and harbored no illusions as to the possible French response. He wrote:

> It seemed to me necessary to remind Paris again of the German Empire. It was not only the extent of our economic and political interests in and about Morocco which decided me to advise the Kaiser to set his face against France, but also the conviction that in the interests of peace, we must no longer permit such provocation. I did not desire war with France either then or later. But I did not hesitate to confront France with the possibility of war, because I had confidence in my own skill and caution. I felt that I could prevent matters coming to a head, cause Delcassé's fall, stem the flow of aggressive French policy, knock the continental dagger [the Entente Cordiale] out of the hands of Edward VII and the war group in England and, at the same time, ensure peace, preserve German honour and enhance Germany's prestige."[24]

Finally on April 19, the French Chamber took alarm at the looming prospect of a Franco-German war and in the course of a passionate debate, Delcasse's unilateral and reckless diplomacy came under heavy fire. Jean Jaurès thundered: *"Since you took the initiative in inaugurating a policy capable of changing the status quo in Morocco, you ought also to have taken the initiative in offering explanations and beginning negotiations."*[25]

The strength and unanimity of the Deputies on this point took Delcassé by surprise and the next day he offered his resignation. The big question in all of this is why would Delcassé insist on violating the 1880 Madrid Convention by ignoring Germany while fully appreciating the likely consequences? Why on earth would he persist in such a policy even when the threat of war between France and Germany became acute?

Théophile Delcassé was described by one biographer as *"a short, thickset, swarthy man, unattractive in appearance and sufficiently conscious of his physical inferiority to feel a need for built-up heels.... Throughout his life cartoonists found him an easy prey."*[26] He was a most ardent admirer of Léon Gambetta and fully shared the latter's passion for the return of Alsace-Lorraine. His daughter said of him that *"The word Alsace-Lorraine was never mentioned by my brother or myself. We had the conscious feeling that it was too sensitive a subject to be spoken of."*[27] For his own part, Delcassé was quite certain that Germany had asked for a recognition of the 1871 Treaty of Frankfurt (which ceded Alsace-Lorraine to Germany) and that this remained Germany's basic condition for any sort of cooperation with France. Delcassé re-stated this belief whenever negotiation with Germany was suggested to him. Georges Bilhourd, the French Ambassador in Berlin, was very nervous about the probable consequences of Delcassé's policy towards Germany. But when he tried to persuade his boss to open talks with Germany after the conclusion of the Entente Cordiale, he again used the same argument. Bilhourd later reported:

> He [Delcassé] declared that he had no fixed prejudice against Germany and that he would not refuse to begin talks with her if he had a guarantee that he would not first of all be asked to sanction the conquest of 1871, for he would not agree at any price to sign the Treaty of Frankfurt a second time. [French President] M. Loubet had already told me, for his part, that he would sooner have his right hand cut-off than countenance such an action.[28]

Early in 1904, Delcassé mirrored the words of Léon Gambetta when he said:

> This liquidation [of Anglo-French disagreements] should lead us, and I desire that it should lead us, to a political alliance with England. Ah, my dear friends, what a beautiful horizon would open before us. Just think! If we could lean both on Russia and on England, how strong we should be in relation to Germany. A Franco-British alliance has always been my dream even during the Fashoda crisis. Now I can believe I am near my goal."[29]

While it is true that Delcassé's most important collaborators shared in varying degrees his hostility to Germany, not a single one agreed with his refusal to negotiate with her and many gave explicit warnings of the inevitable consequences of such a refusal early on. One of Delcassé's close advisors complained in March, 1902:

> The great misfortune is that he finds it repugnant to have talks with Germany. "The Germans are swindlers" he says. But in heaven's name, I'm not asking for an exchange of romantic words or lovers' rings but for a business discussion.[30]

Some months later on August, 1902, Cambon, the French Ambassador in London cautioned:

> Do not forget to take into account the efforts which the Germans will undoubtedly make to thwart an agreement relative to Morocco. It would have been prudent to have talks with them.[31]

On June 20, 1904, Bilhourd, the French ambassador in Berlin, returned to Paris and invited Delcassé to lunch in order to personally persuade him of the need for a written agreement with the German government:

> I did not hesitate to say that in my view we were falling back into the clutches of Germany, and that I hoped for an accommodating and courteous policy towards her. For if war came – and that depended on the good pleasure of Wilhelm II – we should be overrun, and the enemy troops would be in Paris in fifteen days.[32]

Even Eugène Étienne, leader of the French Colonial Party, viewed Delcassé's refusal to negotiate with the Germans over Morocco as "the height of imprudence."[33]

With this forest of red flags and storm warnings, how could Delcassé continue to refuse his obligation under the 1880 Madrid Convention to negotiate with Germany? The astonishing answer is that Delcassé had the strong, unflagging support and encouragement of the King of England, who harbored secret hopes of triggering a war between France and Germany. There had always been a common, albeit unspoken agreement, among French and German statesmen that the main reason for England's newfound friendliness for France was her increasing hostility towards Germany. Cambon wrote: *"The English draw nearer to us in proportion as they feel the hostility between their country and Germany grow and become more acute."*[34]

Anglo-French planning for concerted military action had preceded the reign of Foreign Secretary Edward Grey who took office in December, 1905. Lord Lansdowne admitted that English and French *"military and naval experts … got together and talked about possible schemes of cooperation as was their business, and talked indiscreetly as they always will do."*[35] Edward Grey himself wrote frankly:

> It was not until some time after I entered office [1905] that I discovered that, under the threat of German pressure upon France in 1905 steps had been taken to concert military plans, in the event of war being forced upon France.… Plans for naval and military cooperation had, I found, begun to be made under Lord Lansdowne in 1905 when the German pressure was menacing. The naval conversations had already been direct; the military conversations had hitherto been through an intermediary."[36]

Despite the fact that the *"threat of German pressure forced upon France"* was in fact a legitimate demand that France honor the 1880 Madrid Convention, this policy was nevertheless underlined and given the royal stamp of approval during King Edward's visit to Paris from April 29 to May 4, 1905. The German diplomat, Baron von Eckhardstein, was in Paris during the King's visit and reported to von Bülow that England would support France against Germany and that: *"King Edward had left no doubt on this subject in Paris."*[37] The King's closest French friend, the Marquis de Breteuil, reported that *"M. Delcassé appears to me to have acquired the certainty in his conversation with Edward VII that in this event [war with Germany], all the British forces would come to our aid."*[38]

King Edward's interference in French affairs was so blatant that his biographers struggle vainly for an explanation – any explanation – which stops short of revealing the King's intention of fomenting a war between France and Germany. Straining to account for the King's perilous and reckless intervention in Delcassé's first resignation (which was withdrawn the next day), biographer Gordon Brook-Shepherd throws up his hands:

> Without any hesitation and apparently without consulting his government at home he sent, through the French Governor-General, a personal message in his own name to Delcassé in Paris, calling on the beleaguered Minister to stay at his post. King Edward, this message of April 23 said, would be "personally distressed" by M. Delcassé's departure from office. He "strongly urged" the Foreign Minister to stay on, not only because of the authority he still commanded but also because of the loyal and trusted relations between the Minister and himself.[39]

Brook-Shepherd continues:

> It was a totally unprecedented action for a constitutional monarch to take, or even a non-constitutional one for that matter. Whether the Ministers of foreign governments stayed at their posts or not was no earthly business of the King of England. Moreover, if he had felt compelled to intervene, this should have been done only with the approval of his own Cabinet, and then only through a private message to the French President, whose responsibility it was to accept or reject resignations. In fact, unbeknown to King Edward, M. Loubet had already talked Delcassé out of resigning on April 22, the day before the royal message arrived. But this does not diminish the audacity of the King's action. He was, quite plainly, meddling in the domestic policy of another country, in an attempt to preserve the sacred cause of the Entente. He relied on his prestige to get away with it. It was the greatest tribute to that prestige that he succeeded. There was not a murmur in either London or Paris. Indeed, when King Edward heard that Delcassé was staying on, he topped things off by sending him a telegram, this time of congratulations.

He notes further that *"During these few days, Delcassé seemed closer to this foreign monarch than to his own colleagues. He was behaving almost as though he were one of the King's own Ministers. Indeed, he clung to the royal visitor till the last possible minute of his stay."*[40]

As early as April 5th, Baron Greindl, the Belgian Minister Plenipotentiary at Berlin, who had no doubts as to King Edward's motive, reported to Belgian Foreign Minister, Paul Favereau:

> There is no longer any doubt that it was the King of England who, independently of the Government, incited M. Delcassé to pursue a warlike policy, and that it was he who made the promise to the effect that 100,000 soldiers should be landed in Holstein.... If any doubts could still prevail, they would be dispelled by the singular proposals which Colonel Barnardiston [British Military Attaché in Brussels and The Hague] has made to General Ducarne [Belgian Chief of Staff.][41]

And he reiterated on April 18:

> The offer of 100,000 men, made by the King of England, cannot be forgotten in Berlin. We ourselves need only recollect the singular overtures made by Colonel Barnardiston to General Ducarne.[42]

Another of the King's protégés, who admittedly owed his career and position to the sponsorship and protection of the King, was First Sea Lord, Jacky Fisher. At the height of the crisis and in typically direct terms, the swashbuckling Admiral addressed these words from the Admiralty to Lord Lansdowne:

> This seems a golden opportunity for fighting the Germans in alliance with the French, so I earnestly hope you may be able to bring this about. Of course I don't pretend to be a diplomat, but it strikes me that the German Emperor will greatly injure the splendid and growing Anglo-French Entente if he is allowed to score now *in any way* – even if it is only in getting rid of M. Delcassé.... All I hope is that you will send a telegram to Paris that the English and French fleets are *one*. We could have the German fleet, the Kiel Canal, and Schleswig-Holstein within a fortnight."[43]

This was the same Fisher who, shortly after he was appointed to his high position by the King on Trafalgar Day (October 21, 1904), had suggested to the King that the growing German fleet at Kiel should be "Copenhagened" by a sudden assault without the formality of a declaration of war. It is hardly credible that the First Sea Lord would have sent such a telegram to Lord Lansdowne without the knowledge and approval of the King.

In all of this ominous saber-rattling, neither English nor French statesmen made mention of French obligations under the Madrid Convention of

1880, upon which the legitimate German objections were based. English editors, with a few exceptions, proved themselves more French than the French in placing blame on Kaiser Wilhelm, but the fact that Germany was on solid moral and legal ground in both Moroccan crises was studiously ignored. *"The plain fact is that German policy was open, correct, and perfectly justified: the dishonest and aggressive policy was that pursued by England and France."*[44] Like other biographers, Brook-Shepherd stops short of accusing Edward VII of promoting war in 1905, but the King's extraordinary support of Delcassé allows no credible explanation other than that King Edward aimed at inciting a war between France and Germany, in which England would side with France.

By June, 1905, German forbearance was at an end. German Ambassador Prince Radolin passed a message from Bülow to French Prime Minister, M. Rouvier: *"The Chancellor of the German Empire does not wish to have any further dealings with Monsieur Delcassé."*[45] In response to this throwing down of the gauntlet, Delcassé proposed sending French cruisers to Tangier to enforce France's demands upon the Sultan. But in the course of a tumultuous emergency meeting of the French Cabinet on June 6, Rouvier easily won the day with his impassioned *cri de coeur* that

> Delcassé is leading us into war! Are we in a condition to sustain a war with Germany? No! No! Even with the aid of the British fleet we should be in for a worse catastrophe than in 1870. We should be criminals to indulge in such an adventure. France would not recover.[46]

With this, Rouvier called for a vote, which was unanimous against Delcassé and left him no option but to resign, this time for good.

With Delcasse's humiliating resignation on June 6, Germany had won a significant diplomatic victory and a jubilant Kaiser rewarded Bülow with a promotion to the rank of Prince of the German Empire. Still unresolved from the German viewpoint, however, was that Morocco should be internationalized and the Entente Cordiale be destroyed. Thus French hopes that Germany would now withdraw her demand for an international conference on Morocco were dashed when German Ambassador Prince Radolin informed Rouvier that Germany "absolutely insisted" on the conference and continued:

> It is my duty to declare to you that if France were to attempt to change in any way whatever the status of Morocco, Germany would stand behind the Sultan with all its forces.[47]

An international conference was anathema to the French government since any such conference could hardly be expected to deliver Morocco to

France. But, as with Delcasse's resignation, Rouvier had little choice and on September 28, France and Germany, with Teddy Roosevelt's urging, agreed to the agenda of a conference which formally opened on January 16, 1906, in the picturesque Spanish port city of Algeciras, across the bay from Gibraltar.

The Campbell-Bannerman government, formed in the wake of the resignation of Balfour's Unionist Government, appointed Sir Edward Grey in December, 1905, to succeed Lord Lansdowne as Foreign Secretary. But fond hopes that the new Liberal government (later confirmed in the 1906 landslide UK general election conducted against the backdrop of the Algeciras conference) would pursue a less aggressive foreign policy, were soon disillusioned. Among the first of Grey's official actions was to inform the German Ambassador, Count Metternich, that England would honor its commitment to France at Algeciras. This followed King Edward's blunt, unambiguous instruction to Cambon in London:

> Tell us what you wish, on each point, and we will support you without restriction or reserve."[48]

In the course of the Conference, it was agreed that special responsibilities for preserving order along the Moroccan-Algerian frontier were to be conceded to France and supervision of the police would be shared with Spain under the command of a Swiss Inspector General. This agreement – The Act of Algeciras – was signed on April 7, 1906, and the proceedings were officially closed. Germany had been successful in postponing the French protectorate in Morocco and President Roosevelt congratulated the German Ambassador in Washington, Hermann Speck von Sternburg, on the Kaiser's "epoch-making success" and stated further that *"His Majesty's policy has been masterly from beginning to end."*[49] But it soon became apparent that Germany had failed to "knock the continental dagger out of the hands of Edward VII" and instead pushed it *into* the hands of the King more firmly than ever.

In his mental blueprint for the Triple Entente, the British King had always reckoned on Russia fighting alongside her ally, France. Accordingly, even before the ink was dry on the Entente Cordiale, he called on Alexander Isvolsky who was then Russian minister plenipotentiary in Denmark and whose strong pro-Entente feelings were well known at the English Court, and prepared the way for Isvolsky to succeed Lamsdorff as Foreign Minister of Russia. This was for the purpose of concluding an agreement with Russia similar to that with France. Unfortunately, the intervening Russo-Japanese war and the opposition of Count Witte obliged the King to temporarily suspend his plans for Russia and occupy himself with cruising the Mediterranean and coaxing Italy away from the Triple Alliance with suggestive allusions to Tripoli and Cyrenaica.

Taking advantage of the Czar's resentment at the 1902 Anglo-Japanese Treaty, which he blamed for the present war with Japan, Kaiser Wilhelm cajoled Czar Nicholas into signing the stillborn Treaty of Björkö on July 24, 1905. The Kaiser's improbable notion that France could somehow be persuaded to join Germany and Russia in an anti-British coalition reflected his growing anxiety that the purpose of his royal uncle's radical diplomacy was to impale Germany on the horns of the Franco-Russian dilemma – soon to evolve into the Triple Entente. The Björkö treaty was ignored and soon repealed and forgotten, but the end of the Russo-Japanese war on September 5, 1905, and the temporary resolution of the Moroccan imbroglio on April 7, 1906, finally cleared the diplomatic decks for the long-planned agreement with Russia similar to the Entente Cordiale, thereby putting the finishing touches on King Edward's Triple Entente. But just as the 1904 Entente Cordiale had resulted in the 1st Moroccan Crisis, the 1907 Anglo-Russian Entente would result in the 1908 Annexation Crisis, again pushing Europe to the brink of war ...

***

Endnotes

1. Dugdale, E.T.S., *German Diplomatic documents*, III, 171.
2. Eckhardstein, *Ten Years at the Court of St. James*, 288.
3. Ibid, 230.
4. Lee, *King Edward VII*, II, 241.
5. Tardieu, *France and the Alliances*, 60.
6. Ibid., 60.
7. Nicolson, Sir Harold, *Sir Arthur Nicolson: A Study in the Old Diplomacy*, 188.
8. Massie, *Dreadnought*, 601.
9. Dunlop, Ian, *Edward VII and the Entente Cordiale*, 228.
10. PRO FO 800/92, Grey memorandum, 20 Feb., 1906; Grey, *Twenty-Five Years*, I, 114.
11. Ferguson, Niall, *The Pity of War*, 64.
12. Hamilton, *Great Britain and France*, 331.
13. Details in d'Ombrain, *War Machinery*, 75-96, 103-9.
14. PRO FO 800/100, Grey to Asquith, 16 April, 1911.
15. McCullough, Edward, *How the First World War Began*, 329.
16. Farrar, J.A., *England Under Edward VII*, 111.
17. Woodward, E.L., *Great Britain and the German Navy*, 83.
18. Massie, *Dreadnought*, 129.
19. Haller, *The Kaiser's Friend*, II, 297.
20. Ibid., I, 354.
21. Ferguson, Niall, *The Pity of War*, 62.
22. McCullough, *How the First World War Began*, 85.
23. Ibid., 79.
24. Bülow, *Denkwürdigkeiten*, II, 104.
25. *Journal Officiel de la République Francaise*, 19 April, 1905.

26. Christopher, Andrew, *Théophile Delcassé and the Entente Cordiale*, 10.
27. Nogués, Mme., Unpublished memoirs on Delcassé.
28. Georges Bilhourd, MS, *Memoir* on the first Moroccan crisis, 9.
29. Gooch, *Before the War*, I, 153.
30. Combarieu, *Seven years at the Elysee with President Loubet,* 183-4.
31. Cambon to Delcassé, August 12, 1902.
32. Bilhourd, MS. *Memoir*, 9.
33. Clark, Christopher, *The Sleepwalkers*, 156.
34. DDF2, III, No. 137.
35. Temperly, H., *"British Secret Diplomacy from Canning to Grey"* Cambridge Historical Journal, VI - 1938, 26).
36. Grey, *Twenty-Five Years*, I, 74-6.
37. GP, XXII, No. 6652.
38. Paléologue, *Un Grand Tournant*, 330.
39. DDF., Ser. 2, Vol. VI: Delcassé to Bompard, 23 April, 1905.
40. Brook-Shepherd, *Uncle of Europe*, 247-9.
41. *Belgian Diplomatic Documents*, No. 17.
42. Ibid., No. 29.
43. Marder, *Fear God and Dread Nought*, II, 55.
44. McCullough, *How the First World War began*, 92.
45. Spender, *Fifty Year of Europe*, 245.
46. Gooch, G.P., *Before the War*, I, 179.
47. Spender, *Fifty Years of Europe*, 245.
48. Nicolson, Sir Harold, *Sir Arthur Nicolson: A Study in the Old Diplomacy,* 128.
49. Dugdale, E. T. S., III, 248; DGP, XXI, 312.

Chapter Three

The 1907 Anglo-Russian Entente and the Annexation Crisis

Count Alexander Petrovich Isvolsky was a man with a dream. Born in Moscow on March 6, 1856, to an ancient aristocratic but impoverished Polish family with a long history of service to the House of Romanov, he graduated from the Imperial Lyceum at St. Petersburg with honors and entered the Russian Foreign Office at age nineteen. Showing early promise, he rose quickly through the ranks and distinguished himself by restoring relations between Russia and the Holy See and became good friends with Bernard von Bülow, who was then German Minister to Italy. After further postings to Belgrade, Munich, and Tokyo, Isvolsky was made Minister Plenipotentiary to Denmark [1903-1906] where he continued to voice his determined opposition to the looming Russo-Japanese war. When events vindicated his judgment, his fervent, long-time advocacy of an Anglo-Russian alliance as the best means of gaining control of the Straits, which had already aroused the interested attention of King Edward VII, now came to the fore.

Just as the recovery of Alsace-Lorraine and hegemony in Europe would be the hidden driving force of French foreign policy after 1871, Russian diplomacy also had a secret agenda.

Ever since the days of Peter the Great, Russia had sought to assert her dominance and control over the Bosporus and the Dardanelles leading from the Black Sea to the Mediterranean, collectively referred to as the "Straits." Even a cursory glance at the map shows why this was so. The great industrial and manufacturing centers around the shores of the Black Sea needed an outlet to Europe, Africa, and Asia. But the Powers – particularly Great Britain – were less than eager to see the powerful Russian Black Sea fleet in the eastern Mediterranean from whence it could menace Egypt and India. In the course of building the Trans-Siberian railway, Russia turned her face toward the Pacific and gained – at long last – a warm-water harbor at Port Arthur, but after she was dislodged by a disastrous contest with Japan in 1905, she turned once again to the Atlantic. Seeming to mock her status as a Great Power, Russia's apparent inability to control her own back door, so recently and painfully underscored by the humiliating defeat suffered at the hands of Japan, made her more determined than ever to accomplish her "historic mission" to control the Straits of Constantinople. Czar Alexander

III, the father of Nicholas II, had earlier expressed this secret agenda quite succinctly in the *Arkhiv Vneshnei Politiki* (Archive of Foreign Policy):

> In my opinion we must have one main purpose: the taking possession of Constantinople, in order to establish ourselves once and for all on the Straits and to make sure that they remain permanently in our hands. This is in Russia's interest; and it is to this that our efforts must be directed; everything else that happens on the Balkan Peninsula is of secondary significance from our standpoint. We have had enough of seeking popularity at the expense of the interests of Russia. From now on, the Slavs must devote themselves to the service of Russia, not we to theirs.

Virtually all of the Russo-Turkish wars, beginning in 1776 and ending in 1878, had been fought to loosen the Ottoman grip on Constantinople using the pretext of protecting Ottoman Christians. For much the same reason, Russia had dabbled in the murky and complex affairs of the Balkans by supporting various intrigues in Bulgaria as well as Slavic independence movements in Bosnia and Herzegovina – then controlled by Austria-Hungary. The centuries-old Russian *drang nach Constantinople* was a powerful subterranean political force which perfectly complemented the equally secret objectives of French diplomacy (after 1871) with regard to Alsace-Lorraine. These were the forces which had pulled the two nations inexorably together to form the Franco-Russian Alliance of 1894 which aimed at achieving these twin objectives and was a major cause of the First World War.

Alexander Isvolsky was described as *"A plumpish, dandified man, he wore a pearl pin in his tight-fitting white waistcoat, affected white spats, carried a lorgnette and always trailed a faint touch of eau de cologne"*[1] He was known for his obsession with Russian control of the Straits and his strong advocacy of an alliance with England to bring it about. This soon brought him to the attention of King Edward VII, whose plans for a Triple Entente between England, France, and Russia required a reliable Russian contact, and who therefore proposed a formal meeting with Isvolsky. Immensely pleased and flattered that he should be selected for such a high honor by no less a personage than the King of England, Isvolsky eagerly agreed to meet the King on April 13 at the British Legation just days after the official signing [April 8, 1904] of the historic Entente Cordiale. The King confided to Isvolsky his high hopes that England might smooth out her differences with Russia just as she had done with France. Isvolsky replied heartily that this was his own dearest wish. After the meeting, which lasted most of an afternoon, Isvolsky immediately wired an enthusiastic, almost rhapsodic, report to his boss, Foreign Minister Lamsdorff, extolling the beatific vistas and endless opportunities which would open up through an alliance with England. On

May 12, King Edward likewise, after consultation with Lansdowne, wrote to his cousin (by marriage), Nicholas II, about his latest protégé in Copenhagen and the prospect of a "lasting agreement":

> It gave me great pleasure to make the acquaintance last month of your Minister at Copenhagen, M. Isvolsky. In him you have a man of remarkable intelligence and who is, I am sure, one of your ablest and most devoted servants. I had a long conversation with him at Copenhagen, the substance of which has, I believe, been imparted to you. My earnest desire, which I am convinced you will share, is that at the conclusion of the [Russo-Japanese] war our two countries may come to a satisfactory settlement regarding many difficult matters between us, and that a lasting agreement may be arrived at, similar to the one which we have lately arrived at with France. Believe me, my dear Nicky, you're very affectionate Uncle."[2]
>
> (Signed) Edward R.

This was high praise indeed and would soon have its intended effect, but in the summer of 1904, the moment was not yet ripe. Not until after the stillborn treaty of Björkö [July 24, 1905], the conclusion of the Russo-Japanese war [September 5, 1905], and the resignation of Count Lamsdorff, [May, 1906], was Isvolsky made Foreign Minister and the way finally cleared for an Anglo-Russian Convention. To be sure, British objections to the excesses of Russian autocracy remained strong despite the inauguration of Russia's first Parliamentary Duma on May 6, 1906, but the forward momentum for the long-delayed Anglo-Russian negotiations had become unstoppable. As in 1904, the King's efforts were key. Upon hearing that the Russian Foreign Minister was in Paris, the King wrote from Scotland to Charles Hardinge on October 19, 1906:

> The great M. Isvolsky is at Paris ... I would give anything to see him, and that you and Sir E. Grey could also do so, as there are so many important matters to be discussed ... How is this to be managed? I leave here tomorrow and shall be in town by 7.[3]

Isvolsky was notified at once by Hardinge that King Edward had returned to London and wished to see him. Thrilled to be invited by the King, Isvolsky crossed the Channel and came to London for 48 hours. Hardinge noted that Isvolsky's impromptu visit was entirely due to King Edward's initiative and that it helped materially to smooth the path of negotiations then in progress.[4]

Hitherto insoluble disputes and rivalries about Tibet, Afghanistan, and (mainly) Persia, which had threatened war on more than one occasion, were suddenly resolved through a complicated reshuffling of spheres of interest. After some months of intense negotiations, King Edward was notified that on August 31, 1907, the Anglo-Russian Entente had been officially signed by Alexander Isvolsky, Foreign Minister of the Russian Empire, and Sir Arthur Nicolson, the British Ambassador to Russia. Waving aside Parliamentary objections about the repressive Russian autocracy (but nonetheless agreeing not to set foot on Russian soil), King Edward prepared to weigh anchor for a June 9, 1908, congratulatory *rendezvous* with nephew Nicky at Reval (now Tallinn), a picturesque resort town on the shores of the Gulf of Finland.

> When the King finally set sail to meet his new political partner, the basic structure of the Triple Entente between England, France, and Russia was now standing, even if, in parts, the mortar was still wet and many of the bricks were still loose. For King Edward, a personal vision he had cherished since his youth was becoming reality.[5]

It should here be noted that there was an important, secret meeting between Kaiser Wilhelm and Isvolsky at the German Legation in Copenhagen in July, 1905, which sheds an interesting light on the thinking of the German Emperor:

> The Kaiser alluded to his recent meeting with Nicholas at Björkö Bay (July 24, 1905), but he did not disclose the fact that, without consulting his ally, France, or even his own ministers, the Tsar had at that meeting signed a secret personal treaty of alliance between Germany and Russia. Emperor William then aired at length his conviction that the preservation of peace in Europe depended upon the creation of an alliance between the continental powers, Germany, Russia and France, and directed explicitly against England. A startled Isvolsky replied that France, on account of Alsace-Lorraine would never join such an alliance. William angrily retorted that since France had not picked up the gauntlet which he had thrown down over the Moroccan affair, she had renounced once and for all any claims to the lost provinces in Europe.[6]

Isvolsky in any case admirably played his assigned role in King Edward's grand design for the Triple Entente by adding Russia to the Entente Cordiale. He wrote that in meeting King Edward in Copenhagen, he:

> ... had the opportunity of sketching to the British sovereign, in the course of long conversations, the essentials of the agreement arrived at later, in 1907, between Russia and Great Britain, which has so greatly influenced the course of events in Europe ... My stay in Paris and in London resulted most happily for me, in that it gave me the

> chance to arrive at a complete communion of ideas with M. Nelidoff [Ambassador to France], Count Benckendorff [Ambassador to England], and M. Mouravieff [Ambassador to Italy], as to the policy to be adopted by Russia. It was, in fact, the identical policy that I submitted to the Czar when, only a few weeks later, I became Minister of Foreign Affairs, and it finally developed into the arrangement which became known to the world as the 'Triple Entente.'"[7]

Kaiser Wilhelm had never doubted that the Entente Cordiale was a cocked pistol aimed at Germany. When he was informed at a dinner for the Knights of the Order of St. John, numbering some three hundred guests in Berlin in 1907, that the British Government was negotiating at St. Petersburg for an agreement similar to that with France, he exploded:

> He's a Satan! You can hardly believe what a Satan he is!

Count Zedlitz related that just before this outburst,

> He [the Kaiser] began to talk freely about the policy of England and grew rather excited. He complained bitterly of the intrigues that his uncle, the King of England, was carrying on about him. He said he knew all about them from private letters from France, and King Edward was equally hard at work in every other country."[8]

Still basking in the afterglow of the June, 1908, festivities at Reval, King Edward was startled to be informed of an unanticipated revolution in Turkey. Having been able to survive because of the rivalries between Britain and Russia, the precarious rule of the Ottomans over their Turkish Christian population was suddenly threatened by a Convention between these two Powers. This was the opportunity for which the Turkish revolutionaries had been waiting. Dubbed the Young Turks, they forced the reigning Sultan, Abdul Hamid, to restore the constitution which had been suspended since 1876 and summon a Chamber of Deputies. The Young Turk rebellion was at first hailed with delight throughout the Ottoman dominions and dreams of progressive liberalism filled the air. But, as with many such sudden, flash-in-the-pan revolutions, the Young Turks had underestimated the problems and within weeks fell out in quarrels among themselves. Political chaos soon threatened Turkey with dissolution from within and the Powers prepared to dispose of the remains of the "sick man of Europe." With Turkey thus weakened, Isvolsky saw his chance.

Just as the Entente Cordiale and King Edward's strong support had emboldened Delcassé in his pursuit of a Moroccan protectorate, thereby triggering the 1st Moroccan Crisis, so was Isvolsky inspired by the steadfast support of King Edward with regard to the Straits. He reckoned that the alliance with France and the Entente with England would guarantee their benevolent attitude, and that he could proceed to open the Straits to Russian warships. Germany had already declared that she would have no objection to this, while Austria could be pacified with the offer of Bosnia-Herzegovina. With such thoughts in mind and the new Anglo-Russian Convention now signed, sealed and delivered, and burning a hole in his diplomatic pocket, Isvolsky sent an *aide-memoire* to his Austrian counterpart, Count Aehrenthal, on July 2, 1908, suggesting that the failing Young Turk Rebellion offered an opportunity to resolve the Russian problem of the Straits, as well as the Austrian problem with political unrest in Bosnia-Herzegovina (which Isvolsky had himself secretly helped to foment). Aehrenthal responded with an invitation to Isvolsky to discuss the details at Count Berchtold's castle at Buchlau in Moravia on September 15, 1908. On that day, Isvolsky offered to accept the annexation of Bosnia-Herzegovina by Austria, in return for Austrian agreement to the opening of the Straits to Russian warships.

When Aehrenthal agreed to this (and some further minor concessions), Isvolsky was ecstatic. He had resolved Russia's most intractable problem and he had done it without war. He was confident that Russia's trusted ally, France, and England under his new friend, King Edward VII, would now be agreeable. On September 26, he visited Berchtesgaden and spoke with Schoen, the German Secretary of State for Foreign Affairs. Schoen seemed sympathetic. On September 29 and 30, he visited the Italian Foreign Minister, Tittoni, at Desio, and was again encouraged. But when his train reached Paris, Isvolsky was handed a letter from Aehrenthal which stated that the annexation had been announced in Vienna on October 6th. The news was devastating. He had not anticipated that Aehrenthal would act so precipitately and present the world with a *fait accompli*, while Isvolsky's part of the bargain was still in the balance. He cautioned the Serbians to stay calm,[9] but became alarmed when he could get no backing in Paris for his projected opening of the Straits. French Foreign Minister Pichon was "sympathetic" but remained non-committal until he could ascertain the British attitude.

On arriving in London, Isvolsky's alarm grew into panic upon discovering that Foreign Secretary Grey remained firmly opposed, despite the more friendly relations in the wake of the Entente of 1907. Isvolsky went so far as to threaten a possible collapse of the 1907 Convention which he had advocated against all opposition,[10] but to no avail. He seems never to have grasped that England would under no circumstances consent to opening the Straits as this would expose Egypt and the Suez Canal as well as India to attack by Russian naval forces. It was therefore England's firm policy to preserve Anglo-Russian relations by an outward pretense of sympathy for opening the Straits, while inwardly determined to oppose it at all cost.

Isvolsky's one-sided proposal for opening the Straits to Russian warships, while leaving them still closed to war vessels of the other Great Powers, allowed Grey to tactfully agree with Isvolsky on the condition that the Straits were opened *"on terms of perfect equality to all," i.e,* including the English. Grey argued that any modification of the existing treaties closing the Straits to warships *"must be one which would contain such an element of reciprocity as would, in the event of war, place belligerents on an equal footing."*[11] As Grey well knew, this was not at all what Isvolsky had in mind. Like his predecessors, Isvolsky wanted the backdoor to the Straits bolted from the inside so that Russia and only Russia could control it. No Russian statesman could possibly consent to opening the Straits to all nations thereby exposing Odessa or Sevastopol to attack by enemy naval forces in a future war.

Having now lost all hope of securing the opening of the Straits to Russian warships, Isvolsky was in full panic mode. His only remaining option was to try and put the question of the annexation before a conference of the signatory Powers of the 1878 Congress of Berlin, failing which he faced a humiliating diplomatic defeat and a severe loss of personal prestige. Already there was stinging criticism from Pan-Slavs in Russia and an angry, mounting chorus of Serbian demands for compensation. Even his own ambassadors did not shrink from denouncing his folly in allowing Aehrenthal to outsmart him. Isvolsky's anger knew no bounds. While still in London he *"did not conceal his vexation at Austria and protested most energetically against the affirmation that he had given his approval to the annexation ... He condemned Austria-Hungary, which has entirely lost the confidence of Russia and the Western Powers. He expressed the conviction and the hope that her action in this affair would be avenged upon her in a sanguinary manner."*[12]

As the crisis simmered, it became increasingly clear that Isvolsky's strenuous efforts to have the Annexation Question submitted to a conference of the Powers would not succeed. Meanwhile, demonstrations of defiance against the Hapsburgs continued to escalate while Austria responded with wholesale arrests of agitators and suspected traitors, but when Austria began moving troops to the Serbian frontier, the crisis became acute. Russia was not ready for war so soon after the Russo-Japanese war and was obliged to urge Serbia to submit for now, with promises of future action. Heated rhetoric was, however, very much in evidence. M. Guchkov, the most influential member of the Duma, informed the Serbian Minister in St. Petersburg:

> When our armaments shall have been completely carried out, then we shall have our reckoning with Austria-Hungary. Do not begin any war now, for this would be your suicide. Conceal your purposes and make ready. The days of your joy will come.[13]

A few days later, Guchkov confirmed that this represented the views of Czar Nicholas as well:

> The Tsar said the Serbian sky is overcast with black clouds by this blow. The situation is frightful because Russia is unprepared for war and a Russian defeat would be the ruin of Slavdom. The Tsar has the feeling that a conflict with Germandom is inevitable in the future, and that one must prepare for this.[14]

Finally, with the crisis at its height, Germany stepped forward with a proposal to preserve the peace. The Kaiser had been angry that his ally [Austria] could have taken such a far-reaching step without first consulting him. He expressed his annoyance with such marginalia as *"Vienna will be charged with duplicity and not unjustly. She has duped us in a most unheard of fashion." And "My personal feelings as an ally have been most seriously wounded." And "With a policy of this kind Austria will drive us into a dangerous opposition to Russia."*

But the Young Turks had already accepted a payment of £2,500,000 "for the loss of crown property." This and the imminent threat of an outbreak of hostilities on the Austro-Serb frontier, obliged the Kaiser to accept von Bülow's point of view that the only way to defuse the crisis was to support Austria and to make a confidential offer of mediation to Russia as follows: Germany would invite the Powers to accept the Austro-Turkish agreement involving the nullification of Article 25 of the Treaty of Berlin, provided Russia promised beforehand to give her approval. As explained by Professor Fay:

> This [German] proposal had a threefold advantage: it secured to Austria a recognition by the Powers of the change of status of Bosnia and Herzegovina and deprived Serbia of the legal grounds and hopes that the *fait accompli* would be overturned; it satisfied the Entente demand that no change in a treaty is valid unless formally recognized by all who signed it; and, finally, by omitting any reference to a Conference, it avoided humiliating Russia by a direct rejection of the Conference idea which Isvolsky had been steadily demanding for months. It let Isvolsky easily out of the embarrassing blind alley into which he had strayed.[15]

Recognizing that Isvolsky might continue to press the idea of a conference, Bülow carefully instructed the German Ambassador in St. Petersburg:

> Say to M. Isvolsky that we learn with satisfaction that he recognizes the friendly spirit of our proposal and seems inclined to accept it ... and that we expect an answer – yes or no; we must regard any evasive or unclear answer as a refusal. We should then draw back and let things take their course. The responsibility for further events would then fall exclusively on M. Isvolsky, after we had made a last sincere effort to help him clear up the situation in a way which he could accept.[16]

Czar Nicholas had already telegraphed to the Kaiser that he was heartily pleased that the German proposal had offered a way out of the crisis, and Isvolsky added to this his formal acceptance. But as Fay noted: [17]

> Such were the events which soon became distorted into the legend that Germany had threatened Russia with force and humiliated her with an ultimatum. The legend was exploited in the Russian Press, spread in England by Sir Arthur Nicolson, and used by Isvolsky as a means of saving his face before his critics in Russia. But it was not an ultimatum. It was an attempt on Germany's part to bridge the gulf between Russia and Austria and prevent an outbreak of war between Serbia and Austria. Sir Edward Grey had meanwhile come forward with a similar mediation formula and told Austria in language almost identical with that of Bülow to Russia that, "if this fails, he would draw back and let things take their course."[18]

With this German initiative, the 1908 Annexation Crisis was thankfully relieved. But just as he had done earlier with Delcassé, King Edward staunchly supported Isvolsky throughout the crisis and even advised cousin Nikky that the bumbling Russian Foreign Minister should not be relieved of his duties as he so richly deserved. It marked the 2nd time that King Edward's reckless diplomacy, fully supported by Foreign Minister Grey, had brought Europe to the brink of war. It would not be the last ...

***

Endnotes

1. Massie, *Nicholas and Alexandra*, 263.
2. Lee, *King Edward VII*, Vol II, 289.
3. Hardinge Papers.
4. Hardinge of Penhurst, *Old Diplomacy*, 133.
5. Brook-Shepherd, *Uncle of Europe*, 324.
6. Mathes, *The Politics and Diplomacy of A. P. Izvolsky*, xvii.
7. Isvolsky, *Memoirs of Alexander Iswolsky*, 35.
8. Zedlitz-Trützschler, Count, *Twelve Years at the Imperial German Court.*
9. Report of Vesnitch, the Serbian Minister in Paris, of conversation with Isvolsky, Oct. 5, 1908.
10. Grey to Nicolson, Oct. 14, 1908.
11. Grey's memorandum to Isvolsky, Oct. 14, 1908.
12. Report of Gruitch from London, October 13, 1908; Bogitschevitch 157-161.
13. *Deutschland Schuldig?* 112.
14. Ibid, 114.
15. Fay, *The Origins of the World War*, II, 388.
16. Bülow to Pourtales, Mar. 21, 1909; G.P., XXVI, 693 ff.
17. Fay, *The Origins of the World War*, II, 391.
18. Metternich to Bülow, Mar. 22, 1909.

Chapter Four

THE KING IS DEAD LONG LIVE THE TRIPLE ENTENTE

King Edward and Kaiser Wilhelm did not like each other and the thin veil of cordiality covering their various meetings could not entirely conceal the fact. The Kaiser disapproved of his uncle's womanizing and the fact that gluttony had rendered him too fat to mount a horse, but the King's dislike of his German nephew was so visceral that the multitude of negative qualities so assiduously attributed to him by Anglo historians cannot account for it and we must look elsewhere for an explanation. Certainly, the charge that Kaiser Wilhelm lacked discretion was amply validated by a number of incidents, the most famous being the *Daily Telegraph*[1] interview which appeared on October 28, 1908. In it, the Emperor had made a number of assertions which, much to his surprise, triggered an avalanche of outrage and ridicule from abroad, but his harshest critics were the Germans themselves. Editorial writers and political cartoonists were merciless and actually drove the Kaiser to consider abdication. One cartoon pictured the Emperor as "Little Willy" sitting at a table with ink-stained fingers, while Father Bülow and Mother Germania wagged a chastising finger and said: *"Didn't we tell you, you were not to play at writing letters any more?"* An apocryphal story has it that an anonymous note addressed to Bülow arrived from London with instructions to hand it to the Kaiser:

If your lips you'd keep from slips
Five things observe with care:
Of whom you speak, to whom you speak
And how, and when, and where.

Aside from the perennial naval question, there were other royal vexations as well. The Kaiser's racing yacht, *Meteor II,* proved faster than the King's *Britannia* at the annual Cowes Regatta. The Kaiser was generally acknowledged to be more clever than the King and better informed about world affairs, whilst the King was adjudged to be more likable and socially adept. The mothers of both men, Queen Victoria and the outspoken Empress Frederick (the older sister of the King), disapproved of their eldest sons and expressed serious misgivings about their ability to handle the weighty responsibilities they would someday inherit. They tended to harbor opposite attitudes towards Prussia and world affairs in general.

But such differences simply do not account for the King's determined avoidance of his German nephew and his absolute refusal to discuss politics with him. Even now, in the eighth year of his reign, the King had declined to pay an official state visit to Berlin as his royal duties required, while he had done so in every other capital. When the Kaiser's latest visit to England in November, 1907, had made the King's failure to balance the protocol scales too conspicuous to ignore, it was decided to accept a return invitation to the German capital in the spring of 1908. Alas, before any planning could take place, the visit was called off for ostensible reasons of prior commitments. The real reason was the King's distaste for the whole idea and the Queen's implacable hatred for Germans in general and the Kaiser in particular.[2] Nevertheless, the pressing need for a serious discussion between King and Kaiser, including the dreaded naval question, had to be addressed. On May 4, 1906, Count Metternich, the German Ambassador in London, wired Chancellor von Bülow:[3]

> The Germans are without doubt the most unpopular among the upper circles of English society. This is due to a great extent to the attitude of the Court and to the personal relations between the two sovereigns. If an amicable meeting could be arranged between them, this would change things greatly for the better ...

Pressure from the Foreign Office and the handy pretext of finding a suitable successor for Sir Frank Lascelles for the post of ambassador to Berlin prompted the King on July 13, 1908, to send this handwritten letter to the Kaiser:

> I propose making my annual cure at Marienbad next month, and *en route* have arranged to pay my visit to Emperor of Austria at Ischl on 12th August to congratulate him on his 60th anniversary. I should be very glad if it suited you to give me a rendezvous on 11th at Friedrichshof. Should this proposal suit you, would you kindly send me a telegram so as to enable me to make the necessary arrangements?

The Kaiser replied that he would be delighted and so the important meeting was scheduled. Sir Edward Grey was determined that this time around, the cardinal issue of the German navy should not again be ignored and provided the King with two memoranda about the naval building program. Sir (later Lord) Charles Hardinge, the King's constant companion and diplomatic alter ego, recorded that *"This was really a very interesting innovation, since for the first time in history the British Government briefed the King to act as their spokesman in an interview with the head of a Foreign State, and it serves as indisputable proof of the confidence they felt in the wisdom and tact of the Sovereign in dealing with such matters. It was arranged that I should accompany His Majesty as Minister in attendance."* [4]

For himself, the King was greatly annoyed at the prospect of personally confronting his nephew on a subject upon which the latter was known to be far better informed and he minuted on August 6: *"This is, I believe, the first occasion on which the Sovereign has received instructions from his Government!"*[5] But as one of the King's many biographers has aptly observed:

> The same Sovereign who in 1903 had sailed clean away from the Foreign Office on a self-charted diplomatic course of his own, now made no real attempt to lead the field, and seemed content to leave this tricky bit of navigation to a professional pilot. Why? Was he, in plain language, ducking it?[6]

A better question might have been: why would the King trouble himself with a difficult, technical discussion with the Emperor of a state which he had long ago decided should be confronted with military force?

Nevertheless, on the morning of August 11, 1908, at Friedrichshof, King and Kaiser were closeted alone *tête-à-tête* for three hours. While no official record of that conversation exists, King Edward told Hardinge that every conceivable subject under the sun had been discussed but that once again, the subject of naval estimates and armaments had been ignored. This made it necessary for Hardinge to take up the confounding issue with the Kaiser after lunch that same afternoon. According to Hardinge, the Kaiser had maintained that, *"in a year's time, England would still have sixty-two first-class battleships to Germany's twenty-four,"* so why all the fuss? Hardinge had questioned this comparison, saying that the Emperor must surely be talking about *"every obsolete vessel that could be found floating in British harbours."* The Emperor thereupon sent for a copy of the latest German *Nauticus* handbook to prove his assertions; and, when the volume was put in front of him, Hardinge commented only that he *"'wished very much' he could accept the statistics it contained, which would be studied."*[7] On that afternoon's exchange with Hardinge, the Kaiser sent the following sentence-by-sentence report to his Chancellor, Prince Bülow[8]:

> **He**: [Hardinge] Your construction of Dreadnoughts is now being so accelerated ... say in 1912 you will be equal or even superior to us.
>
> **I**: That is complete nonsense. Who has been telling you such ridiculous tales?
>
> He: It is not nonsense, but authentic evidence from our Admiralty.
>
> I: It's still nonsense, even if your Admiralty produces it ... I can prove I'm right out of the *Nauticus*.

> **He**: You cannot have figures which are more authentic than those the admiralty have given me.
>
> **I**: Your documents are wrong. I am an Admiral of the British Navy which I know all about and understand better than you, who are a civilian with no idea of these matters.

This disagreement about sources escalated to a dramatic climax which was not mentioned by Hardinge but was described by the Kaiser as follows:

> **He**: Can't you put a stop to your building, or build less ships?
>
> **I**: Germany's maritime construction is measured by her own interests and needs. It is defensive and is directed against nobody, least of all against England ...
>
> **He**: But an arrangement must be reached to limit this construction. You must stop or build slower.
>
> **I**: Then we shall fight, for it is a question of national honor and dignity.

Brook-Shepherd records that

> At this point, Hardinge, according to the Kaiser, went brick-red with embarrassment, bowed, and asked the Emperor to regard his last words as a regrettable lapse in a private conversation, which he hoped would be forgiven and forgotten. If the tone and the language had been anything like what the Kaiser recorded immediately afterwards, the apology was certainly called for. It was no way, especially in the year 1908, for a Foreign Office official who was not even a Minister of the Crown, to address the Emperor of Germany.[9]

But by the time King Edward and his party left Friedrichshof Castle for Marienbad, cordiality was restored and the decision had been made that Sir Edward Goschen would replace Sir Frank Lascelles as British Ambassador to Berlin, and that the King, accompanied by Queen Alexandra, would finally pay his oft-postponed state visit to Berlin early the following year. On August 23, Edward Grey praised Hardinge for duty above and beyond[10]:

> You had to take a big fence in broaching the Navy question to the Emperor, but it would never have done to let him discuss relations between England and Germany without bringing this in.... As the matter was not mentioned by the King, an exceptional responsibility fell upon you.

Commenting on a later report from London that, at Friedrichshof, the original intention had been for King Edward – not Hardinge – to discuss the naval problem, the Kaiser wrote *"How nice that would have been!"*[11]

King Edward's strategy of strengthening the Triple Entente necessarily aimed equally at weakening the Triple Alliance and on this account, Spain, Italy, Macedonia and Greece, entered the King's political calculations. Just as Germany and France could never belong to the same coalition on account of Alsace-Lorraine, neither could Austria and Russia belong to the same coalition because of their conflicting ambitions in the Balkans. These were the geo-political fault lines which determined, preserved, and solidified the shape of the coalitions, as well as the disposition of these lesser Powers, which split Europe into opposing camps with the Triple Entente emerging as by far the stronger.

Remembering his pleasure forays to Vienna as the Prince of Wales and grateful to Franz Joseph for his steadfast support of England during the Boer war, Edward VII arrived at Vienna on August 31, 1903, for his first (and last) official visit to the Austrian capital. Franz Joseph's personal Adjutant, Lieutenant-General Baron von Margutti, described the efforts of Edward VII with regard to Austria as follows:

> Edward VII was exerting himself deliberately to secure the isolation of Germany and began by bringing pressure to bear on the Emperor Francis Joseph. In Ischl he [Edward] met with no success, but on the other hand during the following winter, he induced France to refuse to join a Russo-German coalition and at the same time persuaded Russia to turn her back on Germany and ally herself with the western powers. Naturally Francis Joseph expected that the Emperor William would bestir himself, in fact, whatever men may say, he needed the direct support of his ally to meet the further advances of Edward VII with the necessary determination. This was why the visit to Vienna in June, 1906, when another brilliant reception was prepared for William II, announced unmistakably to the world the firmness of the alliance between Germany and the Danube Monarchy."[12]

The King soon relaxed his efforts to detach Austria from Germany as there were few prospects for success in this direction. Instead, he tried during the course of informal summer meetings at Bad Ischl starting in August 1905, to enlist Franz Joseph in an attempt to get the Emperor to downgrade his plans for the German navy – again without success.

On April 8, 1907, at Cartagena, Edward VII met with King Alfonso of Spain and, after rigorous negotiations, secured the adherence of Spain to the soon-to-be-completed Triple Entente (the Convention with Russia would be signed on August 31, 1907) to the great satisfaction of Cambon who reported:

> The link is now established between the three governments ... Spain has been snatched from German influence ... yesterday's arrangement ties her henceforth to France and England."[13]

As for Italy, on April 18, 1907, King Edward steamed into Gaeta harbor. An escort of no fewer than eight battleships, four cruisers, and four destroyers, left little doubt as to the importance of the occasion. King Victor Immanuel, who had arrived the previous evening in his personal yacht, the *Trinacria*, was there to greet him with his own massive escort of twelve Italian warships and their accompanying torpedo-boats. King Edward was the first English sovereign to set foot in Italy since Richard the Lionhearted, who was on his way to the Crusades more than six centuries ago. On April 22, 1864, the Prince of Wales had angered his mother, Queen Victoria, by hosting Giuseppe Garibaldi, the great Italian revolutionary leader. Now forty-three years later, this translated into a hero's welcome for Edward VII by King Victor Emmanuel. Italy was nominally a member of the Triple Alliance and any conversations between Hardinge and Italian Foreign Minister Tittoni had to be circumspect in order to avoid alarming Germany. Nevertheless, the word "encirclement" was beginning to be heard. M. Cartier, the Belgian Chargé d'Affaires in London, reported to the Belgian Foreign Minister on April 12:

> King Edward's visit to his royal nephew at Cartagena was no doubt specially inspired by the desire to strengthen the ties that unite Spain to Great Britain as much as possible to weaken German influence at Madrid.[14]

Baron Greindl, the Belgian Minister in Berlin noted:

> There is some right to regard with suspicion this eagerness to unite, for a so-called defensive object, Powers who are menaced by nobody ... It is no wonder, therefore, that the King of England's proceedings give rise to certain apprehensions here, apprehensions that are shared in Vienna. They have found utterance in an article in the *Freie Presse* which was reproduced and commented on by the *Kölnische Zeitung* the day before yesterday.[15]

Baron Greindl was referring to an editorial in the Austrian *Newe Freie Presse* dated April 15, which enumerated King Edward's recent spate of visits to Paris, Cartagena, and now Gaeta, and went on to state:

> The King of England has not a reputation for caring about parades and shows for their own sake. He is reckoned a clever man of business, who has succeeded in acquiring a determining influence upon the conduct of foreign policy, despite all the obstacles presented by the British Constitution. If the King of England has a meeting with the King of Italy, without circumstances affording any quite external and obvious explanation of it, then it must be a matter of serious politics.... The accident of his traveling to Italy from Spain by sea

> takes away from the meeting nothing of its deliberate and intentional character.... Who can fail to receive the impression that a diplomatic duel is being fought out between England and Germany under the eyes of the world? The King of England, however, is in serious earnest over the duel, and is no longer afraid of appearing to throw the whole influence of his personality into the scales whenever it is a question thwarting the aims of German policy. This meeting at Gaeta is another fact connected with the burning jealousy between England and Germany. Here again an attempt is being made still further to loosen the tie between Italy and Germany. Already people are anxiously asking themselves everywhere: What is the meaning of this continual political labour, carried on with open recklessness, whose object is to put a close ring round Germany? (Deutschland ganzlich einzukreisen)[16]

The King complained to the Prince of Wales about "the damned nonsense" broadcast in the German Press, and some papers, like the *Kölnische Zeitung*, soon denied that the King's purpose was the encirclement of Germany. But the King's nonsensical explanation that the meeting at Gaeta was "informal" was belied by the massive naval presence of some thirty-two British and Italian warships and discrete whispers about the planned Italian conquest of Tripoli. In a few months, moreover, the Anglo-Russian Convention would be officially signed (see above). *Edward the Caresser* was quickly evolving into *Eduard der Einkreiser* (Edward the Encircler).

Greece was yet another object lesson in Edward VII's powerful hold on foreign policy. The strategic island of Crete, nominally a part of Turkey, had been governed since 1898 by Prince George, the second son of the King of Greece, George of the Hellenes. In June, 1904, the British Government was considering withdrawing British forces from Crete as part of a general military evacuation by the Powers in order to placate Turk and Greek factions vying for control until a very stiff and very unconstitutional veto arrived, courtesy of King Edward:

> British troops *will not* be withdrawn from Crete, as Prince George leans on England more than any other country – and especially for advice.[17]

Prime Minister Balfour reconsidered, and British troops were not withdrawn. Years later, when another crisis boiled up in Athens over the issue of Crete, the King ordered that the Royal Navy should stand by in case it was needed. Brook-Shepherd summed up the effects of the King's activist diplomacy as follows:

> Like the movement of his own navy, King Edward's presence each year, first at Biarritz and then on his spring cruises, served as a pal-

> pable reminder of England's interest in what went on in the Iberian Peninsula and throughout the whole Mediterranean area. The effect is impossible to quantify. No one can say what contribution his dynastic diplomacy as conducted, for example with the Kings of Spain and Italy, made to the behavior of their respective countries when the First World War broke out. All that seems clear is that, without all King Edward's personal efforts, England's political position in the area would not have been so strong, or Germany's so doubtful, as they were when the test of alignments came in 1914. Diplomacy, as the King fully realized, was not just a matter of those great and spectacular heaves like the Paris visit of 1903. Much more often, it consisted of a series of small and hidden nudges, patiently planted over the years in the right place and the right time.[18]

During these diplomatic forays around the Mediterranean, Sir Charles Hardinge was the King's *"special man going everywhere abroad with him, and fulfilling the functions appertaining to the Secretary of State as Cabinet Minister"* – as Sir Horace Rumbold told Blunt.[19] *"All the diplomacy of the time", said Sir Horace, "was done by Hardinge and the King; Sir E. Grey, the Foreign Secretary, being only their mouthpiece in the House of Commons."*[20]

The year of 1909 did not bode well for the peace of Europe. It broke under the shadow of King Edward's irresponsible diplomacy at the Seine and the Neva which had lately found expression in the Bosnian Crisis – again bringing Europe to the precipice as it had in 1905. There was also the King's diplomacy at Cartagena, Gaeta, and St. Petersburg, giving rise to German fears of encirclement, whilst the English press speculated darkly about Count Zeppelin's dirigibles and how they could portend a German airborne invasion. Then there was the aftermath of the February 1, 1908, bloody assassination of King Carlos of Portugal; the death on April 22, 1908, of Prime Minister Campbell-Bannerman and his replacement by Chancellor of the Exchequer, Henry Asquith; the tyranny and revolt in Macedonia; the controversy of *The Telegraph* interview; the naval debate.

When Metternich reported to the Chancellor on June 25, 1908, that *"the great mass of English people desire peace, and that this is King Edward's policy,"* the Kaiser added the marginal note: *"Untrue. He aims at war. I am to begin it, so that he does not get the odium."*[21]

In the spring of 1908, First Sea Lord "Jacky" Fisher confided to the King his cherished plan of attacking and destroying the German fleet in a surprise attack, citing the precedent of his hero Horatio Nelson, who on April 1, 1801, had attacked and destroyed the Danish fleet in the harbor of Copenhagen. The King, while admitting the general force of his argument, disapproved and chastised Fisher for his incautious exuberance. Fisher later lamented that *"we possessed neither a Pitt nor a Bismarck to give the order."*[22] The quarrel between Lord Beresford and Fisher, as well as the controversy about the revolutionary Dreadnought, were all resolved in Fisher's favor with the King's help. *"There is not the slightest doubt that but for King Edward's unwavering support, Sir John Fisher would have been unable to go through with his plans."*[23] Fisher himself agrees that he owed his illustrious career to the King:

> When Your Majesty backed up the First Sea Lord against unanimous naval feeling against the Dreadnought ... it just simply shut up the mouths of the revilers as efficiently as those lions were kept from eating Daniel, and they would have eaten me but for your Majesty.

There was also the January, 1907 Crowe Memorandum (see below), secretly solicited by the King, which was so demagogic and inflammatory that it was difficult to believe it had come, not from some unhinged British nationalist, but from top levels of the British Foreign Office. Described by Grey as "most valuable," there was nothing even remotely similar produced by the Wilhelmine Government.

It was against this troubling backdrop that on February 8, 1909, the King and the Queen boarded the *Alexandra,* the smaller of the two royal yachts, to cross the Channel and take the train to Berlin for their first official three-day state visit to Germany. The Queen had lost none of her antipathy against Germans while the King was feeling distinctly out of sorts and pining for the warming sun of Biarritz. He was now within fifteen months of his death. His reception in Berlin the next day by the Kaiser and Kaiserin was magnificent and even blessed by intermittent sunshine. Crowds, at first respectful but cold, soon warmed and even staged enthusiastic demonstrations in response to the King's cordial, tactful speeches, but there was also a growing sense of alarm at the King's pallor and his frequent fits of coughing. On the first day of the visit, the King panicked his hosts when he momentarily lost consciousness. Daisy Pless, an English society beauty with whom the King was chatting described it:

> Suddenly he coughed and fell back against the back of the sofa, and his cigar dropped out of his fingers, his eyes stared and he could not breathe. I thought, My God, he is dying; oh! Why not in his own country. I tried to undo the collar of his uniform ... then the Queen rushed up and we both tried; at last he came to – and undid it himself ... Please God, this dear, kind, able Monarch is not in for a serious illness![24]

James Reid, the King's personal physician, was summoned and after fifteen minutes, everything was pronounced to be in order.

Kaiser Wilhelm had truly bent over backward to make his royal visitors as comfortable as possible and aside from some comical minor technical glitches, the three days went smoothly except for one very odd event. Just before his departure and much to the Kaiser's surprise, the King brought up the naval question. No one had wanted or expected any sort of serious discussion and Count Metternich had even warned from London that any attempt at such talks would be *"highly inappropriate."*[25] Similarly, Sir Edward Grey, in defending his decision not to go to Berlin, had written that, apart from the naval question, there were *"no big issues to negotiate"*[26] in Berlin.

> Why he [Edward] should have suddenly tackled in Berlin in February 1909 what he had avoided at Sandringham, Windsor, Kiel and Cronberg during the previous seven years is a bit of a mystery. Perhaps he sensed, especially after that fainting fit, that he might never see either Berlin or his nephew again. Perhaps he merely felt that the decorum of a full-blown state visit, with the Kaiser as his host, was sufficient guarantee against unpleasantness. Whatever the reason, he picked the very end of his stay in the German capital (presumably on the drive to the station or even on the railway platform itself) to take the initiative.[27]

Hardinge, who had accompanied the King as always, does not mention this highly unusual discussion between uncle and nephew. The Kaiser's version, sent just hours afterwards, is the only version we have. He reported:

> H.M. King Edward VII held his first political talk with me in the last minute before his departure. He expressed his thanks and deep satisfaction with his reception here. The day in the Town Hall had pleased him very much. Then he came to relations between our two countries which, he hoped, would henceforth move into safer channels of mutual trust. On the naval question he said:
>
> I hope people will grow sensible ... and take a quieter view. We are in a different position from other countries; beeing [sic] an island, we must have a fleet larger than all the other ones. But we don't dream of attacking anybody, only we must make sure that our shores are quite safe from danger.

I: It is perfectly natural that England should have a Navy according to its interests and to be able to safeguard them and its shores. The same thing is with us. We have laid down a naval Bill ... adequate to our interests. This implies no aggressive [*sic*] against any Power, certainly not against England.

He: Oh quite so, quite so. I perfectly understand it is your absolute right; I don't for one moment believe you are designing anything against us.

I: This Bill was published 11 years ago; it will be adhere to and exactly carried out, *without restriction.* [Kaiser's italics]

He: Of course that is quite right, as it is a Bill voted by the people and their Parliament, I know that cannot be changed.

> **I**: It is a mistake on the part of some Jingoes in England that we are making a building race with you. That is nonsense. We only follow the Bill.
>
> **He**: Oh, I know that is quite an absurd notion. The situation is quite clear to me and I an in no way alarmed; that is all talk and will pass over.[28]

This final exchange with his nephew was odd indeed. The King had always pooh-poohed the idea that there were significant problems between England and Germany and dismissed the Kaiser's suggestion of an Anglo-German treaty similar to the one with France and Russia as unnecessary. But this marked the first time that he had done so in the context of the serious naval rivalry which divided the two nations and without Hardinge or anyone else being present. The incongruous interview illustrated once more the yawning disconnect between the King's views indicating that all was well, which he expressed privately to his nephew, and his public political associations and actions which expressed the precise opposite.

A much-relieved King and Queen arrived back in London in the midst of a severe constitutional crisis arisen over the question of the authority wielded by the House of Lords, as well as the ongoing Bosnian Crisis. Edward had not recovered from the chronic cough which had afflicted him since before the Berlin visit, and he soon found himself once more installed in the comfortable Hotel du Palais of his beloved Biarritz from whence he sent another letter of his regular correspondence with his financial advisor, Sir Ernest Cassal. Part of the letter went:

> Since you left England, we have had many dark days relating to the state of affairs in the Balkans! I however hope that matters may yet be settled without going to war ... I arrived here on the 6th [of March, 1909] and though our weather has been changeable and strong it has done me much good as I left in deep snow and intense cold with a bronchial catarrh which was not improved by my visit to Berlin, though that visit was in every respect a great success ...[29]

Upon returning to England, the King received Czar Nicholas II at Cowes, who was reciprocating the King's own visit to Reval (Tallinn) the previous year. With the Czar's Baltic fleet residing at the bottom of the Tsushima Strait, King Edward was determined to reassure him and his Foreign Minister, Isvolsky, that Russia had made the right decision in staking her political future on England and France instead of Germany. To that end he had assembled the greatest display of naval might ever seen in the Solent (the strait that separates the Isle of Wight from the mainland of England). The royal Russian yacht, *Standart,* was greeted by no fewer than twenty-four battleships, sixteen heavy cruisers, forty-eight destroyers, and fifty other warships.

The year 1910 dawned with Europe much relieved at Germany's successful resolution of the Bosnian Crisis, but the Act of Algeciras had failed to check the ever-increasing tribal unrest in Morocco; while back home, the vexing constitutional crisis (owing to the Liberal Government campaign to reduce the powers of the House of Lords) seemed more intractable than ever. On Monday, March 7, 1910, King Edward crossed the channel accompanied by the torpedo boats *Mohawk* and *Corsair*, for his annual cure at his beloved Biarritz. The King had never fully recovered from his bronchial catarrh and when the weather turned suddenly cold and windy, the pretense that all was well came to an end with this note from Alice Keppel:

> The King's cold is so bad that he can't dine out but wants us all to dine with him at 8:15 at the Palais, so be there. I am quite worried *entre nous* and have sent for the nurse ...[30]

The King returned to London on April 27 and a week later his throat and chest were inflamed and the chronic cough had returned. In the evening of May 5, the nation learned that the King was ill with bronchitis and that this was the cause of "some anxiety." A further bulletin described his condition as "grave" and another as "critical." In his bedroom suite at Buckingham Palace, surrounded by family members and close friends, King Edward VII died at fifteen minutes before midnight on May 6, 1910.

His funeral on May 20 was an international pageant every bit as glittering and impressive as that of his mother, Queen Victoria, a decade earlier. Kaiser Wilhelm, who was present, gives a detailed and poetic description of the funeral procession in his memoirs. Condolences, tributes, accolades, and homage poured in from around the globe, but there was also heavy criticism and accusations of warmongering – especially from Germany: The *Rheinisch Westfälischezeitung* editorialized:

> To us Germans he was the greatest opponent, who inflicted on us immeasurable injury. We stand at his bier as that of a mighty and victorious antagonist.

In Leipzig, the *Neuste Nachrichten* opined:

> For long years, King Edward wove, with masterly skill, the Nessus robe that was to destroy the German Hercules.

In St. Petersburg, the *Novoye Vremya* commented:

> According to common usage, the monarch of England ... merely reigns without governing. But the late King not only reigned but also

> molded the destinies of his realm ... Bismarck created an overlordship for Germany in Europe. King Edward substituted for this the hegemony of England.

One of the King's legion of biographers weighed-in with this:

> With his death the clouds of war lifted for a moment. During nearly the whole of his reign the world had trembled on the brink of war. On several occasions it had only just been averted; and how closely the King's life was bound up with that condition of things was shown by the sudden relaxation of tension which followed his decease.[31]

Another biographer frankly admits Edward's policy of encirclement, but somehow manages to provide the King with a noble motive for doing so:

> ... the political encirclement of Germany had been consummated by the Franco-Russian treaty of alliance [1894], while Edward was still Prince of Wales, and with no initiative whatever from England. What he did do as King was to help strengthen that circle enormously: first, on its western and eastern arcs, by linking his country with both France and Russia; and second, on its southern arc, by increasing England's influence, and diminishing that of Germany, along the length and breadth of the Mediterranean. Yet, even in becoming the 'Encircler', he still remained the 'Peacemaker'. For the purpose of all these moves was not to create an all-round base from which Germany could be attacked and crushed, but to set up a protective ring which would insulate England and the rest of the Continent from the explosion that Germany might one day produce. The Germans were absolutely correct when they noted that, at all points of the European compass, it was Edward VII and his government who were mainly responsible for frustrating their ambitions. But this weakening of Germany was not so much the aim of the King's policy as the result of it. From the time of the Prussian wars of the 1860s down to his dying day he was, however, genuinely afraid of the Furor Teutonicus in the German people, the German Army and in the German Kaiser. What he sought to do was to sandbag the Continent against it.[32]

This biographer was apparently unaware of Anglo-French military planning, which had for years been conducted by Sir Edward Grey. Nor was he aware of Lord Esher's words: "*The British people are warlike and aggressive, they have for centuries been constantly fighting, and, indeed, until quite recently, it has been difficult to find any single year in which the British Empire has not been at war in some part of the world.*"[33] But the absurdity of the claim that the King was building a wall of containment around Germany to "sandbag" the Continent against Teutonic aggression hardly needs further comment.

The English historian James Anson Farrar wrote this fitting eulogy:

> By the time the King died, almost the whole of Europe stood in battle array against Germany. Hardly a year passed between 1904 and 1910 in which the rival camps of Europe did not narrowly escape from coming to blows. The whole reign was a series of crises, nor is there any evidence to show that any of these, like the Bosnian crisis of 1908 and 1909, were passed in safety in consequence of any action taken by the King. And only four years after his death the war began, with the several combatants ranged against one another in exact accordance with the plan marked out for them.... It is highly probable that, but for our backing, no fresh Franco-German war would have been fought in 1914, and therefore no European war to the undeniable benefit of this country and of the world.[34]

Finally, there was the reaction of Kaiser Wilhelm himself, who expressed few regrets:

> The death of the "Encircler," Edward VII – of whom it was said once, in a report of the Belgian Embassy at Berlin, that "the peace of Europe was never in such danger as when the King of England concerned himself with maintaining it" – called me to London, where I shared with my close relations, the members of the English royal family, the mourning into which the passing of the King had thrown the dynasty and the nation.[35]

Thus in the early summer of 1910, the King was dead, but his political offspring, the Triple Entente, was very much alive ...

***

Endnotes

1. For the full text, see Dr. J. Hill's *Impressions of the Kaiser*, pp. 261-2.
2. G.P., Vol. 24, No. 8212: Metternich to Bülow, June 30, 1908.
3. G.P., Vol. 21, No. 417: Metternich to Bülow, June 7, 1906.
4. Hardinge of Penhurst, *Old Diplomacy*, 158.
5. Hardinge Papers.
6. Brook-Shepherd, Gordon, *Uncle of Europe*, 301.
7. Ibid, 303.
8. G.P., Vol. 24, Nos. 8224-8226.
9. Brook-Shepherd, Gordon, *Uncle of Europe*, 303-4.
10. Hardinge Papers.
11. G.P., Vol. 24, No. 8247, Kaiser's annotation.

12. Margutti, Lieutenant-General Baron, *The Life and Times of the Emperor Francis Joseph*. 224.
13. D.D.F., Ser. 2, Vol. XI, No. 2: Cambon to Rouvier, 17 May, 1907.
14. Morel, E.D., *Diplomacy Revealed*, 74.
15. Ibid., 76.
16. Cited in Lee, *King Edward VII*, Vol. II, 541.
17. Ibid., 517.
18. Brook-Shepherd, *Uncle of Europe*, 286.
19. Blunt, *Diaries*, ii, 183.
20. Ibid., ii, 213.
21. *Die Grosse Politik*, Vol. XXV, II, 479.
22. Fisher, *Memories*, 4-5.
23. Lee, *King Edward VII*, Vol. II, 598.
24. Daisy Pless, *Memoirs*, 176-7.
25. G.P., Vol. 28, No. 10255: Metternich to Bülow, 20 January 1909.
26. B.D., Vol. III, No. 143: Grey to Bertie, 7 January 1909.
27. Brook-Shepherd, Gordon, *Uncle of Europe*, 344.
28. Marginal comment of the Emperor Wilhelm on Bülow's report to him on his general talks with Hardinge. G.P., Vol. 28, No.10260.
29. Papers of Sir Ernest Cassel. Letter to Sir Ernest from the King, 19 March 1909.
30. Soveral Papers.
31. Farrer, J.A., *England under Edward VII*, 265, 5.
32. Brook-Shepard, Gordon, *The Uncle of Europe*, 357-8.
33. Esher, Reginald Baliol Brett, Viscount, *The Influence of King Edward*, 18.
34. Farrar, J.A., *England Under Edward VII*, 261.
35. Wilhelm II, Kaiser *The Kaiser's Memoirs* (Kindle Locations 1408-1411).

AGADIR

Chapter Five

Agadir

When England and France signed off on the 1904 Entente Cordiale they neglected to consult Moroccan natives who were not inclined to trade Moroccan independence for a French protectorate. Tribal unrest was overshadowed by Great Power unrest when France refused to consult with Germany with regard to the latter's commercial interests as she was obliged to do under the 1880 Madrid Convention. When the French refusal, supported by King Edward VII, threatened war with Germany, the crisis was defused with the firing of French Foreign Minister Delcassé and the signing of the Act of Algeciras on April 7, 1906. This temporarily resolved Franco-German problems but angered natives.

> Before the ink was dry on the Act of Algeciras, the French had reinstalled the military mission in Fez which had been dismissed by the Sultan, their customs officers had settled into Moroccan ports, and French and Spanish officers took the Moroccan police in hand in coastal towns. Everywhere they looked, Moroccans saw an influx of Europeans, and they were not pleased. European travelers found that the once-friendly population was now decidedly hostile. Attacks on Europeans increased, and were duly noted by consular officials.[1]

The chain-reaction of political turmoil set in motion by the Entente Cordiale was sometimes interrupted but never stopped. Tribal chieftains resented the subservience of the Sultan to French authority and the continuing encroachments upon Moroccan independence. Mounting tribal discontent provided the pretext for the French Government to send troops into several provinces. This in turn triggered a rebellion against the reigning Sultan, Abdul Aziz, which ended with his deposition by his older brother, Mulai Hafid.

Kaiser Wilhelm, never in sympathy with Bülow/Holstein, had always preferred to allow France to exhaust herself in the Moroccan imbroglio. A few days after being painfully surprised by the Austrian annexation of Bosnia-Herzegovina, he wired the Wilhelmstrasse:

> In view of these circumstances this wretched Moroccan affair must now be brought to a conclusion, quickly and definitely. There is nothing to be made of it, it will be French anyway. So let us get out of the affair with dignity so that we may finally have done with this friction with France, now that great questions are at issue.[2]

Germany readily agreed to the French conditions under which Mulai Hafid was to be the new Sultan. This led to negotiations which resulted in the Franco-German Agreement of February 9, 1909. In this new Agreement *"to facilitate the execution of the Act of Algeciras,"* Germany undertook to recognize *"the special political interests"* of France in Morocco, while France was *"firmly attached to the maintenance of the integrity and independence of the Shereefian Empire"* and was *"resolved to safeguard the principle of economic equality, and consequently not to obstruct German commercial and industrial interests in that country."* But, like the previous two, this latest agreement only served to further inflame tribal passions. French promises to respect the independence and sovereignty of Morocco were not believed and conditions in Morocco went from bad to worse. In 1911, a serious rebellion bordering on civil war caused the Sultan to flee to the French consulate and appeal to Paris for assistance. France agreed and on May 21, a French military column from Casablanca entered Fez, followed by a landing of Spanish troops at Larache. This latest escalation would test the new Chancellor, Theobald von Bethmann-Hollweg, and the equally new State Secretary for Foreign Affairs, Alfred von Kiderlen-Wächter. Kaiser Wilhelm had accepted the resignation of Bülow on July 14, 1909, and that of Holstein (much to the latter's disappointment) in the summer of 1906. (Despite the official reasons given for the resignations of Bülow and Holstein, documents indicate that the real reason for their dismissal was their opposition to the naval ambitions of the Kaiser and Tirpitz.) Germany had not objected to the proposed French occupation of Fez, but Kiderlen issued a warning: *"If you go to Fez, you will not depart. If French troops remain in Fez so that the Sultan rules only with the aid of French bayonets, Germany will regard the Act of Algeciras as no longer in force and will resume complete liberty of action."*[3] And when Kaiser Wilhelm, at the suggestion of Bethmann-Hollweg, raised the issue with King George V on May 16th, the King replied candidly:

> To tell the truth, the Algeciras Convention is no longer in force and the best thing everyone can do is forget it. Besides, the French are doing nothing in Morocco that we haven't already done in Egypt. Therefore we will place no obstacles in France's path. The best thing Germany can do is to recognize the *fait accompli* of French occupation of Morocco and make arrangements with France for protection of German commercial interests.[4]

This is exactly what Germany had been trying to do. In fact, this 2nd Moroccan crisis was a mirror-image of the 1st Moroccan Crisis six years earlier. In 1905, the French Foreign Minister, Delcassé, had felt safe to ride roughshod over German rights under the 1880 Madrid Convention because he was confident of backing by the King of England. Now, six years later, France again felt herself safe to absorb Morocco, while ignoring the

Act of Algeciras and refusing to deal forthrightly with Germany. As early as December, 1910, Bethmann informed the Reichstag: *"Do not doubt that we will energetically defend the rights and interests of German merchants."*[5] Here was yet another standoff between Germany and France over Morocco which had come despite the 1880 Madrid Convention, the 1906 Act of Algeciras, and the 1909 Franco-German Agreement. This latest colonial kerfuffle was summed up by one historian as follows:

> Kiderlen's position was strong. Germany had commercial interests and treaty rights in Morocco; France clearly intended to alter the basis of her position in the country; France knew that Germany was entitled to consideration and compensation based on France's action; yet no offer of compensation had been forthcoming. Kiderlen could, of course, simply continue to register complaints with [Jules] Cambon and hope that sooner or later, France would take cognizance of Germany's appeals. The Wilhelmstrasse did not see this as the way great states responded when their interests were challenged. Nor was this course likely to appeal to the vociferous nationalists in the Reichstag and in the press.[6]

The Russian Ambassador in Paris, Alexander Isvolsky, agreed and weighed in with this assessment:

> The Berlin Cabinet has chosen a very advantageous and skillful position: without protesting as yet against the French manner of action, it reserves the power of announcing at any moment that the Algeciras Act has been infringed. In this way German diplomacy dominates the situation and can, not only according to development of events on the spot, but also according to the general trend of her domestic or foreign policy, suddenly render the Moroccan question more acute.[7]

The German position had already been stated in a lengthy May 3 memorandum drawn up by Kiderlen (greatly condensed):

> Three years have shown that the independence of Morocco, as contemplated in the Algeciras Act, cannot be maintained in the face of native rebellion and imperialistic pressure from France and Spain. Sooner or later Morocco will inevitably be absorbed by these two neighbors. It is unlikely that a walled city like Fez can be captured by the natives and the revolt seems to be on the ebb. But the French fear for its safety and are preparing to send an expedition. This they have a right to do, and one must await the development of events. But if they march to Fez, it is hardly likely that they will withdraw; even if French public opinion approved withdrawal, it would be regarded as

> a sign of weakness. This would lead to new uprisings and new French military expeditions. The course of events show that the provisions of the Act of Algeciras cannot be carried out. A Sultan who can only assert his authority with the aid of French bayonets cannot maintain the independence which was the purpose of the Algeciras Act. Germany must recognize these facts and readjust her policy in accordance with them. After the French have been in Fez for awhile, we shall ask them in a friendly way when they expect to withdraw. When they say that they cannot withdraw, we shall say that we understand this perfectly, but we cannot longer regard the Sultan as a sovereign independent ruler as provided by the Act of Algeciras; and since this is a dead letter, the Signatory Powers regain their freedom of action. It will do no good to protest against the French absorption of Morocco. We must therefore secure an object which will make the French ready to give us compensation. Just as the French protect their subjects in Fez, we can do the same for ours at Mogador and Agadir by peacefully stationing ships there. We can then await developments and see if the French will offer us suitable compensations. If we get these, it will make up for past failures and have a good effect on the coming elections to the Reichstag.[8]

On June 21, Cambon told Kiderlen that he hoped the German Empire would not insist on a partition of Morocco because *"French opinion would not stand for it.*[9] But," he added suggestively, *"one could look elsewhere."*[10] Responding to this hint, Kiderlen declared himself ready to listen to "offers." Cambon replied that he would go to Paris and discuss it with his Government. He departed with Kiderlen urging him to *"Bring something back from Paris."*[11]

Cambon returned to Paris with a Government in chaos. Prime Minister Ernest Monis had been replaced by Joseph Caillaux, who in turn appointed M. De Selves, a local Government official with no national experience, as his Foreign Minister. The German Kaiser, having recognized that France, as a result of being backed by England, would be inclined to offer nothing more than an irreducible minimum as compensation, authorized Kiderlen to send ships to Agadir to underscore legitimate German demands. On July 1, 1911, the German gunboat, *Panther,* steamed slowly into the Bay of Agadir and dropped anchor a few hundred yards from the beach. The *Panther,* built for colonial service and two years past her scrapping date, was armed with one 4-inch gun forward, one aft, and included a brass band for ceremonial purposes. The ship itself was short (211 feet long) and fat (32 feet in beam) and the term "gunboat" was therefore a bit of a misnomer. Nevertheless, her symbolic importance recalled the Kaiser's visit to Tangier six years earlier and the news of the *Panthersprung* (Panther's leap) raised eyebrows in the British Foreign Office and *The Times*. Arthur Ponsonby, however, rose in the House of Commons and pointed out that England had taken a magnanimous view of Russian troops pouring into Persia, Italy's seizure of Tripoli, the French occupation of Fez, and offered no protest. *"But immediately a German man-of-war goes to Agadir we are told that we are on the eve of a very great crisis."*[12]

Kiderlen and Bethmann had always believed that the issue of compensation for Morocco should be settled between Germany and France alone. Thus, when Sir Edward Grey called upon Count Metternich on May 4 to discover Germany's intentions, the Ambassador had neither information nor instructions. Grey issued a warning to the startled Ambassador that

> A new situation has been created by the dispatch of a German ship to Agadir. Future developments might affect British interests more directly than they had been hitherto affected; and, therefore, we could not recognize any new arrangement which was come to without us.[13]

The problem with Grey's statement was that Kiderlen, Bethmann, and the Kaiser had all been bent on carrying on the discussion of compensation with France alone, and had intimated politely that intervention by others was not desired.[14] More importantly, Grey was mistaken that "a new situation" had been created by the arrival of the *Panther*. In fact, the "new situation" had been created by the French occupation of Fez to which the *Panther* was the German response. Even Isvolsky, the Russian Ambassador in Paris agreed: *"In her action in Morocco, France is stepping beyond the bounds of the Act of Algeciras, and is placing the Morocco question on a completely new footing."*[15]

Grey's statement to Metternich on this was worse than a mistake, it "was a misrepresentation of the Cabinet's position, as its report to the King shows that it clearly understood that the new situation had been created by France and Spain." Furthermore, *"Sir Edward Grey's attitude should have warned Metternich, and through him the German Government, that he intended to seize the opportunity for a confrontation with Germany and that it was necessary to take every precaution to thwart this intention."*[16]

This assertion is startling, but strongly underscored by the events of July 21. On that day, Grey summoned the German Ambassador and told him that a Franco-German agreement seemed unlikely, and as serious British interests were involved, he wanted to suggest to Metternich that it was time for a discussion à trois between France, Germany, and England. But that very same evening, without giving Metternich time to receive a response from Berlin, Grey, with the permission of Asquith, allowed Lloyd George, Chancellor of the Exchequer, to announce to the world the new English demand that henceforth she should be consulted about Morocco. In this infamous Mansion House speech, Lloyd George explicitly warned Germany that:

> If a situation were to be forced upon us in which peace could only be preserved by the surrender of the great and beneficent position Britain has won by centuries of heroism and achievement, by allowing Britain to be treated, where her interests were vitally affected, as if she were of no account in the Cabinet of nations, then I say emphatically that peace at that price would be a humiliation intolerable for a great country like ours to endure.[17]

This was uncomfortably close to a declaration of war. No surprise, the speech triggered a fierce firestorm of protests and counter threats in Germany and a war-scare throughout Europe. On September 14, Sir Arthur Nicolson reported on conversations with Haldane, Lloyd George and Churchill, and that he was relieved to find that all three were *"perfectly ready – I might almost say eager – to face all possible eventualities."*[18] Sir Henry Wilson, the director of military operations wrote that the possibility of England being involved in a European war caused grave anxiety in the Cabinet for several weeks.[19] There were similar preparations in France and Russia.

Kiderlen seethed: *"If the English Government had intended to complicate the political situation and to bring about a violent explosion, it could certainly have chosen no better means than the speech of the Chancellor of the Exchequer."*[20]

But Grey stubbornly maintains in his memoirs that Lloyd George's Mansion House speech *"had much to do with preserving the peace in 1911"* and that it made *"German Chauvinists there doubt whether it would be wise to fire the guns."*[21] This statement by Grey is outrageously false, as there is not a shred of evidence that Germany had any such intentions. One historian summed it up as follows:

> All these [Grey's] statements are completely untrue. The first serious threat to peace was the Mansion House speech. No person in a responsible position in Germany had any intention of firing the guns; and the German Government answered Metternich's dispatch reporting Grey's démarche of July 21 immediately. Lloyd George's speech was everywhere interpreted as a threat of war directed against Germany, and in fact it was Lloyd George's intention to warn Germany that if war came, England would fight along with France.[22]If Wilhelm II had aimed such a belligerent speech at England, the resulting storm would have darkened the English sky for a month, and the incident would still be cited today as an example of the megalomania engendered by a withered arm."[23]

On November 4, 1911, after further negotiations which did not include England, France agreed to cede 100,000 square miles of the French Congo, giving Germany two much needed river outlets to the Congo for the export of their Cameroon product, in return for German acknowledgment of a French protectorate in Morocco. The Agadir Crisis was over.

Meanwhile, Alexander Isvolsky, the disgraced former Russian Foreign Minister, had not let the crisis go to waste in his persistent quest to advance historic Russian designs on the Straits. He had already made two futile efforts to open the Straits to Russian warships. The first came in 1907 during negotiations for an Anglo-Russian Convention, and the second in 1908 with his Buchlau Bargain with Vienna. Both failed on account of opposition from Sir Edward Grey, but the changed European situation in 1911, Isvolsky believed, made a successful effort possible.

The Russian Foreign Minister, Sasonov, was absent from early July to mid-December, 1911, due to illness, leaving the direction of foreign affairs to Isvolsky in Paris and Neratov in St. Petersburg. Isvolsky was counting upon the Franco-German dispute about Morocco and the double-dealing conducted by the duplicitous Italian Foreign Minister, Tittoni, at Racconigi in October, 1909, with regard to Tripoli, to get approval from Italy, Austria, France and Germany for Russian plans for the Straits. After some very complex and deceitful diplomacy, mainly by Tittoni, these nations agreed in principle to support Russian control of the Straits, with the exception of England. As in 1908, Sir Edward was ready to see the Straits opened, provided they were opened to the warships of all nations alike, but not if they were opened only to Russia, thus converting the Black Sea into a potential Russian naval fortress.[24]

Neither Isvolsky nor any other Russian statesman seems to have figured out that England would under no circumstances allow the powerful Russian Black Sea fleet access to the eastern Mediterranean, whence it could threaten India, Afghanistan, Egypt and the Suez Canal from the safe harbor of the Black Sea, while at the same time maintaining a vigorous pretense of support for Russian ambitions for the purpose of keeping her aligned with the Triple Entente. With this latest failure, Isvolsky finally accepted that Russian control of the Straits could not be achieved short of "European complications," which he intended to help produce from his new post as Russian Ambassador in Paris, in concert with a quickly rising star in the French political firmament, Raymond Nicolas Landry Poincaré ...

***

Endnotes

1. Porch, Douglas *The Conquest of Morocco,* 143.
2. G.P., XXIV, 440f.
3. Schmitt, Bernadotte, E., *England and Germany, 1740-1914,* 313.
4. Wilhelm II, *My Memoirs,* 141.
5. Jarausch, Konrad H, *The Enigmatic Chancellor,* 120.
6. Massie, *Dreadnought,* 722.

7. Isvolsky to Sasonov, May 11, 1911.
8. G.P. XXIV, 101-108.
9. Gooch, *Studies in Diplomacy and Statecraft*, 145.
10. Schmitt, Bernadotte, E., *England and Germany, 1740-1914*, 315.
11. Gooch, *Studies in Diplomacy and Statecraft*, 145.
12. HCD, XXXI, cols 2615,6.
13. G.P., XXIV, 167; Grey, I, 214.
14. G.P., XXIV, 155 ff.
15. Stieve, *Isvolsky and the World War*, 30.
16. McCullough, Edward, *How the First World War Began*, 145.
17. George, Lloyd, *War Memoirs*, 26.
18. Nicolson, Harold, *Lord Carnock*, 347.
19. Callwell, Major General, *Field Marshal Sir Henry Wilson*, 97, 8.
20. Schmitt, Bernadotte, *England and Germany*, 331.
21. Grey, I, 217.
22. George, Lloyd, *War Memoirs*, 25.
23. McCullough, Edward, *How the First World War Began*, 150.
24. P. Cambon to de Selves [early in Oct.]; L.N., I, 149 f.

Chapter Six

The Triple Entente Prepares for War

Repeated suggestions by the German Ambassador Metternich in London, to the effect that Germany and England should come to an agreement with regard to naval policy, led in early 1912 to the Haldane Mission. According to Grey, Haldane was *"to find out whether Germany's recent overture was serious or not. He was also to attempt to gather information about the Bagdad Railway. But there is no question of entering upon negotiations. We desire only to learn the intentions of the German Government and to inquire about its plans for a naval program."*[1] Clearly, these instructions limited Haldane to little more than a messenger boy and despite Lord Haldane's cordial reception in Berlin on February 7, 1912, *"This attitude on Sir Edward Grey's part in itself foredoomed the Haldane Mission to failure."*[2]

Far more ominously, in that same year – 1912 – French nationalism was reborn when Poincaré took both the Premiership and Foreign Affairs portfolios. Diminutive and intense, he was born in Lorraine in 1860 within sight of the new border established by victorious Prussian troops in 1870. One biographer wrote of him: *"The scar of mutilated Lorraine was too near at hand ever to be forgotten by Raymond Poincaré."*[3] Another wrote: *"For his enemies, in France and abroad, the amputation of much of his homeland ingrained in him a rabid anti-Germanism, a ceaseless longing for 'revanche', an intemperate desire to restore the 'lost provinces' to France by any means, even war."*[4] In Verdun, Poincaré addressed a national teacher's congress in August, 1911, and told them: *"Two steps away from a grievous frontier, in a province which is the bulwark of France, how could one find a teacher who would listen to the enervating counsel of the internationalists or who would yield to the insidious suggestions of a gaping pacifism?"*[5] Writing two years after the War for the magazine *Revue d l'Université de Paris* (October, 1920), Poincaré asserted:

> In my years at school, my thought, bowed before the spectre of defeat, dwelt ceaselessly upon the frontier which the Treaty of Frankfurt had imposed upon us, and when I descended from my metaphysical clouds I could discover no other reason why my generation should go on living except for the hope of recovering our lost provinces![6]

When, as a result of the 2nd Moroccan Crisis in 1911, the Caillaux Cabinet fell in January 1912, Poincaré was swept into office on a wave of national and patriotic feeling. That same month, he told a journalist:

> I have one firm conviction ... that every time we have desired to show ourselves conciliatory toward Germany she has abused our goodwill; and on the other hand every time that we have shown ourselves firm toward her, she has given way. Germany does not understand the language of right and wrong; she only understands strenuous measures.[7]

Leaving no doubt as to the new direction in which he was taking his country, he warned the Chamber that *"profoundly pacific though our country may be, it is not master of every eventuality, and it intends to remain equal to all its duties. The army and the navy will be the object of our attentive solicitude ... "*[8]

In his new capacity as Premier, he suited action to words by traveling to Russia and signing the Franco-Russian Naval Convention of July 16, 1912, and confided to Russian Foreign Minister, Sasonov, that:

> ... although there does not exist between France and England any written treaty, the Army and Navy Staffs of the two countries have nevertheless been in close contact. This constant exchange of views has resulted in the conclusion between the French and English Governments of a verbal agreement, by virtue of which England had declared herself ready to aid France with her military and naval forces in case of an attack by Germany.[9]

Poincaré then urged Sasonov to take advantage of his upcoming visit to England to discuss the possibility of an Anglo-Russian naval agreement which would complete the naval cooperation of the three Triple Entente Powers. Sasonov duly followed Poincaré's suggestion. After his September, 1912 visit to Balmoral he sent this revealing report to his sovereign:

> As a favorable opportunity occurred I felt it useful, in one of my conversations with Grey, to seek information as to what we might expect from Great Britain in the event of a conflict with Germany. What the director of British foreign policy said to me as to this, and King George himself later, I think is very significant. Your Majesty is aware that during M. Poincaré's visit to St. Petersburg last summer he expressed to me a wish that I would clear up the question of the extent to which we might count on the co-operation of the British fleet in the event of such a war.
>
> I informed Grey confidentially of the main points of our naval convention with France, and remarked that under the treaty con-

> cluded, the French fleet would endeavor to safeguard our interests in the southern theatre of war by preventing the Austrian fleet from penetrating into the Black Sea; and I then asked whether Great Britain for her part could perform the same service for us in the north, by keeping the German squadrons away from our Baltic coasts. Grey declared unhesitatingly that should the anticipated conditions arise Great Britain would make every effort to strike a crippling blow at German naval power. On the question of military operations he said that negotiations had already taken place between the competent authorities concerned, but in these discussions the conclusion had been reached that while the British fleet could easily penetrate into the Baltic, its stay there would be very risky. Assuming Germany to succeed in laying hands on Denmark and closing the exit from the Baltic, the British fleet would be caught in a mousetrap. Accordingly Great Britain would have to confine her operations to the North Sea.
>
> On his own initiative Grey then gave me a confirmation of what I already knew through Poincaré – an agreement exists between France and England, under which in the event of war with Germany, Great Britain has accepted the obligation of bringing assistance to France not only on the sea but on land, by landing troops on the Continent. The King [George V] touched on the same question in one of his conversations with me, and expressed himself even more strongly than his Minister. When I mentioned, letting him see my agitation, that Germany is trying to place her naval forces on a par with Britain's, His Majesty cried out that any conflict would have disastrous results not only for the German navy but for Germany's overseas trade, for he said, 'We shall sink every single German merchant ship we shall get hold of.' These words appeared to me to give expression not only to His Majesty's personal feelings but also to the public feeling predominant in Great Britain in regard to Germany.[10]

Poincaré's innate skills, mainly his eloquence and gift for Churchillian oratory, enabled him to easily vanquish his opponents in the Chamber of Deputies and to dominate his colleagues in the Cabinet. In his world vision and the capacity and determination to impose it, he had no equal since Bismarck. His controversial replacement of the pacific-minded Georges Louis by the Germanophobe Théophile Delcassé as Ambassador to Russia raised eyebrows and outright alarm throughout Europe. His biographer notes:

> Poincaré knew enough about politics to realize what the nomination of Delcassé, coincident with his own inauguration [as President], would mean in the eyes of Frenchmen. He must have foreseen also the agitation and anger in Berlin and Vienna, the "lively satisfaction" in Russia and Serbia. To take such a resounding step on the morrow of his inauguration was to draw European attention to the French Presidency.[11]

German overtures to France, including a generous offer of far-reaching autonomy for Alsace-Lorraine were harshly rejected by Poincaré. He complained that the German Government

> ...seems to be pursuing with tireless obstinacy a *rapprochement* which only a complete break with the past would allow ... We would fall out with England and with Russia, and we would lose all the benefits of a policy that France has been following for many years. We would obtain for Alsace only illusory satisfactions and we would find ourselves the following day isolated, diminished, and disqualified.[12]

S.B. Fay provides this description of Poincaré's political activities:

> Such was the man who mainly directed and controlled French foreign policy from 1912 to 1914. In his memoirs he frequently denies that he pursued a personal policy as Minister of Foreign Affairs or exceeded his constitutional position after he became President of the Republic in February, 1913, by imposing his wishes on the Ministers of Foreign Affairs who succeeded him. But with his ability, energy, and strong personality, it was inevitable that he should be the guiding spirit. In spite of his denials, we believe that he exercised a strong influence in the direction of an aggressive and dangerous policy, which was not a reflection of the wishes of the great majority of the truly peace-loving French people from 1912 to 1914, and which they would not have approved, had they been fully aware of it and the catastrophe to which it was leading.[13]

In a confidential report to Sasonov on February 25, 1913, the Russian Ambassador in London, Count Benckendorff, gives this telling assessment of the French readiness for war:

> Recalling his [M. Cambon's] conversations with me, the words exchanged, and, adding to that the attitude of M. Poincare, the thought comes to me as a conviction that, of all the Powers, France is the only one which, not to say that it wishes war, would yet look upon it without great regret.... The situation as I regard it, seems to be that all the Powers are sincerely working to maintain peace. But of all of them, it is France who would accept war most philosophically. As has been said, France 'stands erect once more.' Rightly or wrongly, she has complete confidence in her army. The old ferment of animosity has again shown itself, and France would very well consider that the circumstances to-day are more favorable than they will ever be later.[14]

While France was getting on her hind legs under the stewardship of Poincaré, Russia had been doing the same under Isvolsky and, later, Sasonov. Still seething with resentment over his failed Buchlau Bargain with Aehrenthal in 1908, Isvolsky arranged for the Czar to visit the King of Italy, Victor Emmanuel, at the castle of Racconigi, south of Turin, in October, 1909. From this meeting emerged the very important and very secret Russo-Italian Agreement signed by Isvolsky and Italian Foreign Minister, Tittoni. After the usual pious boilerplate about preserving the *status quo* in the Balkans, it came to the point with the fourth and fifth clauses:

> 4. If Russia and Italy wish to make agreements concerning the European East with a Third Power, beyond those which exist at present, each will do it only with the participation of the other.
>
> 5. Italy and Russia engage themselves to regard with benevolence, the one Russia's interests in the question of the Straits, the other Italian interests in Tripoli and Cyrenaica.[15]

This, along with the facile Tittoni's earlier agreements with Austria as well as King Edward VII, set the stage for the Tripolitan war and Italy's eventual defection to the Triple Entente. In a new proposal to King Ferdinand of Bulgaria, Isvolsky promised Russian support in case of wars against Turkey and Austria and suggested a military convention in which Article V declared:

> The realization of the high ideals of the Slav peoples upon the Balkan Peninsula, so near to Russia's heart, is possible only after a favorable outcome of Russia's struggle with Germany and Austria-Hungary.[16]

While these negotiations did not result in the signing of a military convention, they were continued during the visit of King Ferdinand to St. Petersburg in 1910, and are indicative of the ultimately successful Russian efforts in the formation of the Balkan League which (it was hoped) would ultimately help the Triple Entente to triumph over the Triple Alliance. While in favor of these energetic efforts, Czar Nicholas worried about Russian preparedness. He warned Nekliudov, Russian Ambassador in Bulgaria, that

> Everything which might lead to war must be avoided. It would be out of the question for us to face a war for five or six years – in fact till 1917 ... Though if the most vital interests and the honour of Russia were at stake, we might, if it were absolutely necessary, accept a challenge in 1915, but not a moment sooner – in any circumstances or under any pretext whatsoever."[17] (On this comment from the Czar, one historian wrote: "Had this remark been the Kaiser's instead of the Tsar's all our war historians would have been citing it as a definitive proof of the guilt, and the sole guilt of Germany).[18]

Not so much worried about preparedness as about the secrecy of Russian dabbling in murky Balkan affairs, Poincaré was concerned that Russia might act imprudently and provoke Austria-Hungary with the serious prospect of France being dragged into a Balkan quarrel in which Germany was not involved. He warned Isvolsky that *"It is not enough that you inform us, it is necessary that we should concert beforehand."*[19] When in August, 1912, Poincaré learned the full text of the Serbo-Bulgarian Treaty, he exploded:

> I did not conceal from him [Sasonov] that I could not well explain to myself why these documents had not been communicated to France by Russia ... The [Serbo-Bulgarian] Treaty contains the germ not only of a war against Turkey, but a war against Austria. It establishes further the hegemony of Russia over the Slav kingdoms, because Russia is the arbiter in all questions. I observed to M. Sasonov that this convention did not correspond in any way to the definition of it which had been given to me; that it is, strictly speaking a convention for war, and that it not only reveals mental reservations on the part of the Serbs and Bulgarians, but that it is also to be feared lest their hopes appear to be encouraged by Russia, and that the eventual partition will prove a bait to their covetousness.[20]

The progressive decay of the Ottoman Empire, made acute by the 1908 Bosnian crisis, gave rise to the on-again off-again grand notion of a Balkan League which aimed at the destruction of Turkey and, hopefully, Austria-Hungary. Always hampered by the distrust between Serbia and Bulgaria, the idea of a Balkan League was galvanized by news of Italy's September, 1911, Tripolitan war on Turkey and, as a result, came finally to fruition under the leadership of the Ministers Neratov, Nekliudov, and Hartwig, under the patronage and control of Russia. The main obstacle to the formation of the Balkan League was that Bulgaria had little interest in seeing Serbia acquire Bosnia and Herzegovina or other Hapsburg territory, while Serbia was adamantly opposed to any Bulgarian acquisitions in Macedonia or Thrace. But when these heretofore insurmountable obstacles were finally resolved by the top secret Serbo-Bulgarian Treaty on March 13, 1912, the Balkan League was ready to proceed to "active measures." Russia was ready as well. On the previous day, March 12, the following order was issued to the Russian army:

> In accordance with his Majesty's decision, a telegraphic order for mobilization in the European military commands on account of political complications on the western frontiers is to be interpreted as an order also for the commencement of hostilities against Austria and Germany.[21]

And on March 30, 1912, Sasonov informed the Russian ambassadors in London and Paris of the Serbo-Bulgarian alliance and instructed them that "the conclusion of the alliance must be kept absolutely secret," and:

> You may add that as a special secret clause binds both parties to ascertain Russia's view before they proceed to active measures, we are of the opinion that this puts into our hands a means of bringing pressure on both parties, and that we have at the same time taken a protective step enabling us to oppose the extension of the influence of a great Power [Austria] in the Balkans.

On October 8, 1912, Montenegro declared war on Turkey; on the 17th and 18th Bulgaria, Serbia, and Greece followed. Still worried, Poincaré complained to Cambon that:

> It is certain that she [Russia] knew all about the [Serbo-Bulgarian] Treaty, and, far from protesting it she saw in this diplomatic document a means of assuring her hegemony in the Balkans. She perceives today that it is too late to wipe out the movement which she has called forth, and, as I said to MM. Sasonov and Isvolsky, she is trying to put on the brakes, but it is she who started the motor.[22]

But Poincaré needn't have worried. The Balkan League astonished themselves and the world with spectacular victories on every front. In little more than a month's campaigning, victorious Balkan armies stood at the very gates of Constantinople. French anxieties about the Balkans was very much reassured. Impressed and delighted by the unexpected military prowess of the Balkan League, Poincaré had a change of heart which Isvolsky was only too happy to report to Sasonov:

> Nothing succeeds like success. Under the influence of recent events one notices here a marked change in feeling in favor of the Balkan States and the Russian point of view.[23]

Just a week later (Nov. 7), Isvolsky reports:

> Whereas France up to the present has declared that local, so to speak, purely Balkan events could not induce her to take any active measures, the French Government now appears to admit that an acquisition of territory on the part of Austria in the Balkans would effect the general European equilibrium and consequently also the special interests of France ... Poincaré is perfectly conscious of the fact that France may thus become involved in a warlike action. For the present, of course, he submits this question merely for our consideration, but in a conversation with me, Paléologue plainly admitted that the proposed agreement might lead to some kind of active step.[24]

On November 17, 1912, Poincaré actually hints that Russia should start the ball rolling:

> "It is," said Poincaré, "for Russia to take the initiative in a matter in which she is the most closely interested party. France's task is to accord to Russia her most emphatic support. Were the French Government to take the initiative, it would be in danger of forestalling the intentions of its Ally ... Broadly", added M. Poincaré, "it all comes to this: if Russia goes into the war, France will do the same, as we know that in this matter Germany would stand at Austria's back.[25]

It is hardly surprising that this damning statement was severely criticized by Poincaré in his memoirs as being inaccurate, but the interpretation of Poincaré's legion of French critics is almost certainly correct and is strongly supported by Poincaré's subsequent dismissal of the pacific-minded Ambassador, Georges Louis, and his replacement by the very militant Delcassé and then Paléologue. Friedrich Stieve commented on this truly astonishing statement from Poincaré as follows:

> This is a document of the greatest importance in the history of the process that led to the world war. Germany has been blamed for allowing Austria a free hand after the Sarajevo assassination in her dealings with Serbia, a free hand, that is, in a war which Berlin hoped would be localized. More than eighteen months before this, the French Prime Minister, in saying that 'if Russia goes into the war, France will do the same,' allowed the Tsarist Empire a much wider measure of unquestioned plenary power, envisaging not a local but a general European conflict. From now onwards, St. Petersburg was assured of the intervention of the French army in any struggle for predominance in the Balkans. That is the immense and inestimable significance of Poincaré's statement quoted above.[26]

The general aims of Russia and the Balkan League are amply revealed in the statements of Pasitch, the Serbian Premier, and Sasonov. While dividing up the spoils of the 2nd Balkan War at the Bucharest Peace Conference, Pasitch told his Greek colleague:

> The first round is won; now we must prepare the second against Austria.[27]

A few days later, in a meeting at Marienbad, he informed the Serbian Chargé d'Affaires at Berlin that

> Already in the first Balkan War I could have let it come to a European war, in order to acquire Bosnia and Herzegovina: but as I feared that we should then be forced to make large concessions to Bulgaria in Macedonia, I wanted first of all to secure the possession of Macedonia for Serbia, and only then to proceed to the acquisition of Bosnia.[28]

Similarly, on May 6, 1913, Sasonov wrote to Hartwig in Belgrade:

> Serbia has passed only through the first stage of her historical career. To reach her goal she must endure another frightful struggle, in which her very existence will be staked ... Serbia's Promised Land lies in the territory of the present Austria-Hungary, and not there where she is now making efforts and where the Bulgarians stand in her way. Under these circumstances it is of vital interest to Serbia to maintain her alliance with Bulgaria on the one hand, and, on the other, to accomplish with steady and patient work the necessary degree of preparedness for the inevitable struggle of the future. Time works on the side of Serbia and for the ruin of her enemies, who already show evident signs of decay. Explain all this to the Serbians! I hear from all sides that if ever any voice can have full effect at Belgrade, it is yours.[29]

A week later the Serbian Ambassador in St. Petersburg reported to Belgrade:

> Sasonov told me again that we must work for the future, as we shall get a great deal of territory from Austria-Hungary. I replied that we shall gladly give Monastir (Bitolin) to the Bulgarians if we can get Bosnia and other Austrian provinces.[30]

Nicolai Hartwig was Russia's point man in Belgrade. Having lost his bid to succeed Lamsdorff as Foreign Minister to Isvolsky due to the latter's promotion by King Edward VII, he lost a second bid to become Isvolsky's successor to Sasonov, due to the latter's support by Stolypin. One of Sasonov's first official acts was to assign Hartwig to the vacant Russian Ministry in Belgrade. A fanatical Pan-Slav who had earned his spurs as Russian Ambassador to Persia, Hartwig's self-appointed task was to fashion the 'Greater-Serbia' movement into the spearhead of Russia's campaign to control the Balkans – a role embraced and cherished by Pasitch – and was soon recognized as the power behind the Serbian throne. The Serbian nationalist publication *Pijemont* (Piedmont) had already in September 28, 1911 described the Russian Minister as being the real ruler of Serbia,[31] while Franz Joseph said of him in 1914: *"Hartwig is master at Belgrade, and Pasitch does nothing without him."*[32]

After Bulgaria's treacherous attack upon Serbia at the end of June, 1913, thereby inaugurating the 2nd Balkan War, Austria grew seriously alarmed. But when Berchtold twice expressed growing Austrian anxiety to the German Ambassador, Germany responded with this warning:

> Austria-Hungary from the outset declared that in the present Balkan crisis she is striving after no territorial conquests. She has defined

> her interests as to the outcome of the Balkan War to the effect that Serbia must not reach the Adriatic, and that a viable Albania must be delivered ... the hostilities which have now broken out between Bulgaria and Serbia-Greece in no wise disturb as yet the rule of policy hitherto traced by Austria-Hungary ... How the present hostilities between Bulgaria and Serbia will end, no man knows. But this is certain, that whichever wins, both will be weakened and filled with hatred against one another. Austria-Hungary should not interfere in this result. Even if Serbia should win, it is still a long way to a Great Serbia ... Should Austria-Hungary now try by diplomatic means to chase Serbia out of her newly-won territories, she would have no luck, but would certainly rouse deadly hatred in Serbia. Should she try to do this by force of arms, it would mean a European war ... I can therefore only express the hope that the people in Vienna will not let themselves be upset by the nightmare of a Great Serbia, but will await further developments from the Serbo-Bulgarian theatre of war. Only insistently can I warn against the idea of wanting to gobble up Serbia, for that would simply weaken Austria.[33]

This effectively put an end to Austrian plans for military intervention against Serbia. *"This speedy and decisive warning from Germany on July 6 effectually deterred Berchtold and Conrad from rashly entering upon any reckless adventure which would have endangered the peace of Europe"*[34]; and marked the second time that German intervention had preserved the peace in Europe. But Austria was unhappy. During the course of the Conference of Ambassadors convened in London under the leadership of Sir Edward Grey at the request of Berchtold, Austria had only managed to block Serbia's access to the Adriatic by the establishment of Albania, but Serbia would be allowed to retain the conquests which had almost doubled her size to the lively dissatisfaction of Vienna.

Generally, in the course of two Special Conferences on December 31, 1913, and on January 13, 1914, Sasonov made very clear the thrust and purpose of Russian foreign policy, never forgetting to dress his proposed policies with the pieties of preserving the peace and the *status quo*. At yet another Special Conference on February 21, 1914, presided over by himself, and including military and naval experts and also M. Giers, the aggressive Russian Ambassador at Constantinople, Sasonov called attention to his report of December 5, approved by the Czar:

> ...that account must be taken of the possibility of the occurrence, perhaps even in the immediate future, of events which might radically alter the international situation of the Straits of Constantinople, and that it was therefore necessary to proceed without delay, in collaboration with the appropriate departments, to the preparation of a programme, elaborated in every direction, which should aim at

> the assurance of a solution in our favor of the historic question of the Straits. Sasonov expressed the firm conviction that should events result in the Straits slipping from Turkish control, Russia could not permit any other Power to establish itself on their shores. Russia might thus be compelled to seize possession of them, in order to secure in one shape or another, a state of things along the Bosphorus and the Dardanelles corresponding to her interests. The success of this operation would depend in large degree on the rapidity with which it was carried out. He therefore asked for a technical discussion of measures for expediting the mobilization and transportation of a sufficiently strong landing force; the strengthening of the Black Sea fleet, so as to be able, jointly with landing force, to occupy the Straits; and the construction of strategic railways in the Caucasus. Renewing the wish expressed above for the prolongation as far as possible of the status quo, it is also necessary to repeat that the question of the Straits can hardly be advanced a step except through European complications. These complications, to judge from present conditions, would find us in alliance with France, and in a possible, but not at all assured, alliance with England, or at least with her as benevolent neutral.[35]

It is hardly necessary to point out that the "*status quo*" and "European complications" are mutually exclusive, but this didn't stop Sasonov from pretending to pursue the first while actually pursuing the latter. Russian foreign policy as seen and executed by Sasonov is summarized by Fay as follows:

> From the minutes of this Special Conferences one sees clearly that Sasonov sided fully with the militarists in being ready to adopt measures of compulsion to oust General Liman from command of the Turkish Corps in Constantinople. While not desiring war with Germany and preferring a diplomatic victory, he was nevertheless quite ready to adopt measures which would probably lead to war with Germany, provided he was sure of the support of the Entente. He was ready to use a threat of force, and 'to translate the threat into action,' if the threat did not prove to be an effective bluff. This was his attitude in July, 1914, and it led to war. In January, 1914, it did not lead to war, because Germany made timely conciliatory concessions in the Limon von Sanders affair, and because M. Kokovtsev used his influence to prevent any over-hasty action on Russia's part, like the occupation of Trebizond or Bayazid. This Conference reveals sharply the contrast between Kokovtsev's moderate, conciliatory, and restraining influence on the one hand, and, on the other, the dangerous policy of military pressure urged by Sasonov and the military and naval officials.[36]

Strengthened by the Balkan baptism of fire, the Triple Entente stood strong and ready for "European complications." Dr. Stieve gives this summary:

> It is evident from all this how comprehensive were already the war preparations of the Entente Powers. A close network had been placed around the Central Powers. In the North Sea, British and French fleets were to act together. On top of this a British land army of 100,000 men was to join on in Belgium to the left wing of the French army, which had to carry out from there to Lorraine the speediest possible advance against Germany. In the Mediterranean the French fleet recently transferred thither aimed at holding the Austrian naval forces in check, and on the Russian frontier all conceivable measures were to be taken to expedite as far as possible the advance of the troops of the enormous Tsarist Empire if the emergency arose. These were, indeed, gigantic plans, covering all Europe, which, as we have just seen, were in important respects developed and promoted by Poincaré's initiative in Russia.[37]

Indeed, Edward Grey had prepared well:

> By the spring of 1914 the joint work of the French and British General Staffs was complete to the last billet of every battalion, even to the places where they were to drink their coffee. The number of French railroad cars to be allotted, the assignments of interpreters, the preparation of codes and ciphers, the forage of horses was settled or expected to be consummated by July. The fact that Wilson and his staff were in constant communication with the French had to be concealed. All the work on Plan W, as the movement of the expeditionary force was called by both Staffs, was done in utmost secrecy, confined to half a dozen officers, who did even the typing, filing, and clerical work. While the military prearranged the lines of battle, England's political leaders, pulling the blanket of "no commitment" over their heads, resolutely refrained from watching them.[38]

It is important to note that the massive and detailed preparations by the Triple Entente were conspicuously absent on the side of the Triple Alliance:

> After 1896, the contact between the two General Staffs [German and Austrian] was virtually reduced to the exchange of New Year greetings.[39]

And while personal relations between Moltke and Hötzendorf improved,

> There nevertheless remained an incredible lack of planning as to how the two allies would coordinate their wartime strategies.[40]

Similarly:

> The antagonism that developed between the German and the Austrian Chiefs of the General Staff was not reduced until 1908 when Moltke and his Austrian counterpart Franz Conrad von Hötzendorf began a correspondence that lasted until the outbreak of war. However, even Moltke never discussed with Conrad the important issue of establishing a unified allied military command, despite the fact that the next war would have to be an alliance war.[41]

Of course, in order to subvert British public opposition and get Tommy Atkins to the recruiter, England's coming holy war would need a noble, altruistic motive and the conscientious Sir Edward had taken care of this as well:

> Belgium's rigid purity confirmed what the British never tired of repeating to the French – that everything depended on the Germans violating Belgian neutrality first. "Never, no matter on what pretext," Lord Esher cautioned Major Huguet in 1911, "let the French commanders be led into being the first to cross the Belgian frontier!" If they did, England could never be on their side; if the Germans did, they would bring England in against them. M. Cambon, the French Ambassador in London, expressed the condition the other way around; only if Germany violated Belgium, was the burden of his dispatches, could France be sure of Britain's support.[42]

In the digital age of computers and internet, it is easy to forget that public opinion at the turn of the 20th century was formulated mainly by newspapers. It was the American publisher, William Randolph Hearst, who gave America her "splendid little war" with Spain, and it was mainly Lord Northcliffe who prepared the British public for a war against Germany. On May 24, 1907, The Belgian Minister in London, Count Lalaing, wrote to M. Davignon, the Belgian Foreign Minister, with this description of Lord Northcliffe's journalistic activities:

> A certain category of the Press, known here as the Yellow Press, is to a large extent responsible for the hostility which is observable between the two countries [England and Germany]. What, indeed, can be expected from a journalist like Mr. Harmsworth (Lord Northcliffe), proprietor of the *Daily Mail, Daily Mirror, Daily Graphic, Daily Express, Evening News,* and *Weekly Dispatch,* who, in an interview which he has granted to the Matin, says: 'Yes, we detest the Germans cordially. They make themselves odious to the whole of Europe. I will not allow my paper [*The Times*] to publish anything which might in any way hurt the feelings of the French, but I would not like to print anything which might be agreeable to the Germans.' Journalists of this stamp, publishers of cheap and widely read newspapers, are

> able to poison at pleasure the mind of an entire nation. It is evident that official circles in England are pursuing in silence a hostile policy which aims at the isolation Germany, and that King Edward has not disdained to place his personal influence in the service of this idea.[43]

While it is true that the German Press reciprocated in kind, the initiative for this sort of Yellow journalism almost always came from the British side. German feelings were illustrated by Herr von Jagow, the German Foreign Minister, who, in the course of a dinner on October 23, 1915, blurted out to Princess Blücher:

> But is there nobody who will shoot Lord Northcliffe? He is his own country's worst enemy as well as ours. And he is more answerable for all this bloodshed and carnage than any other single individual throughout the world.[44]

Despite the end of the Balkan Wars and improving Anglo-German relations, the dawn of 1914 did not augur well for the peace of Europe. The Grey-Cambon exchange of letters on November 22-23, 1912 in lieu of a formal commitment and approved by the British Cabinet, fixed the parameters of Anglo-French cooperation in case of a war with Germany no matter how the war arose. These letters allowed Grey to continue to cherish the illusion that he had his "hands free." Austria-Hungary was determined to tolerate no further nonsense from Serbia and ill-disposed to settle any future Balkan problems with another Conference of Ambassadors. Serbia was determined with Russian backing to continue nipping at Austria's racial Achilles heel. Russia herself was determined to not back down again as in 1909. The Balkan fuse was now primed and ready to ignite powder-keg Europe ...

***

Endnotes

1. Poincaré, *Au Service de la France*, I, 166, (Abridged English Trans.), Cited in Fay, I, 304.
2. Fay, *The Origins of the World War*, II, 304.
3. Wright, Gordon, *Raymond Poincaré and the French Presidency*, 18.
4. Keiger, J.F.V., *Raymond Poincaré*, 3.
5. *Le Temps*, August 8, 1911.
6. Dupin, *M. Poincaré et la Guerre de 1914*, 101, 2.
7. Lauzanne, Stéphane, *Great Men and Great Days*, 48.
8. *Chamber Debates*, January 6, 1912, 22-23.
9. Sasonov's Report to the Czar of August 17, 1912.
10. *Krasnyi Arkhiv*, III, 18.
11. Wright, Gordon, *Raymond Poincaré and the French Presidency*, 71.

12. Poincaré to J. Cambon, 27 March, 1912, MAE; Jules Cambon Papers, 16.
13. Fay, *The Origins of the World War*, II, 315.
14. *Un Livre Noir*, Vol. II, 303, 306.
15. Cf. G.P., XXVII, 403 ff., 425.
16. Proposed Russo-Bulgarian Military Convention of Dec. 1909.
17. Nekliudov, *Diplomatic Reminiscences Before and During the World War, 1911-1917*, 5.
18. Dickinson, Lowes, *The International Anarchy*, 303.
19. Poincaré to P. Cambon, 13 March, 1912, DDF, 3e serie, vol. II,.No. 193.
20. Note by Poincaré of his conversation with Sasonov in August, 1912.
21. Montgelas, Count Max, *The Case for the Central Powers*, 54.
22. Poincaré to P. Cambon, Oct. 15, 1912; *Affaires Balkaniques*, I, 112.
23. Isvolsky to Sasonov, Oct. 28, 1912, M.F.R., 292.
24. M.F.R., 296; L.N., I, 342.
25. Stieve, *Isvolsky and the World War*, 113.
26. Ibid., 114.
27. Bogitschevitch, *Kriegsursachen*, (Eng. Trans., 1919), 65.
28. Ibid, 65.
29. Deutsche Weisbuch, (Eng. trans., 1924), *Deutschland Schuldig?*, 99.
30. Bogitschevitch, *Causes of the War*, 100.
31. Dedijer, *The Road to Sarajevo*, 431.
32. Tschirschsky to Bethmann, July 2; K.D., 9, 11.
33. Bethmann to Szögyényi, and Zimmermann to Tschirschsky, July 6, 1913.
34. Fay, *The Origins of the World War*, II, 452.
35. Minutes of the Special Conference of Feb. 8/21, 1914; Pokrovski, *Drei Konferenzen*, 46 ff.
36. Fay, *The Origins of the World War*, II, 535-6.
37. Stieve, *Isvolsky and the World War*, 90.
38. Tuchman, Barbara, *The Guns of August*, 74.
39. Herwig, Holger, From Tirpitz Plan to Schlieffen Plan, *Journal of Strategic Studies*, 58.
40. Ibid., 56.
41. Mombauer, Annike, *Moltke and the Origins of the First World War*, 82.
42. Tuchman, Barbara, *The Guns of August*, 74.
43. *Belgian Diplomatic Documents*, No. 30.
44. Blücher, Princess, *English Wife in Berlin*, 81.

Chapter Seven

Lord Grey and The World War

Edward Grey, 1st Viscount Grey of Fallodon, was born on April 25, 1862, at the family estate at Northumberland near the Scottish border within sight of the North Sea. Edward was the eldest of the seven children of Colonel George Henry Grey and Harriet Jane Pearson. He was twelve when his father, a retired Colonel who fought in the Crimean war and the Indian Mutiny and then served for fifteen years as one of the Prince of Wales' [later Edward VII] rotating equerries, died unexpectedly of pneumonia at Sandringham. His grandfather, Sir George Grey, promptly retired from an active and distinguished political career and devoted himself to raising his seven grandchildren.

An undistinguished education at Winchester and Balliol College (a constituent college of Oxford University) proved Grey to be an exceptional tennis player but little else. The master at Balliol noted that *"Sir Edward Grey, having been repeatedly admonished for idleness, and having shown himself entirely ignorant of the work set him during the vacation, was sent down."*[1] Grey was elected in November, 1885, as the youngest member of the House of Commons, and in that same year he married Dorothy Widdrington. The marriage was remarkable in that shortly after the honeymoon, the newly-minted Mrs. Grey informed her husband that she had an aversion to both the physical side of marriage and children. Even more remarkable was Edward Grey's response that in that case, the two of them could live together as brother and sister. Grey apparently felt that their common passion for fishing, hiking, and birdwatching was a sufficient basis for marriage. But Grey was young, good looking, athletic, and independently wealthy. Could he really be happy with a life of voluntary celibacy? The answer seems to be 'no' as there were rumors of more than one love child and secret romantic dalliances, but Grey was nothing if not discrete and the rumors remain little more than idle gossip.

Like King Edward VII, Grey's Germanophobia started early on. In his memoirs he wrote:

> I remember being asked by my father, at the outbreak of the Franco-Prussian War in 1870, on which side I was. My age was then about 8¼ years and I had little feeling in the matter; but, moved probably by what I had heard of Waterloo ... I replied that I was on the side of the Germans. My father had been in the Rifle Brigade and had fought in alliance with the French in the Crimea. My answer did not

> please him; he reproved me for my preference, and I relapsed into the indifference from which, but for his question, I should never have emerged.
>
> It must have been a few months later that I was called out on to the balcony at Fallodon on a winter evening to see a display of Aurora Borealis. A great part of the sky was not only irradiated with light, but suffused with pink. The recollection of the apparition has always been very positive to me.... It may be, therefore, that imagination has enhanced the glory and beauty of it, but it remains in memory as a wonderful vision. I remember my grandfather saying, as we stood on the balcony, that if Paris had not been so distant we might have thought that the Prussians were burning it and that this was causing the illumination of the sky."[2]

Grey duly blamed Prussia for the war as well as for the earlier 1864 and 1866 wars with Denmark and Austria respectively and retained these opinions throughout his tenure as Foreign Secretary. It was the prolonged turf war between Commons and Lords and the baffling Irish Question that first drew Grey to politics. After serving as Under Secretary of State from August, 1892, until June, 1895, Grey was elected to the House of Commons where he quickly caught the eye of Liberal leaders such as Morley and Rosebery. He wrote: *"Of the first six years spent in the House of Commons little need be said."*[3]

But while this may be true, his evolving political predilections brought him into alignment with a group of "radical" thinkers in the Liberal party who would in due time become known as the "Liberal Imperialists." The central core of this group was Edward Grey, Richard Haldane, and Henry Asquith. This was the imperialist triumvirate – Grey as Foreign Secretary, Haldane as War Minister, and Asquith as Prime Minister – along with a small cadre of lesser lights (led by the brilliant but somewhat reluctant political warrior, Lord Rosebery) who carried out and executed King Edward's radical diplomacy, mainly at the Seine and the Neva, thereby creating the Triple Entente which took the field against the Central Powers in 1914.

After some complex haggling with Campbell-Bannerman to banish him to the House of Lords, Edward Grey was selected to succeed Lord Lansdowne as Foreign Secretary: *"On the afternoon of [a very foggy] Monday, December 11, 1905, the Liberal Ministers received the seals of office from the King"*[4] and immediately inherited the 1st Moroccan Crisis, which was about to enter its Algeciras phase.

The reclusive Sir Edward's eleven-year reign as Foreign Secretary was most prominently marked by a policy of secrecy and hostility to Germany. The lethal policy was aptly summed up by Lord Loreburn, who wrote:

> On the formation of the Liberal Government on 12th December 1905, three Ministers, Mr. Asquith, Mr. Haldane, and Sir Edward

> Grey, laid the foundation for a different policy, namely, a policy of British intervention if Germany should make an unprovoked attack on France. They did this within a month, probably within a few days of taking office, by means of communications with the French Ambassador and of military and naval conversations between the General Staffs of the two countries, who worked out plans for joint action in war if Great Britain should intervene. They did it behind the back of nearly all their Cabinet colleagues, and, what really matters, without Parliament being in any way made aware that a policy of active intervention between France and Germany was being contemplated.[5]

It is difficult if not impossible to underestimate the importance of this policy as it created the conditions which brought about the July Crisis of 1914 and allowed it to devolve into a European war. It did not take long for Grey's Germanophobia to assert itself in his very first experience with Germany as Foreign Minister. He recalled the experience in his memoirs as follows:

> British firms were applying for railway concessions in Asia Minor, and the British Ambassador supporting them. German firms were also applying, and the German Ambassador supporting them. Suddenly there came a sort of ultimatum from Berlin, requiring us to cease competition for railway concessions in Turkey for which Germans were applying, and stating that, unless we did so, the German Consul at Cairo would withdraw support from the British Administration in Egypt. Instructions in this sense were actually sent without delay to the German Representative at Cairo, and the German ultimatum was followed – almost accompanied – by a despairing telegram from Lord Cromer pointing out that it would be impossible to carry on his work in Egypt without German support in the face of French and German opposition.
>
> It was the abrupt and rough peremptoriness of the German action that gave me an unpleasant impression.... This was the German method. It cannot be said that in substance the contention was absolutely unreasonable; the Germans were, at any rate, entitled to ask that, in return for German support in Egypt, we should not oppose some specified German interests elsewhere. Had this been suggested we could not fairly have refused to consider an arrangement, if one had been proposed, that on the face of it was reasonable. But the method adopted by Germany in this instance was not that of a friend. There was no choice for us but to give way, unless we were ready to face the opening of the whole Egyptian question without a single Great Power on our side. Lord Rosebery withdrew competition for the railway concession in Turkey; things in Egypt resumed their normal course, and the incident was over. But it left a sense of discomfort and bad taste behind.[6]

The incident clearly made a deep impression on Grey, but not surprisingly, the German version was a bit different. Various British diplomats have acknowledged the value and importance of German support for English policy in Egypt. There was, for instance, Sir William Harcourt, who told Count Herbert Bismarck that the German Chancellor had:

> ...rendered such services to the British Government in the policy followed towards it in the past two years that it could never be grateful enough for them.[7]

A few weeks later, Mr. Chamberlain, President of the Board of Trade, put the matter even more strongly:

> Prince Bismarck has rendered such great services to us that I can only hope he will rest assured that there is no country to which we so gladly show favours as Germany. Without Germany's favourable attitude we should have got into great difficulties.[8]

But the conspicuous lack of any British reciprocity caused Herbert Bismarck to complain on March 26, 1887 to the German Ambassador, Count Hatzfeldt, in London:

> If Great Britain is unwilling even to show the measure of complaisance that we ask in fields of so little importance to British power as Zanzibar and Samoa, we shall adjust our attitude accordingly and oppose her where her most vital interests are at stake. In recent years we have found ourselves every few months in the position of having to use a sharp tone in discussing colonial matters with England, and it is nothing short of exasperating to have this occur again and again and to find that the readiness of the British Government to show consideration to us only lasts in the case of the Government up to its first friendly communication from here and in the case of its agents is never evidenced at all.[9]

And when England continued to offer no concessions in Asia Minor despite repeated hints from Berlin, Baron Marschall, the Foreign Secretary, sent a telegram to the Imperial Consul-General in Cairo:

> Should the declaration which you were requested to make in regard to the increase of the Egyptian troops not yet have been made by you in official and binding form, will you please postpone it, as the offensive and inimical attitude of the British Embassy in Constantinople, which defends even French interests against German in all questions of railway construction in Asia Minor, is incompatible

> with the accommodating spirit which has been shown for years past on the German side in regard to British interests, even sometimes when, as in the Eastern Asiatic treaty, they were in competition with German interests. You may also explain to Lord Cromer the reasons for our changed attitude in the future.[10]

This is the "ultimatum" to which Grey refers in his memoirs and is typical of his biased recollections. Grey is upset by the German "ultimatum" but makes no attempt to show what British actions had led to it, even while admitting frankly that Germany was "entitled to ask" for reciprocity from London and that her request was "reasonable" but not that the request was entirely ignored.

Similarly, in describing the Jamison Raid and the Kaiser's Krüger telegram, Grey wrote:

> In the first months of Lord Salisbury's Government, in which Mr. Chamberlain took the Colonial Office, there occurred the Jamison Raid upon the Transvaal. When all the fact were known many people at home felt indignant that an act of gross aggression should have been perpetrated by any British persons or organized on British territory; they were disgusted by the hollow pretext, put forward by those who defended it as necessary to protect women and children in Johannesburg; to everybody the collapse of the raid showed it was an act of folly. We could not, therefore, be surprised that the raid was condemned by foreign opinion, nor could we justly resent that condemnation. But why should the German Emperor make it his business, and his alone, to appear as the friend and even champion of President Krüger? The German Emperor's telegram to President Krüger did undoubtedly cause both surprise and resentment in Britain. It passed, however without incident, for the raid had put Britain clearly in the wrong and President Krüger in the right, and our business was to clear up the mess as best we could ...[11]

In other words, Britain, in Grey's words, stood *"condemned by foreign opinion"* and the British people themselves *"were disgusted"* and Britain *"was clearly in the wrong and President Krüger in the right,"* but despite all of this, it was the Kaiser's telegram congratulating President Krüger on resisting a surprise attack by a heavily armed regiment of volunteers which almost succeeded, that arouses Sir Edward's righteous indignation. Grey admitted that

> The war was regarded as aggression upon a small State and sympathy with the Boers and dislike of Britain found free and even vehement expression. In Germany this feeling was as pronounced as in other countries – if anything, it was even stronger. This was particularly resented in Britain, and I have heard a German complain that we

> should have resented so strongly in the case of Germany, a manifestation of feeling that was generally shared and expressed in other countries.[12]

Nevertheless, it may be noted that after gold was discovered in the Transvaal, Sir Edward had no trouble in supporting a full scale British assault upon the Boer republics on the same pretext used by Jamison. The bloody war that followed caused the independent and sovereign Transvaal and the Orange Free State to be swallowed whole by the Empire of John Bull and disappear forever from the map of Africa.

Again, in explaining the First Moroccan Crisis, Grey is true to form:

> The German Emperor made a visit that was like a demonstration at Tangier, and in 1905 the German Government forced the French, by what was practically a challenge, to dismiss M. Delcassé (their Minister for Foreign Affairs) who had made the Franco-British Agreement and to agree to an international conference about Morocco.... The French were being humiliated because of an Agreement that we had made with them.[13]

This recollection is so false it is hard to know where to begin. Sir Edward makes no mention of Delcasse's adamant refusal to consult with Germany despite the 1880 Madrid Agreement (to which England was a signatory) which obligated France to do so. Neither does Sir Edward mention the many warnings to Delcassé by his own colleagues, including Cambon, the French Ambassador in London, that his irresponsible policy could lead to war with Germany. Finally, Sir Edward fails to mention the most important fact; namely, that Delcassé persisted in his reckless policy almost to the point of war because he had the steadfast backing and encouragement of King Edward VII. (see Chapter 2)

Grey writes that

> In June 1895 the Government of Lord Rosebery was defeated in a division on the War Office vote in the House of Commons and resigned. I was set free, and left office with the expectation and the intention of never returning to it. Ten years and a half were now to pass before I entered the Foreign Office again.

Grey entered the Foreign Office again in December, 1905, and from that time to the outbreak of war in 1914, France never ceased to demand of Grey, what, exactly, was England prepared to *do* in case of a Franco-German war. Grey's usual response was to hide behind the strictly technical circumstance that there was nothing in writing which might be construed as legally binding and that therefore there was no commitment except as might in the future be made by the Cabinet. But Grey was always quick to add that in any conflict with Germany arising out of the Entente Cordiale, British opinion would be on the side of France. After receiving a letter from Colonel Repington [the Military Correspondent of *The Times*] about a conversation with Major Huguet [the French Military Attaché in London] about Anglo-French cooperation inaugurated by Lansdowne, Grey responded: *"I am interested to hear of your conversation with the French Military Attaché. I can only say that I have not receded from anything Lord Lansdowne said to the French, and I have no hesitation in confirming it."*[14] Thus began the extensive, detailed military planning between the British and French General Staffs:

> As the Franco-Russian Entente of 1891 was followed by a secret Military Convention, so the Anglo-French Entente of 1904 was soon supplemented by momentous but very secret naval and military arrangements, or, as Sir Edward Grey euphemistically calls them, "conversations." These lacked, at first, the rigid and binding character of the Franco-Russian Alliance, but they gradually came to be, in fact if not in form, a most vital link in the system of secret alliances. In spite of the meticulous nicety with which Sir Edward Grey was careful to state that "England's hands were free," and that "it would be left for Parliament to decide," he allowed the French to hope confidently that, in case Germany caused a European war, England would take the field on the side of the French. He permitted the English and French Naval and Military Staffs to elaborate technical arrangements for joint war action, which became the basis of the strategic plans of both countries. These came to involve mutual obligations which were virtually as entangling as a formal alliance. It is always dangerous to allow the military authorities of two countries to develop inter-dependent strategic plans. They come to make arrangements which, by their very nature, necessarily involve obligations which are virtually binding upon the political authorities. Here is where Sir Edward Grey's great responsibility and mistake began.[15] It was not until 1912 that circumstances caused the military "conversations" to be revealed to the whole Cabinet, and not until Grey's speech on August 3, 1914, that Parliament and the British public had any inkling of them. At any rate, he concealed the matter from the majority of his colleagues in a way which seems hardly to accord with the seeming honesty and frankness of his memoirs.[16]

But Grey's secrecy was no "mistake." Grey knew perfectly well that if his policy had become known (to other than Asquith, Haldane, and the King), he would have been ordered at once to cease and desist. His remorse that: *"I have always regretted that the military conversations were not brought before the Cabinet at once. This would have avoided unnecessary suspicion,"*[17] was another self-serving lie and a foretaste of his double role in the 1914 July Crisis. His response to anxious German inquiries was more lies. Fay explains:

> In view of Haldane's own statement of how he saw Colonel Huguet [the French Military Attaché in London], personally authorize the direct negotiations between the French and British Staffs represented by Huguet and Grierson, and at once organized the British Army for cooperation with the French, a sinister light is thrown on the obliquity of the British secret preparations and the denials of their existence, by a statement which Lord Haldane made himself to the German Ambassador in London. According to Metternich's report of this statement:[18]
>
> Mr. Haldane replied most definitely that a military conversation between France and England did not exist, and had not existed, and also that no preparations had been made for the conclusion of one. Whether non-committal conversations between English and French military persons had taken place or not, he did not know. [Kaiser: "Impudence! He, the Minister of a Parliamentary country, not supposed to know that! He lies!"] At any rate, no English officer has been authorized by the English Government [Kaiser: "Indeed! He did it himself!"] to prepare military arrangements with a French military person for the eventuality of war. It was possible that a General Staff Officer of one country might have expressed himself to the General Staff Officer of another country as to war-like eventualities. He, the Minister of War, however, knew nothing of this. [Kaiser: "Magnificent lies!"][19]

The Kaiser's marginal comments were, if anything, understated. In fact, Anglo-French military planning was detailed and comprehensive to the point of British and French Staff Officers thoroughly reconnoitering the ground upon which their armies were to fight in Belgium and in France. Sir Henry Wilson was known to have an entire wall of his London office covered by a gigantic map of Belgium, indicating the most likely travel routes which future armies might follow, and spent his holidays personally inspecting these routes on his bicycle. *"He [Wilson] was deeply in the secrets of the French General Staff. For years he had been laboring with one object, that, if war came, we should immediately act on the side of France. He was sure that war would come sooner or later."*[20]

Sir Edward did not forget about Belgium which would have the important task of raising Britain's *casus foederus.* Fay tells us:

> The Anglo-Belgian military conversations began on Jan. 18, 1906, upon instructions from General Grierson, between the English Military Attaché, Col. Bernardiston, and the Belgian Chief of Staff, Gen-

> eral Ducarne. They had the express sanction of the Foreign Ministers of both countries, as well as of the military authorities. They quickly led to an agreement for the landing of 100,000 British troops on the continent for the defense of Belgium (cf. B.D., III 186-203; and Carl Hosse, Die Englisch-Belgischen Aufmarschpläne gegen Deutschland vor dem Weltkrieg, Vienna, 1930). Hosse prints for the first time interesting details of the technical railway schedules worked out for the British; he uses photographs of Belgian documents which were taken by the Germans during the war, (but restored after the Treaty of Versailles). General Wilson, who succeeded General Grierson as Chief of Military Operations in August, 1910, arranged with Belgium and France for the rapid transport of 160,000 British, who were to take a position on the French left wing. In 1912 there were some doubts for a while about Belgium's readiness to cooperate with the French and British (cf. D.D.F., 3e Serie, I, No. 522), and the British Foreign Office, in spite of its obligation to observe Belgian neutrality, appears to have considered the question of marching British troops into the little country, without invitation and even against Belgium's consent "in order to meet the approach of German troops on the other side."[21] In 1913 Belgium increased her army and was again ready to enter into close military relations with the French and British at the outbreak of the war.[22]

So much for Belgian "neutrality." Under the secret auspices of Grey's Foreign Office, the military requirements for hitching the Franco-Russian horse to the British cart soon reached across the pond to Russia.

> Not only the French, but the Russians also, soon came to count upon Haldane's Expeditionary Force as a certain and essential part of their strategic plans in case of a war against Germany.... In August, 1911, at Krasnoe-Selo, General Dubail was able to assure his Russian colleagues, as a matter of course, "that the French army would concentrate as quickly as the German army, and that from the twelfth day it would be in a position to take the offensive against Germany[23] with the aid of the English army on its left wing,"[24] that is, on the Belgian frontier.

Both King and Secretary were ever ready to squelch any notion of a *rapprochement* with Germany. Kaiser Wilhelm gives this example, which occurred during the visit of Edward VII to Kiel, just before the commencement of the Algeciras Conference:

> It took place on board the royal English yacht after a breakfast to which I and the Chancellor [Bülow] were invited. Both gentlemen sat for a long time alone over their cigars. Afterward Bülow reported

> to me what had transpired at the interview. In discussing the possible conclusion of an alliance between Germany and England, the King, he told me, had stated that such a thing was not at all necessary in the case of our two countries, since there was no real cause for enmity or strife between them. This refusal to make an alliance was a plain sign of the English "policy of encirclement," which soon made itself felt clearly and disagreeably at the Algeciras Conference. The pro-French and anti-German attitude of England, which there came out into the open, was due to special orders from King Edward VII, who had sent Sir D. Mackenzie Wallace to Algeciras as his "supervising representative," equipped with personal instructions. From hints given by the latter to his friends it turned out that it was the King's wish to oppose Germany strongly and support France at every opportunity. When it was pointed out to him that it might be possible, after all, to take up later with Germany this or that question and perhaps come to an understanding, he replied that, first of all came the Anglo-Russian agreement; that, once that was assured, an "arrangement" might be made with Germany also. The English "arrangement" consisted of the encirclement of Germany.[25]

Grey was always in full agreement with the King. Grey was a Liberal while the King was a Conservative but when it came to Germany, the two men were birds of a feather. Keith Robbins, a later biographer, quotes a private letter from Grey to his good friend and Liberal MP, the poet Henry Newbolt:

> I have come to think that Germany is our worst enemy and greatest danger. As a matter of fact the German Government have behaved very badly to us in China. I believe the policy of Germany to be that of using us without helping us: keeping us isolated that she may have us to fall back on. Close relations with Germany mean for us worse relations with the rest of the world especially with the US, France and Russia.[26]

As early as August of 1905, Grey declared to the Liberal MP Ronald Munro-Ferguson:

> If any Government drags us back into the German net, I will oppose it openly at all costs.

Some months later, he underscored this commitment:

> I am afraid the impression has been spread with some success by those interested in spreading it, that a Liberal Government would

> unsettle the understanding with France in order to make up to Germany. I want to do what I can to combat this.[27]

And he informed a "City" audience that

> Nothing we do in our relations with Germany is in any way to impair our existing good relations with France.[28]

Loyalty to the Entente was the Grey mantra endlessly repeated:

> Ultimately, Grey had steered his colleagues and the nation to war, in line with his own endlessly repeated conviction that fidelity to the Entente was indispensable. For instance, way back in 1907, Grey had expressed this, almost as a vow, to his astonished ambassador Frank Lascelles in Berlin: "no wavering by a hair's breadth from our loyalty to the Entente."[29]

Lascelles, a strong believer in reconciliation with Germany, who had previously complained about the "anti-German current" dominating at the Foreign Office, quoted the line in his reply to Grey, promising he had told the Germans that Britain could not *"leave France in the lurch"* and *"that the Entente is the key-stone of our policy and that we do not intend to abandon it."*[30]

One historian properly observed that

> It was very clear that "Grey's Germanophobia and his zeal for the Entente with France were from the outset at odds with the views of the majority of the Liberal Cabinet. This division ought to have caused trouble much sooner than it did."[31]

Grey is particularly culpable because he knew well, as the result of his close dealings with Cambon, Delcassé, Clemenceau, and other French leaders, that no reconciliation between France and Germany was possible unless Alsace and Lorraine were restored to France; and this of course was never going to happen without war.

It is true that Prime Minister Asquith, normally content to follow in Grey's wake, did raise a mild objection. Grey records it and his reply as follows:

> My dear Grey, – Conversations such as that between Gen. Joffre and Col. Fairholme seem to me rather dangerous; especially the part which refers to possible British assistance. The French ought not to be encouraged, in present circumstances, to make their plans on any assumptions of this kind. Yours always,
>
> H. H. A.

To this I replied:

> My Dear Asquith,– It would create consternation if we forbade our military experts to converse with the French. No doubt these conversations and our speeches have given an expectation of support. I do not see how that can be helped.[32]
>
> Yours sincerely
>
> E. Grey

But Grey's lethal policy was approved by King Edward and Prime Minister Asquith and therefore caused no further trouble until August 3, 1914, when he was finally obliged to partially reveal it to the House. As already noted, Grey was intimately acquainted with any number of prominent French statesmen and thus knew well that any Franco-German *rapprochement* could never happen without the return of Alsace-Lorraine to France.

> All of this makes German fears of encirclement seem less like paranoia than realism. When Bülow denounced in the Reichstag the efforts to "encircle Germany, to build a circle of powers around Germany in order to isolate and render it impotent," he was not – as British statesmen subsequently insisted in their memoirs – fantasizing.[33] ... And what, after all, had prompted the so-called 'war council' summoned by the Kaiser in December 1912? A communication from Haldane via the German Ambassador to the effect that "Britain could not allow Germany to become the leading power on the continent and it to be united under German leadership." The Kaiser's inference "that Britain would fight on the side of Germany's enemies," was not wrong. As Bethmann said, this "merely reflected what we have known [for some time].[34]

Bethmann further noted in his memoirs:

> ... to deny that King Edward aspired to and attained our encirclement is mere playing with words. The fact of the matter was that the communications between the two Cabinets were confined essentially to the dispatch of such formal business as was required by the mutual relations of two States not at war with one another. Further, that Germany found itself opposed by a combine of England, Russia and France in all controversial questions of World policy. Finally, that this combine not only raised every obstacle to the realisation of German ambitions, but also laboured systematically and successfully to seduce Italy from the Triple Alliance. You may call that "encirclement," "balance of power," or what you will; but the object aimed at and eventually attained was no other than the welding of a serried and supreme combination of States for obstructing Germany, by diplomatic means at least, in the free development of its growing powers.[35]

But there was a problem. Despite the best efforts of Edward Grey to prevent it, the many advocates of improved relations with Germany persisted in trying to promote an Anglo-German *rapprochement.* Fearing that such efforts might prove successful and prevent a European war, it was decided that something had to be done. The British diplomatist/publisher/politician Edmund Dene Morel described it:

> The anxiety caused by these manifestations of improved relations between Britain and Germany at the very moment when the conspirators in Petrograd, Belgrade, and elsewhere were reckoning that the plum was almost ripe enough for plucking, is evident in the Russian dispatches we now possess. Thus the Russian Ambassador in Berlin, reporting to Sasonov, February 13, 1914, remarks that [Jules] Cambon "is very much worried by these constant rumors of an improvement in Anglo-German relations, since he agrees that there is a possibility of *rapprochement* between these two countries in the future." Cambon's Russian colleague did not "fully share these fears," yet his dispatches show that he was disturbed and uneasy. But the uneasiness of the French and Russian ambassadors in Berlin was as nothing compared with that which reigned in Petrograd and Paris. We obtain corroboration from totally different sources of this deep disquiet, lest Britain slip from the meshes of the net so patiently and closely drawn around her. Sasonov had been almost equally disquieted a year before, when Tirpitz [Chief of the German Admiralty], had made a speech in the Reichstag, which was a virtual recognition of British naval superiority. On that occasion, Sasonov wired to Benckendorff about this "alarming symptom" and his uneasiness at the "effort of German diplomacy to bring about a *rapprochement* with England." He wanted to know "in what degree machinations of that sort might find favorable soil in London.

Having thus defined the problem, Mr. Morel relates the Entente solution:

> But now something obviously had to be done, and quickly to grip the British nation still more tightly in the vise into which certain British Ministers by their secret actions had placed us. The entire policy of eight laborious years was trembling in the balance. Was there consciousness of this among the protagonists of that policy in London? Read carefully the inspired *Times* throughout the months of February to June. Assuredly was there consciousness of it at Krasnoe-Selo and at the Quai d'Orsay. If the inconceivable happened and the British salmon should slip out of the net at the last moment, the fishers in troubled waters were down and out. If a section of the British Cabinet should clearly perceive almost at the last moment the rocks ahead, and force the hands of the other section by some public ref-

> erence that would suddenly electrify the British public into a sense of imminent peril leading to insistent inquiry as to their true relationship with the rival continental groups – then indeed, all might be lost. For, without Britain, Sukhomlinoff might shout through his newspaper that he was ready till all was blue – there would be nothing doing. Something had to be done – and this is what was done, in the silence and secrecy of the diplomatic closet.
>
> Sasonov led off with a series of dispatches to the Russian ambassadors in London and Paris, urging that "a further reinforcement and development of the so-called Triple Entente, and, if possible, its transformation into a new triple alliance appears to me to be a demand of the present situation." Lord Grey and King George were going to Paris; Poincaré and Doumergue [French Foreign Minister] should urge upon the former a "closer agreement between Russia and England." Doumergue agreed. He thought the task would be easy, "because it is most obvious that, inasmuch as France has a special military and naval understanding with Russia and England, this system must be coordinated and completed by corresponding understandings between Russia and England." The scheme as finally worked out was this. When Lord Grey reached Paris the French Government would urge him to (a) communicate officially to the Russians, the text of the Grey-Cambon exchange notes, of November 22, 1912, and the text of the military and naval conventions; (b) draw up a naval convention with Russia, active cooperation between the British and Russian armies being obviously impracticable.
>
> Such were the events which preceded Lord Grey's visit to Paris three and a half months before the outbreak of war.
>
> The results of the conference, which were duly reported in great detail by Isvolsky to Sasonov, exceeded the expectations of the French negotiators:
>
> "All three of those present at the conference – Messrs. Doumergue, Cambon, and de Margerie – told me they were astonished at the clearly stated and definite readiness to enter upon a closer approach to Russia, which Sir Edward Grey had expressed."
>
> Lord Grey, indeed, may be fairly said to have leaped at the bait, and to have swallowed it without a moment's hesitation, merely pointing out that there were certain elements in the Cabinet prejudiced against Russia. But he hoped to win over Mr. Asquith and the whole Cabinet. Thereupon he returned to London. The fish was fairly landed.[36]

It is not at all surprising that Grey's attitude about Germany should attract others with similar views. The most influential among these were Eyre Crowe, Arthur Nicolson, Francis Bertie, and Charles Hardinge. At King Edward's request, Eyre Crowe produced the infamous January, 1907 "Crowe Memorandum" on the state of Anglo-French-German relations. But instead of the cogent, intelligent analysis of the European geo-political situations that might have been expected from the British Foreign Office, Crowe produced an unseemly schoolboy's eruption of bile, wrath, and vitriol.

Here is a small sample of Mr. Crowe's analytical skills:

> To give way to the blackmailer's [Germany's] menaces enriches him, but it has long been proved by uniform experience that, although this may secure for the victim [England] temporary peace, it is certain to lead to renewed molestation and higher demands after ever-shortening periods of amicable forbearance … The blackmailer's trade is generally ruined by the first resolute stand made against his exactions and the determination rather to face all risks of a possibly disagreeable situation than to continue in the path of endless concessions.

By way of illustrating general anti-Germanism in Great Britain, Christopher Clark (*The Sleepwalkers*) provides this comical description of the infamous 1907 Crowe Memorandum:

> The Germanophobes were rarely very specific about their case against the Germans. They spoke in general terms of the vaunting ambition and bullying 'demeanour' of Germany, the unpredictability of the Kaiser and the threat German military prowess posed to the European balance of power, but they were coy about identifying actual German offences against good international practice. The fullest account of British grievances can be found in a famous "*Memorandum on the Present State of British Relations with France and Germany*" [solicited by King Edward and] composed by Eyre Crowe, then senior clerk in the Western Department at the Foreign Office, in January 1907. Crowe was one of the most extraordinary figures in the British foreign-policy world. His father had worked for the British consular service, but his mother and his wife were both German, and Crowe himself, born in Leipzig, was seventeen and not yet fluent in English when he first visited England to cram for the Foreign Office entrance exam. Throughout his life, he spoke English with what contemporaries described as a 'guttural' accent – one subordinate recalled being dressed down with the words 'what you have wr-r-ritten on this r-r-report is utter r-r-rot'. The perception that Crowe, though admirably efficient and industrious in his handling of departmental business, remained irredeemably Germanic in style and attitude ensured that he never ascended as far through the ranks of the service as his talent warranted. Despite or perhaps in part because of these personal attributes, Crowe became one of Whitehall's most implacable opponents of a rapprochement with Germany.
>
> The memorandum of 1 January 1907 opened with a brief overview of the recent Moroccan crisis … [As Crowe described it] …

The German bully had threatened France in the hope of 'nipping in the bud' her 'young friendship' with Britain. But the bully had underestimated the pluck and loyalty of France's British pal; he 'miscalculated the strength of British feeling and the character of His Majesty's ministers.' Like most bullies, this one was a coward, and the prospect of an 'Anglo-French coalition in arms' was enough to see him off. But before he retreated, the bully further disgraced himself by crudely currying favour with the British friend, 'painting in attractive colours a policy of cooperation with Germany'. How ought Britain to respond to this unlovely posturing?

As the pre-eminent world power, Crowe argued, Britain was bound by what amounted to a 'law of nature' to resist any state that aspired to establish a coalition opposed to British hegemony. Yet this was exactly what German policy intended to do. Germany's ultimate objective was 'German hegemony, at first in Europe and eventually in the world'. But whereas British hegemony was welcomed and enjoyed by all and envied and feared by none on account of its political liberality and the freedom of its commerce, the vociferations of the Kaiser and the pan-German press showed that German hegemony would amount to a "political dictatorship" that would be "the wreckage of the liberties of Europe."

Of course Crowe could not and did not object in principle to the growth in German power and influence. The problem lay in the abrasive and provocative way in which Germany pursued its objectives. But of what exactly did Germany's provocations consist? They included such enormities as "dubious proceedings" in Zanzibar, and the seizure of the Cameroons at a time when London had already announced its intention to grant the inhabitants of that country a British protectorate. Everywhere they looked – or so it seemed to Crowe – the British found themselves stumbling over the Germans.

The list of outrages continued, from German financial support for the Transvaal Republic, to complaints at London's conduct of the South African war, to vexatious meddling in the Yangtze Valley region, 'then considered to be practically a British preserve'. And to make matters worse, there was the "somewhat unsavoury business" of German efforts to influence the international press, from New York, to St Petersburg, Vienna, Madrid, Lisbon, Rome, Cairo and even London, "where the German Embassy entertains confidential and largely unsuspected relations with a number of respectable and widely read papers." There is much one could say about this fascinating document, which Grey circulated as recommended reading to Prime Minister Sir Henry Campbell-Bannerman and other senior ministers. First there is Crowe's almost comical tendency to view the wars, protectorates, occupations and annexations of imperial Britain as a natural and desirable state of affairs, and the comparatively ineffectual manoeuvres of the Germans as gratuitous and outrageous breaches of the peace. How impossible of the Germans to pester

> Britain on the Samoa question when London was on the point of 'submitting' its quarrel with the Transvaal 'to the arbitrament of war'! Then there was the tendency to see the long arm of German policy behind every inter-imperial conflict; thus, it was the Germans who 'fomented' Britain's 'troubles with Russia in Central Asia' and 'carefully encouraged' the European opposition to Britain's occupation of Egypt.
>
> Wherever there was friction between Britain and its imperial rivals, the Germans were supposedly pulling strings in the background. As for German press manipulations from Cairo to London, there was more than a pinch of paranoia in Crowe's handling of this issue: German press work paled into insignificance beside the much larger and better-financed subsidy operations run by St Petersburg and Paris. Perhaps the offensive incidents were ultimately of secondary importance; the core of the argument was Crowe's nightmarish psychogram of the German nation-state, imagined as a composite person conniving to gain concessions by "offensive bluster and persistent nagging," a "professional blackmailer," 'bullying and offending' at every turn, manifesting a "heedless disregard of the susceptibilities of other people."
>
> Whether there was any underlying plan behind all the bluster, or whether it was 'no more than the expression of a vague, confused, and unpractical statesmanship, not fully realizing its own drift' made little difference. The upshot was the same: only the firmest discipline would teach the Germans good behaviour. The French too, Crowe recalled, had once been very annoying, gratuitously challenging Britain at every turn. But Britain's adamant refusal to yield an inch of ground on Egypt and the Sudan, followed by the threat of war over Fashoda, had put an end to all that. Now Britain and France were the best of friends. It followed that only the most 'unbending determination' to uphold 'British rights and interests in every part of the globe' would win 'the respect of the German government and the German nation'. This was not a scenario that left much room to accommodate the rising power of Europe's youngest empire.

Mr. Clark's light-hearted treatment should not distract from a very important fact. The Crowe Memorandum, while sounding like a deranged British ultra-nationalist rant, came from the highest levels of the British Foreign Office. If the German Foreign Office had produced anything even remotely similar, it would have been held up to this day as proof positive of "Prussian militarism." Perhaps most alarming of all is Grey's assessment of the Crowe Memorandum as "very valuable." These, in other words, were the sentiments that were driving British foreign policy. Despite Crowe's exalted status in Grey's Foreign Office, S.B. Fay gives this startling assessment of Crowe's reliability:

> Many English officials even believed that Germany was secretly making plans for the invasion of England. One of the most suspicious of these officials was Sir Eyre Crowe. As Senior Clerk in the Foreign Office it fell to him to write the first long comments on the despatches as they came in from Germany's diplomatic representatives abroad. Inevitably his hostile dissection of the reports from Germany greatly influenced Sir Edward Grey and the other officials who next read them, and who generally endorsed with brief comments Crowe's long criticisms. Crowe, whose mother and wife were both German, appears to have been accepted as an infallible authority on Germany.
>
> But unfortunately he was prone to accept baseless gossip as gospel truth. For instance, he cites in 1908 three alleged circumstances as evidence that Germany was making plans for the invasion of England. (1) "So great an authority as Moltke regarded the invasion of England as practicable. It is certain that the Great General Staff at Berlin is of the same opinion." (2) "It is only 2 or 3 years ago [in reality, seven years earlier, in 1901] that Baron von Edelsheim, then a captain of that Staff, published, with the authorization of his chief, a pamphlet dealing in detail with the measures to be taken for that purpose." (3) "Some 2 or 3 years ago, I think, the Emperor with his own hand made a number of blue pencil corrections or alterations in the designs of 2 new liners [of the Hamburg-America Line], then about to be built, because His Majesty maintained that the designs as submitted to him would not permit of these ships taking their allotted part in the transport of 2 divisions to England" (B.D., VI, 117). The statements in regard to Moltke, the General Staff, and the Emperor are untrue; and Edelsheim was dismissed from the General Staff because he had published his pamphlet without the approval of his chief, General von Schlieffen, and because the views expressed in it were in contradiction with those of the General Staff.[37]

Clark in any case goes on to provide this telling analysis of British fears:

> Lurking beneath these apprehensions, though only indirectly alluded to in Crowe's text, was the spectacle of Germany's titanic economic growth. In 1862, when Bismarck had become minister-president of Prussia, the manufacturing regions of the German states accounted, with 4.9 per cent, for the fifth-largest share of world industrial production – Britain, with 19.9 per cent, was well ahead in first place. In 1880–1900 Germany rose to third place behind the United States and Britain. By 1913, it was behind the United States, but ahead of Britain. In other words, during the years 1860–1913, the German share of world industrial production increased fourfold, while the British sank by a third. Even more impressive was Germany's expanding share of world trade. In 1880, Britain controlled 22.4 per cent of world trade; the Germans, though in second place, were well behind with 10.3 per cent. By 1913, however, Germany, with 12.3

per cent, was hard on the heels of Britain, whose share had shrunk to 14.2 per cent. Everywhere one looked, one saw the contours of an economic miracle: between 1895 and 1913, German industrial output shot up by 150 percent, metal production by 300 per cent, coal production by 200 per cent.

By 1913, the German economy generated and consumed 20 per cent more electricity than Britain, France and Italy combined. In Britain, the words 'Made in Germany' came to carry strong connotations of threat, not because German commercial or industrial practice was more aggressive or expansionist than anyone else's, but because they hinted at the limits of British global dominance. German economic power underscored the political anxieties of the great-power executives, just as Chinese economic power does today.

Yet there was nothing inevitable about the ascendancy of Germanophobe attitudes in British foreign policy. They were not universal, even within the upper reaches of the Foreign Office itself, and they were even less prevalent across the rest of the political elite. Hard work behind the scenes was needed to lever Bertie, Nicolson and Hardinge into the senior posts from which they were able to shape the tone and course of British policy. Bertie owed his rapid ascent after years of frustration in low-level positions to his energetic politicking with the private secretary to King Edward VII. Hardinge, too, was a seasoned courtier and intriguer, who pushed Bertie's candidacy for the Paris ambassadorship in 1905. Hardinge employed his connections at court to 'override' a 'certain amount of obstruction at the top of the F.O.' Bertie and Hardinge in turn cooperated in levering Arthur Nicolson into senior ambassadorial posts, despite the fact that his wife was said to shun society and to "dress like a housemaid."

British policy could have taken a different course: had Grey and his associates failed to secure so many influential posts, less intransigent voices, such as those of Goschen and Lascelles or of the parliamentary under-secretary Edmond Fitzmaurice, who deplored the "anti-German virus" afflicting his colleagues, might have found a wider hearing. Instead, the Grey group gradually tightened their grip on British policy, setting the terms under which relations with Germany were viewed and understood.

The "invention," as Keith Wilson has put it, of Germany as the key threat to Britain reflected and consolidated a broader structural shift. The polycentric world of the 'great games' in Africa, China, Persia, Tibet and Afghanistan, a world in which policy-makers often felt they were lurching from crisis to crisis and reacting to remote challenges rather than setting the agenda, was making way for a simpler cosmos in which one enemy dominated the scene. This was not the cause of Britain's alignment with Russia and France, but rather its consequence. For the restructuring of the alliance system facilitated – indeed it necessitated – the refocusing of British anxieties and paranoia, which were riding high in the years around the Boer War.

> British foreign policy – like American foreign policy in the twentieth century – had always depended on scenarios of threat and invasion as focusing devices. In the mid-nineteenth century, French invasion scares had periodically galvanized the political elites; by the 1890s, France had been displaced in the British political and public imagination by Russia, whose Cossack hordes would soon be invading India and Essex. Now it was Germany's turn. The target was new, but the mechanisms were familiar.[38]

Despite the best efforts of the Grey-Crowe-Nicolson-Hardinge clique at the Foreign Office, Anglo-German relations continued stubbornly to improve. On July 25, 1912, Prime Minister Asquith described relations between England and Germany to the House:

> Our relations with the great German Empire are, I am glad to say, at this moment, and I feel sure they are likely to remain, relations of amity and goodwill. Lord Haldane paid a visit to Berlin early this year; he entered upon conversations and an interchange of views there which have continued since in a spirit of perfect frankness and friendship, both on one side and the other.[39]

Grey himself was obliged to admit:

> In the early months of 1914 the international sky seemed clearer than it had been. The Balkan clouds had disappeared. After the threatening periods of 1911, 1912, and 1913, a little calm was probable, and, it would seem, due. Surely after so much disturbance there would be a general wish to enjoy the finer weather.[40]

The British Documents prove beyond any doubt that despite his frequent assertions that he knew in 1914 that Germany was determined upon war, Grey was in fact well aware that Germany did not wish a European war and that he was fully informed as to the war-like actions of Russia and France during July of 1914; especially the Russian general mobilization. The list of Grey's critics grows exponentially with the release of documents, but even before this one of the greatest authorities on diplomatic history, the distinguished British historian, C. Raymond Beazley, delivered the following devastating judgment on Lord Grey:

> An eminent historian has well remarked that although Lord Grey, in his *Twenty-Five Years,* disclaims animosity against Germany, his whole book (to say nothing of his policy) shows that Germany was to him very much of a *terra incognita* (and indeed, *inimica*). What a distorted picture of German politics and culture he gives us! He

believes in a Germany thirsting to become mistress of the world by means of war, and dominated by an all-powerful military party in Berlin. He even repeats the threadbare legend of a war of the pure Liberal West against militaristic, despotic and wicked Germany and Austria, leaving Russia comfortably out of his reckoning. Anyone really acquainted with Germany knows that this picture is deeply misleading. Anyone who has with moderate care studied the evidence (which Lord Grey appears to entirely ignore) knows the same.

When Viscount Grey tells us again that the idea of *revanche* had entirely disappeared in France, and that the political and other leaders in France and Russia desired nothing but peace and security against German attack, we know, and we have known all along from our acquaintance with France and Russia before the war, that this is not true. And now we have deeper and fuller knowledge of the same from the Russian archives. Lord Grey appears to know little and to care less about this new light. He does not seem to have read any of the Isvolsky correspondence, so abundant and so illuminating. Nor has he, apparently, explored certain other dossiers scarcely less valuable than Isvolsky's. Has he perused the materials given us by Bogitschevitch? Has he any adequate acquaintance with the priceless documents of Die Grosse Politik? The name of Raymond Poincaré is not mentioned by Lord Grey in his account of the origins of the war. Isvolsky is only once named, with the remark that he could not have had any noteworthy war responsibility, for he had ceased to direct Russian policy before the war, and it is well known that an ambassador has little influence upon the policy of his government. Could indifference to Continental political fact be more naively expressed? As Eric Brandenburg well asks: "Can Sir Edward have been so simple-minded as he pictures himself?" Lord Grey seems likewise to ignore the attempts of the German Government to draw back Austria-Hungary in the final days of the crisis of July, 1914, as he ignores their efforts to start and develop direct negotiations between Austria and Russia in those final days.[41]

Incredibly, Grey was speaking of the same Isvolsky who just hours before the assassination of Jean Jaurès, and with only slight exaggeration, exclaimed: *"This is my war!" "My war!"*[42]

The most eloquent of Grey's many critics was David Lloyd George who spent an entire chapter of his *War Memoirs* describing what he considered to be Sir Edward's failures. He wrote:

In the policy which led up to our participation in the War, Sir Edward Grey, amongst British statesmen, played the leading part. His navigation of foreign waters was not seriously challenged. Whether he could have steered Europe clear of the rocks must always be a matter of conjecture and inference from the facts. Men who are at all interested in that aspect of the problem will for some time draw differing conclusions. I am inclined to believe that the verdict of posterity will be averse to his handling of the situation. Of one thing there can be no doubt; he failed calamitously in his endeavours to avert the Great War.

As to Sir Edward Grey's hesitations during the fateful days when the thunderclouds were deepening and rapidly darkening the sky, I have endeavoured to give an accurate summary of the facts. They tell their own tale of a pilot whose hand trembled in the palsy of apprehension, unable to grip the levers and manipulate them with a firm and clear purpose ... Had he warned Germany in time of the point at which Britain would declare war— and wage it with her whole strength—the issue would have been different. I know it is said that he was hampered by the divisions in the Cabinet. On one question, however, there was no difference of opinion—the invasion of Belgium. He could at any stage of the negotiations have secured substantial unanimity amongst his colleagues on that point. At the very worst there would have been only two resignations, and those would have followed our entry into war, whatever the issue upon which it was fought. The assent of all the Opposition leaders was assured, and thus in the name of a united people he could have intimated to the German Government that if they put into operation their plan of marching through Belgium they would encounter the active hostility of the British Empire. And he could have uttered this warning in sufficient time to leave the German military authorities without any excuse for not changing their dust-laden plans. When the ultimatum was actually delivered, war had already broken out between Germany and her neighbours, and the German staff were able with some show of reason to inform the Kaiser that it was then too late to alter their arrangements without jeopardising the German chance of victory. As a matter of fact, the Kaiser was even then anxious, in order to avoid a conflict with us, to divert his forces from the Belgian frontier, and turn their faces towards the East. Von Moltke gave him the answer which I have already indicated...

He [Grey] was the most insular of our statesmen, and knew less of foreigners through contact with them than any Minister in the Government. He rarely, if ever, crossed the seas. Northumberland was good enough for him, and if he could not get there and needed a change, there was his fishing lodge in Hampshire. This was a weakness—and it was a definite weakness in a Foreign Secretary, and especially in a Foreign Secretary with no imagination—which accounted for some of his most conspicuous failures. He had no real understanding of foreigners—I am not at all sure that for this purpose he would not include Scotland, Ireland and Wales as foreign parts...

A Cabinet which was compelled by political and economic exigencies to concentrate its energies on domestic problems left the

> whole field of foreign affairs to Sir Edward Grey. Anyone reading with care and impartiality the record of the way in which he missed his opportunities must come to the conclusion that he lacked the knowledge of foreign countries and the vision, imagination, breadth of mind and that high courage, bordering on audacity, which his immense task demanded.[43]

But it was not true that Grey "failed calamitously." Like the rest of Grey's critics, Lloyd George was mistaken in his assumption that Grey was working for peace. With the benefit of hindsight, we know that Grey was neither ignorant nor incompetent. It was not incompetence that led Grey to remain silent in the face of the Russian general mobilization whilst knowing the consequences. Nor was it ignorance that led to Grey's failure to warn Germany in good time with regard to Belgium – especially as he was all but certain that any Franco-German war would start with a German advance through Belgium. These were seen as "failures" because Grey's critics wrongly assumed that he aimed at preserving the peace. Neither Lloyd George nor the rest of his legion of critics perceived Grey's true purpose.

The fact is that Sir Edward Grey succeeded brilliantly. He had incurred a binding "obligation of honour" to France because he had come to the decision that *"a danger greater than Napoleon"* could only be defeated by war. This key conviction was the reason for Grey's unquestioning endorsement of Edward VII's radical diplomacy, his secret "conversations" with France and Belgium, and his "deliberate ambiguity" during the July crisis when his deafening silence encouraged France and Russia to the point of no return; that point was the Russian general mobilization on July 30. Far from being incompetent, Grey played his cards with the deftness and skill of a carnival huckster. Pretending to pursue peace, he subtly guided the opposing camps into collision with "deliberate ambiguity" and used the Belgian imposture to shift the blame from British to German shoulders.

His policy during the July Crisis of 1914 – most especially his very conspicuous failure to moderate Russia – was a compact, microcosm of his previous nine years in the Foreign Office described above. It therefore deserves a chapter of its own.

***

Endnotes

1. Trevelyan, G. M., *Grey of Fallodon*, 20.
2. Grey, *Twenty-Five Years*, I, xxiii.
3. Ibid., xxvii.
4. Ibid., 67.
5. Loreburn, Robert, *How The War Came* (Kindle Locations 2889-2899).
6. Grey, *Twenty-Five Years*, I, 10-11.

7. G.P., Vol. 4, doc. 747.
8. G.P., doc. 748.
9. G.P., doc. 1816, 2017.
10. G.P. Gooch, doc. 1816, 2017.
11. Grey, *Twenty-Five Years*, I, 36.
12. Ibid., 45.
13. Ibid., 51.
14. Repington, *The First World War*, 4.
15. Fay, *The Origins of the World War*, I, 192, 3.
16. Ibid., 208, 9.
17. Ibid., 210.
18. Ibid., 212.
19. Metternich to Bülow, Jan. 31, 1907; G.P., XXI, 469.
20. Churchill, *The World Crisis*, 53.
21. Nicolson, Harold, *Lord Carnock*, 399.
22. Fay, I, 555.
23. Ibid., I, 213.
24. Protocol of the 7th annual Franco-Russian Military Conference, Aug. 31, 1911.
25. Wilhelm II, Kaiser, *The Kaiser's Memoirs* (Kindle Locations 1267-1277).
26. Waterhouse, Michael, *Edwardian Requiem*, (Kindle Locations 1761-1765).
27. Wilson, *Policy of the Entente*, 11.
28. Monger, *End of Isolation*, 260.
29. Grey to Sir F. Lascelles, 18 Sept. 1907, cited by Wilson, *Policy of the Entente*, 36.
30. Lascelles to Grey, 20 Sept. 1907, Lascelles Papers.
31. Ferguson, *The Pity of War*, 58.
32. Grey, I, 92-3.
33. Geiss, *Der Lange Weg*, 249.
34. Fischer, F., *War of Illusions*, 160-165 - cited in Ferguson, *The Pity of War*, 68.
35. Bethmann Hollweg, Theobald von, *Reflections on the World War* (Kindle Locations 36-42).
36. Morel, E.D., *The Secret History of a Great Betrayal*, 22-24, 27-8.
37. Fay, II, Supplementary Notes.
38. Clark, Christopher, *The Sleepwalkers: How Europe Went to War in 1914*, 206.
39. Ibid., 14.
40. Grey I, 269.
41. Beazley, R.C., *Foreign Affairs*, October, 1927.
42. Florinsky, *The End of the Russian Empire*, 1290; Mansergh, *The Coming of the First World War*, 136.
43. Lloyd, David George, *War Memoirs*, Vol I, Kindle Locations 1683-1753.

Chapter Eight

Sir Edward Grey And The July Crisis

It is often alleged that in the summer of 1914, European statesmen in a haze of confusion and miscalculation stumbled blindly, unwitting and unwilling, into war. Nothing could be further from the truth. In fact, during the month after the Sarajevo murders, events played out with such uncanny predictability that it seemed as if they had been pre-ordained.

Trouble between Serbia and Austria-Hungary had been long predicted and the consequences forewarned. Here is the British Ambassador at Vienna, Sir Fairfax Cartwright, writing to Arthur Nicolson, January 31, 1913:

> Serbia will someday set Europe by the ears and bring about a universal war on the Continent. I cannot tell you how exasperated people are getting here at the continual worry which that little country causes to Austria under encouragement from Russia. It will be lucky if Europe succeeds in avoiding war as a result of the present crisis [Balkan Wars]. The next time a Serbian crisis arises, I feel sure that Austria-Hungary will refuse to admit of any Russian interference in the dispute and that she will proceed to settle her difference with her little neighbor coûte que coûte.[1]

A little later, on May 23, Sir Fairfax issued a second warning:

> This country [Austria] cannot allow any dismemberment of her provinces without incurring the danger of the whole edifice crumbling down. We have all the elements in the near future of another violent crisis in this part of the world.

The result of ignoring the Serbian menace was described by the British political scientist/philosopher, G. Lowes Dickinson:

> For years the little State of Serbia had been undermining the Austrian Empire. What was the Empire to do in self-defence? One can conceive a world in which Austria would not have wished to hold down a nationality against its will. But that would not be the world of history, past and present. Never has an empire resigned before the disruptive forces of nationality. Always it has fought. And I do not

> believe there was a State in existence that would not, under similar circumstances, have determined as Austria did, to finish the menace, once for all, by war. So long as power is the object of States, so long will such policies be pursued, and in the mouth of what State does it lie to blame another? The pertinent question is, therefore, why was the war not localized, as Austria and Germany intended and desired? There is only one answer to this: because Russia did not choose to allow it. Why not? … The answer is that she wanted Constantinople and the Straits; that she wanted access to the Mediterranean, that she wanted extension of territory and influence; that she had a 'historic mission'; … France entered … to recover Alsace-Lorraine and her technical success in waiting till the declaration of war came from Germany does not alter the position … And England? … She had military and naval commitments to France which were like a suction-pipe to draw her, whether she would or no, into war. And that approximation to the other two Powers of the Entente was made for no other reason than the maintenance of the balance of power. We had become more afraid of Germany than of our traditional enemies, France and Russia. After all of our commitments to France it would have been base to desert her. Agreed! But what were the objects for which those commitments were made? Our own power, our own empire, our own security.[2]

On August 3, 1914, The *Manchester Guardian* editorialized:

> Of all the small powers of Europe, Serbia is, quite decidedly, the one whose name is most foully daubed with dishonour. The record of her rulers and her policy in recent years is an unmatched tissue of cruelty, greed, hypocrisy, and ill-faith … If one could tow Serbia to the edge of the ocean and sink it, the atmosphere of Europe would be cleared.

When news of the Sarajevo murders hit European embassies on Monday, June 29, the three assassins had already been subjected to twelve hours of rigorous interrogation by Austrian authorities. The trio were proud of what they had done and spoke freely about their methods and motive. Austria was quickly able to trace the pistols and bombs used by the assassins to a Serbian Government armory, identify Major Tankositch, the go-between Milan Ciganovitch, as well as two frontier guards, all of whom assisted the assassins in their journey from Belgrade to Sarajevo. Austria had good reason from the start to suspect the Serbian Government. Thus it was immediately understood everywhere in Europe that (1) Austria would make demands upon Serbia, and (2) if Serbia refused and was backed by Russia, a European war would likely ensue. This was the frightening prospect that was instantly apparent to all the Powers great and small. It was thus the Russian attitude that would make the difference between a localized Austro-Serb dispute and a larger European war. But the Russian attitude in turn depended on France and England. This central fact was keenly appreciated throughout Europe and – especially – at Number 10, Downing Street.

The desirability of maintaining British – and thus Franco-Russian – neutrality was therefore forcefully stated by a number of British politicians and newspapers. Typical was the *Manchester Guardian* which editorialized on July 28th and July 30th:

> Not only are we neutral now, but we could and ought to remain neutral throughout the whole course of the war. We have not seen a shred of reason for thinking that the triumph of Germany in a European war in which we had been neutral would injure a single British interest, however small, whereas the triumph of Russia would create a situation for us really formidable. If Russia makes a general war out of a local war it will be a crime against Europe. If we, who might remain neutral, rush into the war or let our attitude remain doubtful, it will be both a crime and an act of supreme and gratuitous folly.

Other British publications weighed-in with similar warnings, but the most brilliant and cogently argued editorial was submitted by A.G. Gardiner of the London *Daily News*.

Alfred George Gardiner (1865-1946) was one of England's most distinguished author/journalist/publicist. In 1902 he was appointed editor of the *Daily News* which he made into one of the leading Liberal journals of the day. His prestige and eloquence were such that no one in a position of power or rival publishers could afford to ignore him. On the morning of August 1st, 1914, the following lead editorial appeared in the London *Daily News*. It was written by Gardiner himself and sets forth the crisis as it was on the eve of war and England's central part in preserving the peace. Please note the timeline: the editorial was written on July 28, but published on August 1 when the clock was still ticking on Germany's July 31 ultimatum to Russia to suspend mobilization:

> The greatest calamity in history is upon us – a calamity so vast that our senses are numbed with horror. We hardly dare look into the pit that yawns at our feet and yet any hour, any minute may plunge us in beyond any hope of return. Every step at this hour may be irrevocable. The avalanche trembles on the brink and a touch may send it shattering into the abyss.
>
> The peace of every land, the happiness of every home in Europe, the very bread by which we live, hang at this moment upon the will of one man, the Czar of Russia. It is he whose hand is on the avalanche.

It is he who with one stroke of the pen, one word of the mouth, one motion of the head can plunge Europe into a sea of blood and bury all the achievements of our civilization in anarchy.

And at St. Petersburg, there sits the man who has every one of these lives and millions more at his mercy, and who can at one word let hell loose upon the face of Europe. Is he a man we can trust with this momentous power? Is he the man for whom we are going to shed our blood and our treasure?

The question is for us! For though the Czar has his hand on the avalanche, it is we who have our hand on him. It is we who in the last analysis must say whether Europe is to be deluged with blood. We see the Czar with his hand on the avalanche looking toward England for the one assurance that he needs. Let England say: 'No, you touch it at your own risk and peril,' and his hand will drop. Let England falter, temporize, equivocate, and he will plunge us into ruin with the rest.

We are told that we must be quiet. That we may encourage Germany by making her believe that she has not to reckon with us. But the move is not with Germany. The move is with Russia. It is she whom we encourage or discourage by every word that is said and every other action that is taken. It is she who has the issues of peace and war in her hand.

If we are free – and we know that we are free – what ground is there for involving ourselves in this unspeakable calamity? On the immediate cause of the quarrel we can have no sympathy with Servia. The assassination of the Crown Prince and his wife was a brutal and cold-blooded crime, the fruit of a conspiracy laid with infinite care and deliberation and wholly inspired by Servia. Why is a European war threatened to save Servia from punishment? Because Servia is the instrument of Russia. It was in Belgrade that that most mischievous of Russian diplomatists, M. Hartwig, carried on his machinations throughout the Balkan Wars. It is through Belgrade that Russia hopes to establish her domination of the Balkan Peninsula. Have we any interest in helping her?

It is our neutrality which is the only protection that Europe has against the hideous ruin and combustion on the brink of which it trembles. Let us announce that neutrality to the world! It is the one hope. There is no other. We can save Europe from war even at the last moment. But we can only save it by telling the Czar that he must fight his own battles and take the consequences of his own action.

If the British government does this, it will do the greatest service to humanity in history. If it does not do it, it will have brought the greatest curse to humanity in history. The youngest of us will not live to see the end of its crime.

History records that the British Government did *not* do it. The British Government – that is to say, Sir Edward Grey – gave the green light to the

Russian general mobilization in the full knowledge of what was to follow and then used the Belgian imposture to defeat the near-unanimous public opposition to the war.

Anticipating the Austrian declaration of war upon Serbia, The *Daily Citizen* on Monday. July 27, published a large, front-page picture of Sergei Sasonov. The caption declared bluntly *"Upon Russia and her action rests the fate of Europe."*[3]

Russia's key role was recognized by Germany as well. German Ambassador Pourtales received the following telegram from Bethmann on July 26:

> After Count Berchtold has declared to Russia that Austria does not aim at any territorial acquisitions in Serbia, but only wishes to secure repose, the maintenance of the peace of Europe depends on Russia alone. We trust in Russia's love of peace and in our traditional friendly relations with her, that she will take no step which would seriously endanger the peace of Europe.[4]

In the case against Sir Edward Grey, the Russian general mobilization is Exhibit One. It was ordered on July 30, 1914, at six P.M., when Russia was in no military danger from Austria (and certainly not from Germany) and, most importantly, at the very time when the dangerous crisis was on the cusp of a diplomatic solution as the result of heavy pressure upon Austria exerted by the German Chancellor, Theobald von Bethmann-Hollweg.

In 1914, Great Britain was the largest and most powerful Empire in the history of the world, fully capable of imposing a stranglehold naval blockade anywhere in the world, anytime she chose to do so. For this reason, the attitude of Great Britain was the chief determinant of the Austro-German and Franco-Russian attitudes after the Sarajevo murders. This is proven by Franco-Russian doubts about their ability to defeat the Central Powers by themselves, and the unending requests from French Ambassador Cambon and (later) Russian Ambassador Benckendorff, that Grey should make a binding commitment to them in writing. When Isvolsky reported in 1912 that Poincaré had told him that the French General Staff felt that Russia and France together could defeat Austria and Germany, Sasonov had strongly disagreed. He argued at a secret Conference on December 31, 1913, that:

> In reality, a Russian initiative supported only by France would not appear particularly dangerous to Germany. The two States would hardly be in a position to deal Germany a mortal blow, even in the event of military successes which can never be predicted. A struggle, on the other hand, in which Great Britain participated might be disastrous to Germany, who clearly realizes that if Great Britain were drawn in, the result might be social disturbances of a catastrophic nature within her frontiers in less than six weeks. Great Britain is

> dangerous to Germany, and the consciousness of this is to be found in the explanation of the hatred with which the Germans are filled in the face of Great Britain's growing power. In view of this it is essential that before taking any decisive steps, the Tsar's Government shall assure itself of the support of the London Cabinet, whose active sympathy does not seem, in the Minister's view, to be certain."

And just before Poincaré's arrival at St. Petersburg on July 20, 1914, Czar Nicholas told the French Ambassador:

> There is one question which preoccupies me above everything else; our Entente with England. We must get her to enter our [Franco-Russian] alliance.... It is all the more important that we should be able to count upon the English in case of a crisis."[5]

The entire history of the Franco-Russian Alliance since 1894 shows that France and Russia were not confident of victory over the Central Powers by themselves, but on the other hand were supremely confident of victory if Great Britain participated. For the same reason, Germany was equally anxious to keep Britain neutral. Thus the power to stop the war rested with Great Britain.

> Great Britain was the dominant factor for both sides, and was in control of the situation; had she immediately and clearly stated her position world peace would have been saved.[6]
>
> Kaiser Wilhelm stated: "He [Grey] knows perfectly well that if he were to say one single, serious, sharp and warning word at Paris and St. Petersburg, and were to warn them to remain neutral, that both would become quiet at once. But he takes care not to speak the word, and threatens us instead! Common cur! England alone bears the responsibility for peace and war, not we any longer! That must be made clear to the world."[7]

But instead of stating the British position in a forthright manner – by telling Russia that any general mobilization was premature and might cause England to reconsider her position; and/or by telling Germany that any violation of Belgium would raise the British *casus foederus* – Sir Edward Grey played his cards close to the vest. He gave none-too-subtle hints to France and Russia that England would intervene, while into the Austro-German ear he whispered neutrality. As Sir Edward intended, this "deliberate ambiguity"[8] coaxed the opposing coalitions onto a collision course. The greatest tragedy of the Great War is the ease with which Sir Edward Grey could have prevented it had he wished to do so.

> Great Britain, with her enormous weight, had indisputably the controlling power.[9] Grey failed to use it as it could and should have been used for peace. Instead, as we have seen, he took sides with Russia from July 25th onward.[10]

Historians generally acknowledge that Bethmann-Hollweg attempted to moderate Austria but assert that these efforts were "too little, too late." But in fact, when it became clear on Tuesday, July 28, that Russia intended to intervene, the German policy of supporting Austria, aimed at keeping the dispute localized, turned 180 degrees and immediately put heavy pressure on Austria to submit to arbitration. What follows here is a summation of that pressure.

When the Kaiser read the Serbian reply to the Austrian Note (early on July 28), he added this annotation:

> A brilliant performance for a time limit of only 48 hours. This is more than one could have expected! A great moral success for Vienna; but with it every reason for war drops away, and Giesl ought to have remained quietly in Belgrade! After such a thing, I should never have ordered mobilization.[11]

The Kaiser followed this with his own plan to end the crisis and sent this note to Foreign Secretary Jagow:

> I propose that we say to Austria: Serbia has been forced to retreat in a very humiliating manner and we offer our congratulations. Naturally, as a result, no more cause for war exists (Kaiser's italics) but a guarantee that the promises will be carried out, is probably necessary; that could probably be secured by a temporary military occupation of a portion of Serbia, similar to the way we left troops in France in 1871 until the billions were paid. On this basis I am ready to mediate for peace with Austria ... Submit a proposal to me, along the lines sketched out, to be communicated to Vienna.[12]

Bethmann had meanwhile expressed his exasperation at hearing conflicting reports from London about Austrian intentions with regard to Serbia. He noted indignantly:

> This duplicity of Austria's is intolerable. They refuse to give us information as to their program and state expressly that Count Hoyos's statements which suggested a partition of Serbia were purely personal; at St. Petersburg they are lambs with not a wicked thought in their hearts, and in London their Embassy talks of giving away portions of Serbian territory to Bulgaria and Albania.

In the evening of that same Tuesday, July 28, Bethmann sent the Kaiser's "Pledge Plan" to Tschirschky, the German Ambassador at Vienna, with a very stern warning:

> The Austro-Hungarian Government, in spite of repeated questions as to its purpose, has left us in the dark. The reply now at hand of the Serbian Government to the Austrian ultimatum makes it evident that Serbia has in fact met the Austrian demands in so wide-reaching a manner that if the Austro-Hungarian Government adopted a wholly uncompromising attitude, a gradual revulsion of public opinion against it in all Europe would have to be reckoned with ... [Russia will presumably be satisfied] if the Vienna Cabinet repeats in St. Petersburg the definite declaration that territorial acquisitions in Serbia lie far from its purpose, and that its military measures aim solely at a temporary occupation of Belgrade and other definite points of Serbian territory in order to compel the Serbian Government to a complete fulfilment of the demands, and to serve as guarantees for future good behavior, to which Austria-Hungary unquestionably has a claim after her experience with Serbia.
>
> The occupation could be regarded like the German occupation in France after the Peace of Frankfurt, as security for the demand of war indemnity. As soon as the Austrian demands were fulfilled, a withdrawal would follow ... You are immediately to express yourself emphatically in this sense to Count Berchtold and have him take the proper step in St. Petersburg. You are carefully to avoid giving the impression that we wish to hold Austria back. It is solely a question of finding a method which will make possible the accomplishment of Austria's purpose of cutting the vital nerve of Greater Serbia propaganda without at the same time unchaining a world war, and in the end, if this is unavoidable, of improving as far as practicable the condition under which it is to be waged. Wire reply.[13]

Bethmann at once informed Russia that he was striving to persuade Vienna to have a frank discussion with St. Petersburg and to explain Austria's procedure.[14] He likewise told the British, Ambassador at Berlin, Goschen, that *"he was doing his very best both at Vienna and at St. Petersburg to get the two Governments to discuss the situation directly with each other in a friendly way and lead to a satisfactory result."* His last words to Goschen were: *"A war between the Great Powers must be avoided."*[15]

The next day, Wednesday, July 29, Bethmann-Hollweg waited for an answer, but when Vienna failed to respond, he fired-off another telegram in severe disapproval of Austria:

> I regard the attitude of the Austrian Government and its unparalleled procedure toward the various Governments with increasing aston-

> ishment. In St. Petersburg it declares its territorial disinterestedness; us it leaves wholly in the dark as to its programme; Rome it puts off with empty phrases about the question of compensation; in London Count Mensdorff hands out part of Serbia to Bulgaria and Albania and places himself in contradiction with Vienna's solemn declaration at St. Petersburg. From these contradictions I must conclude that the telegram disavowing Hoyos [who, on July 5 or 6 at Berlin had spoken unofficially of Austria's partitioning of Serbia] was intended for the gallery, and that the Austrian Government is harboring plans which it sees fit to conceal from us, in order to assure itself in all events of German support and to avoid the refusal which might result from a frank statement.[16]

This second telegram added: *"Answer by wire immediately whether telegram 174 of yesterday [concerning the 'pledge plan'] has arrived. I await immediate carrying out of telegram 174."* In fact, Tschirschky had promptly carried out Bethmann's instructions on the morning of July 29 but was informed that

> ... as to further declaration concerning military measures Count Berchtold says that he is not in a position to give me a reply at once. In spite of my representations as to the urgency of the matter, I have up to this evening received no further communication.[17]

To this, Bethmann responded with yet another, even more urgent telegram, in which he went so far as to threaten Austria with abandonment if she refused to negotiate:

> The refusal of every exchange of views with St. Petersburg would be a serious mistake, for it provokes Russia precisely to armed interference, which Austria is primarily interested in avoiding. We are ready, to be sure, to fulfil our obligations as an ally, but must refuse to allow ourselves to be drawn by Vienna into a world conflagration frivolously and in disregard of our advice. Please say this to Count Berchtold with all emphasis and with great seriousness.[18]

When Bethmann was informed by Lichnowsky that news had come from Rome to the effect that Serbia was now ready, *"on condition of certain interpretations, to swallow even articles 5 and 6, that is, the whole Austrian ultimatum,"*[19] Bethmann embraced it eagerly and sent it on to Vienna and added:

> Please show this to Berchtold immediately and add that we regard such a yielding on Serbia's part as a suitable basis for negotiation along with an occupation of a part of Serbian territory as a pledge.[20]

Finally, on Thursday, July 30, Tschirschky had lunch with Berchtold and submitted this report:

> Berchtold listened, pale and silent, while they [Bethmann's telegrams] were read through twice; Count Forgách took notes; finally Berchtold said he would at once lay the matter before the Emperor.

After Berchtold had departed for an immediate audience with Franz Joseph, Tschirschky spent the remainder of the day closeted with Berchtold's advisors, Forgách and Hoyos, to further explain Bethmann's telegrams but was informed by them that,

> ... in view of the feeling of the army and in the people, any checking of the military operations in progress was out of the question ... Conrad von Hötzendorf [Austrian Chief of Staff] would lay before the Emperor this evening the order for general mobilization, as a reply to the measures already taken.

He was finally informed that Berchtold could not give any final answer until the following morning, for the reason that Tisza, who would not be in Vienna until then, had to be consulted.[21]

Just prior to these German efforts, Sir Eyre Crowe had the unmitigated gall to write:

> So far as we know, the German Government has up to now said not a single word at Vienna in the direction of restraint or moderation. If a word had been said, we may be certain that the German Government would claim credit for having spoken at all. The inference is not reassuring as to Germany's goodwill.[22]

This was hypocritical chutzpah at its height. Mr. Crowe seems to have forgotten that Grey had "up to now said not a single word in the direction of restraint or moderation" at Paris or St. Petersburg. Nor does Crowe remember Sasonov's statement that *"In case it is a question of exercising a moderating influence at St. Petersburg, we reject it in advance..."*[23] and Isvolsky's response that *"According to my conversation yesterday at the Quai d'Orsay, the acting Minister of Foreign Affairs does not for a minute admit the possibility of exercising a moderating influence in St. Petersburg ..."*[24] Finally, the supreme irony of Crowe's own minute of July 25 (see below) advising Grey to make no "representation" in St. Petersburg seems to escape Mr. Crowe altogether.

> Grey, who in the whole crisis did not send a single word of warning to St. Petersburg or Paris, has the coolness to write in his memoirs

> that Bethmann-Hollweg and Jagow spoke 'only in whispers' in Vienna when a decisive word was wanted.[25]

In stark contrast to these strenuous efforts by Bethmann-Hollweg, France had actively encouraged Russia from the start and merely cautioned her to avoid alarming Germany as long as possible:

> Margerie [Policy Director at the Quai d'Orsay] told me that the French Govt. without wishing to interfere in our military preparations, would consider it extremely desirable, in view of the negotiations still pending for the preservation of peace, that these preparations should be carried on in the least open and least provocative manner. The Minister of War [Messimy], on his part, expressing the same idea, told Count Ignatiev [Russian Military Attaché in Paris] that we could declare that, in the higher interest of peace, we were willing to slow down temporarily our mobilization measures, which would not hinder us from continuing and even strengthening our military preparations, while refraining, as much as possible, from the transportation of masses of troops.[26]

And just hours later:

> The French Minister of War [Messimy], has declared to me with hearty high spirits the firm decision of the French Government for war, and begged me to confirm the hope of the French General Staff that all our efforts will be directed against Germany, and that Austria will be treated as a quantité négligeable.[27]

The German Chancellor seems never to have grasped that the Russian decision for war had long been made. Ten days earlier, July 20, French President Raymond Poincaré and Prime Minister René Viviani arrived in St. Petersburg for a three-day summit with Czar Nicholas. The French Ambassador in St. Petersburg, Maurice Paléologue, kept a daily diary, and has provided a detailed record of the meeting that leaves little doubt as to its purpose. He begins with a poetic description of the arrival of the French leaders aboard La *France,* the largest, fastest, state-of-the-art battleship in the French navy:

> It was a magnificent spectacle. In a quivering silvery light, the *France* slowly surged forward over the turquoise and emerald waves, leaving a long white furrow behind her. Then she stopped majestically. The mighty warship which had brought the head of the French State is well worthy of her name. She was indeed France coming to Russia. I felt my heart beating. For a few minutes, there was a prodigious

din in the harbor; the guns and the shore batteries firing, the crews cheering, the *Marseillaise* answering the Russian national anthem, the cheers of thousands who had come from St. Petersburg on pleasure boats.

Paléologue records that the business between Nicholas and Poincaré was serious indeed:

> As soon as the presentations are over, the imperial yacht steers for Peterhof. Seated in the stern, the Czar and the President immediately enter into conversation. One should perhaps say into discussion, for it is obvious that they are talking business, firing questions at each other and arguing. As is proper, it is Poincaré who directs the dialogue. Before long, it is he alone who speaks. The Czar simply acquiesces, but his whole appearance shows his sincere approval ...

The emotional atmosphere of excitement and anticipation which permeated these three days (July 20-23) at St. Petersburg is starkly illustrated by Paléologue's description of a dinner conversation with the Montenegrin Duchesses, Anastasia and Melitza, the wives of Grand Dukes Nicholas (who would soon be appointed Commander-in-Chief of the Russian army) and Peter. Both women were passionate, politically active supporters of 'Greater Serbia' and were always present at the highest functions of the Russian Court:

> Anastasia cried enthusiastically, "Do you know we are passing through historic days, blessed days ... at tomorrow's review, bands will play nothing but *Marche Lorraine* and *Sambre et Meuse* ... I have had a letter from my father [the King of Montenegro] today, in a code we agreed on; he tells me we shall have war before the month is out ... what a hero my father! He is worthy of the Iliad. Stop a minute; look at this little box – it never leaves me. It has Lorraine soil in it. Lorraine soil, which I brought over the border when I was in France two years ago with my husband. And now look at this table of honor! It is entirely decorated with thistles. I would not have any other flowers put on it. Now then! They are from Lorraine! Melitza, go on telling the ambassador all today means to us while I go and receive the Czar."
>
> After dinner I was sitting next to the Grand Duchess Anastasia and the dithyrambics continued, mixed with prophecies: "war is going to break out ... there will be nothing of Austria left ... you will get Alsace-Lorraine back ... our armies will meet in Berlin. Germany will be annihilated ..."
>
> Then, suddenly—"I must control myself, the Czar is looking at me."

In a flurry of speeches and toasts, there was a prolific use of the code words "dignity" and "firmness." All knew what it meant: Russia would now act with "dignity" and not back down as she had done in her 1908 dispute with Austria; Russia was also to act with "firmness" as this was the only language Germany understood. The purpose of the visit was summed up by Paléologue when he recalled Poincare's advice: *"Sasonov must stand firm, and we must support him."*[28] By the time Poincaré departed in the evening of July 23, Russia and France were on the same page. Summarizing Poincaré's three-day visit to St. Petersburg, the young French historian, Alfred Fabre-Luce, concluded the following:[29]

> There is, then, no possible doubt about the attitude taken by Poincaré at St. Petersburg between the 20th and the 23d of July. Without any knowledge whatever of the Austrian demands or of the policy of Germany in the circumstances, he assumed a position of energetic opposition to the Central Powers, gave this opposition a very specific character, and never modified it in the slightest degree to the very end. From that time on there was a very slight chance indeed of averting war; and, moreover, Poincaré had given Russia *carte blanche* to initiate hostilities any time she wished to do so, as we know from the fact that two days after Poincaré's departure from St. Petersburg, Paléologue, following his instructions, promised Sasonov, without any reservations after the delivery of the Austrian ultimatum, that France would fulfill all the obligations of the alliance. Further, Viviani, who accompanied Poincaré, declared to Nekliudov at Stockholm on July 25 that "if it is a war for Russia, it will be, most certainly, a war for France also."

The very next morning [July 24], after receiving a copy of the Austrian Note delivered by Austrian Ambassador Giesl to the Serbian Premier, Sasonov ordered Baron Schilling to summon the Ministers of War, Navy, and Finance, to a Council of Ministers at 3 P.M. that same day. Sasonov then consulted personally with General Ianushkevitch, the Chief of the General Staff, and proposed a partial mobilization of the Russian army directed exclusively at Austria. The response of General Dobrorolski to Sasonov's initiative is revealing. Dobrorolski is described by Fay as follows:

> Dobrorolski was Chief of the Mobilization Section of the General Staff in 1914, and therefore in a position to know authoritatively all the technical details and preparations of Russia's mobilization measures. Driven into exile by the Bolshevist revolution, and writing his narrative in Belgrade in 1921 without access to his notes and papers, he made a few minor slips of memory. But his remarkable frankness, authoritative information, and general accuracy is confirmed by all the documents which have come to light, as well as by the talks

which the present writer [Fay] was privileged to have with him in 1923. Dobrorolski writes:[30]

> On July 24 [1914], St. Olga's Day, between 11 o'clock and noon, the Chief of the General Staff, General Ianushkevitch, called me on the service telephone and told me to come immediately to his office.
>
> The situation is very serious, he said, as I entered, Austria has delivered a wholly unacceptable ultimatum to the Serbian Government and we cannot remain indifferent. It has been decided to announce this publicly and decisively. Tomorrow there will appear in the Russkii Invalid a short official warning, saying that all Russia is following with close attention the course of the negotiations between the Austro-Hungarian and the Serbian Governments, and will not remain inactive if the dignity and the integrity of the Serbian people, our blood brothers, are threatened with danger. Have you everything ready for the mobilization of our army?
>
> Upon my replying in the affirmative, the Chief of the General Staff said to me: In an hour bring to me all the documents relative to preparing of our troops for war, which provide, in case of necessity, for proclaiming partial mobilization against Austria-Hungary only. This mobilization must give no occasion to Germany to find any grounds of hostility to herself.
>
> I pointed out that a partial mobilization was out of the question. But General Ianushkevitch ordered me anew to make a detailed report to him after an hour in accordance with his decision already made ... The absolute impossibility of a partial mobilization of the army was evident." [Dobrorolski then explains that on account of the system of alliances, Russia was convinced that a war between Austria and Russia would inevitably involve Germany, and therefore no mobilization plan had been worked out for war against Austria alone.]

The next day, Saturday, July 25, a key Ministerial Council took place which implemented the following decisions which had been agreed upon the previous day:

> 1. All-Highest approval of the decision for contingent "partial mobilization" against Austria.
>
> 2. Recall all troops to their standing quarters.
>
> 3. Promote cadets to be officers.
>
> 4. Proclamation of the "*State of War*" in towns containing fortresses and in the frontier sectors facing Germany and Austria.
>
> 5. Secret orders for the "*Period Preparatory to War.*"

There was no mistaking the results of these key Russian decisions. Before retiring that evening (July 25th) Paléologue recorded in his diary:

> At seven in the evening I went to the Warsaw station to bid farewell to Isvolsky who was leaving to rejoin his post. Great activity at the terminus, the trains crowded with officers and troops. All this points to mobilization. We hurriedly exchanged our views of the situation and both arrive at the same conclusion: this time it is war!" [*Cette fois, c'est la guerre*][31]

When Sasonov learned of the Austrian ultimatum late on July 23, his response was: *"This means a European war!"* (*"C'est la guerre Européenne!"*) This fully comports with Dobrorolski's own candid admission that Russian military leaders, including the Czar and Sasonov, considered the war a foregone conclusion. He said:

> The following days [after Sasonov had been informed of the Austrian ultimatum] are well known to everybody through the 'colored books' and documents published by the European Governments. The war was already a settled matter [*Voina byla uzhe predrieshena*], and the whole flood of telegrams between the Governments of Russia and Germany represented merely the stage setting [*mise en scène*] of a historical drama.[32]

All of this took place *before* Austria's partial mobilization (which came in response to Serbia's full mobilization on July 25), and leaves no doubt whatsoever that the Russian decision for war was made by the time Poincaré and Viviani departed from St. Petersburg in the evening of July 23. All of the subsequent decisions and preparations by Russian leaders confirm it: Mother Russia was gearing up for war! But the most important event of the entire July Crisis by far, also occurred on this fateful day: Saturday, July 25.

Much has been written about Germany's so-called 'blank cheque' to Austria on July 5. Far less has been written about the passel of French blank cheques to Russia, and almost nothing about the one blank cheque that really counted. Professor Fay explains:

> This telegram, indicating that 'Russia, secure of support from France, will face all risks of war,' might well have prompted Sir Edward Grey to the conclusion that it was high time to attempt to exercise a moderating influence at St. Petersburg, if he preferred to place the preservation of peace above the maintenance of the Triple Entente. But he did not. Although Buchanan at St. Petersburg in the early part of the crisis attempted to exercise restraint upon Russia, no such effort was made from London. The British Foreign Office took the stand expressed in a minute by Sir E. Crowe on July 25: [33]
>
>> The moment has passed when it might have been possible to enlist French support in an effort to hold back Russia.

> It is clear that France and Russia are decided to accept the challenge thrown out to them. Whatever we may think of the merits of the Austrian charges against Serbia, France and Russia consider that these are the pretexts, and that the bigger cause of Triple Alliance versus Triple Entente is definitely engaged.
>
> I think it would be impolitic, not to say dangerous, for England to attempt to controvert this opinion, or to endeavor to obscure the plain issue, by any representation at St. Petersburg and Paris ...
>
> Our interests are tied up with those of France and Russia in this struggle, which is not for the possession of Serbia, but one between Germany aiming at a political dictatorship in Europe and the Powers who desire to retain individual freedom.[34]

Here was the magic moment. Here was the consent of silence from the British Foreign Office for which Sasonov and the militarists had been waiting. With this all-important green light from London, the Russian decision to order general mobilization was duly made and scheduled for midnight, July 29. When the order was downgraded to partial mobilization at the last moment by Czar Nicholas, a frustrated Sasonov determined to return to Peterhof to personally, once-and-for-all, get the Czar's authorization for the fatal order.

Of such value to France and Russia was British participation in a European war (as noted above), that both nations would have felt obliged to stand down, if Grey had announced a policy of neutrality. This is why even a whispered caution from Grey to either France or Russia would have stopped the countdown to war in its tracks. For this reason Grey understood that he would have to answer before the bar of history, the key question of why he failed to moderate Russia when doing so might well have prevented the War, and he prepared an answer – sort of. His plan was to suggest a Conference of Ambassadors which he knew was certain to be rejected by Austria and Germany, and he would then use that rejection as the reason for his very conspicuous failure to moderate Russia. He wrote:[35]

> Germany ceased to talk of anything but the Russian mobilization. I could do nothing to stop that. The rejection of a Conference [of Ambassadors] struck out of my hand what might have been a lever to influence Russia to suspend military preparation. If a Conference had been agreed to, if even Germany had said that a Conference could only be agreed to on condition that Russia did not mobilize more than Austria, I should have had some *locus standi* on which to work at St. Petersburg. But throughout these negotiations I had been given nothing that would help me at St. Petersburg.

Of course Grey never explains why he would need *"a lever to influence Russia."* The military might of the British Empire was the biggest lever he could ask for and he apparently needed no lever to "help me" at Vienna or

Berlin. And did Sir Edward not know that a Conference of Ambassadors was anathema to Austria given her traumatic experience with this method in the 1912 London Conference conducted by Sir Edward?

> The decisions of the [1912] London Conference had brought her [Austria] little or nothing, in her own opinion, except disappointments and illusions. Its delay and ineffectiveness in protecting Albanian interests, when defied by the Montenegrins at Scutari and the Serbians at Dibra, explain to some extent why Austria was absolutely unwilling, after the murder of Archduke Franz Ferdinand at Sarajevo, to submit her latest of complaint against Serbia to another Conference of the Powers. 'The course of the London Conference was so horrible to recall to memory, that all public opinion would reject the repetition of such a spectacle.'[36] On the other hand, when Austria had quickly and energetically on her own account, by sending a peremptory ultimatum [in 1909], Serbia had heeded her demands immediately, Russia had not interfered, and the Vienna Foreign Office had accomplished its immediate purpose.[37]

Did Grey not remember that his Conference idea was also rejected by Benckendorff, the Russian Ambassador in London, as Grey himself admitted?

> I was therefore very much surprised, even dismayed, when Benckendorff, on my telling him that the proposal had been made, expressed the opinion that the Russian Government would not agree to it.[38]

...and that France expressed similar reservations? Nevertheless, Sir Edward continues to harp on the Conference and hammer home his alleged "reason" for not moderating Russia:

> Now they [Germans] vetoed the only certain means of settlement without, as far as I knew, even referring it to Austria at all ... The complacency with which they had let Austria launch the ultimatum on Serbia was deplorable, and to me unaccountable; the blocking of a Conference was still worse. I remember well the impulse to say that, as Germany forbade a Conference, I could do no more, and that it was on Germany that the responsibility must rest if war came.[39]

Grey goes on to make the absurd argument that it was dangerous for Russia to delay her mobilization even though Russia was in no military danger from either Germany or Austria:

> I felt impatient at the suggestion that it was for me to influence or restrain Russia. I could do nothing but express pious hopes in general terms to Sazonof [sic]. If I were to address a direct request to

> him that that Russia should not mobilize, I knew his reply; Germany was much more ready for war than Russia; it was a tremendous risk for Russia to delay her mobilization, which was anyhow a slow and cumbrous affair. If Russia took that risk, in deference to our request, would Britain support her, if war did ultimately come and she found herself at a disadvantage owing to following our advice?[40]

"Germany was much more ready for war than Russia?" Here is another lie from Sir Edward. Neither Ambassador Goschen in Berlin, nor the Consuls in the larger cities, nor the Foreign Office archives, nor the later release of the British Documents, provide the slightest basis for any such assumption. Sir Edward could not have been this ignorant. He was simply providing a cover, however false, for his failure to moderate Russia. Was he not informed by his own Ambassador in St. Petersburg, Sir George Buchanan, of extensive Russian mobilization measures, especially the *"Period Preparatory to War"* ordered on July 25? Was he unaware that these extensive secret mobilization measures undertaken by Russia had been intercepted by Germany? To wit:

> The German Foreign Office in fact received, as the *Kautsky Documents* show, between the morning of July 26 and the evening of July 30 twenty-eight reports of Russian military preparations, no less than sixteen of which related to the Russian frontier against Germany; and the German General Staff and Navy Department received many more such reports. But is spite of this, Germany refrained from corresponding preparatory measures [*Drohender Kriegsgefahrzustand* – Threatening Danger of War] until she received on July 31 official news that Russia had taken the final military step of openly announcing by placards throughout the streets of St. Petersburg a general mobilization of the whole Russian army and navy. These secret "preparatory measures," which had been decided on at the Ministerial Council on the afternoon of the 25th, and implemented before dawn of the 26th, enabled Russia, when war came, to surprise the world by the rapidity with which she poured her troops into East Prussia and Galicia.[41]

By now, Sir Edward had been informed of the efforts of Bethmann and the possibility of a resolution by Serbian acceptance of Points 5 & 6, as well as Austrian concessions, but continues his self-serving discourse:

> But besides this I did most honestly feel that neither Russian nor French mobilization was an unreasonable or unnecessary precaution.[42]

"Precaution?" Sir Edward was perfectly well aware that in 1914, mobilization meant war. This was commonly understood by virtually every Gen-

eral Staff in the world and had been specifically defined as meaning war by the authors of the Franco-Russian Alliance, Czar Nicholas, and General Dobrorolski.

> The decision for European war was made by Russia on the night of 29 July 1914, when Tsar Nicholas II, advised unanimously by his advisers, signed the order for general mobilization. General mobilization – as he knew, as Sazonov knew, as Schilling knew; as Krivoshein, Rodzianko, and Duma leaders knew; as Sukhomlinov, Yanushkevitch, and Dobrorolskii knew – meant war. So clearly did the tsar know this that, on being moved by a telegram from Kaiser Wilhelm II, he changed his mind. "I will not be responsible for a monstrous slaughter" is the key line of the entire July crisis, for it shows that the tsar, for all his simplicity – or expressly because of his guileless, unaffected simplicity – knew exactly what he was doing when he did it. He knew exactly what he was doing when he did it again, sixteen hours later, after agonizing all day about it. Sazonov knew it, which is why he told Yanushkevitch to "smash his telephone" so that the tsar could not change his mind again.[43]

In his tireless, seemingly endless efforts to explain his deafening silence in the face of the Russian general mobilization, Sir Edward verges on the conspiratorial:

> But now something that had always been an uncomfortable suspicion in the background came to the front and took more definite and ugly shape. There were forces other than Bethmann-Hollweg in the seat of authority in Germany. He was not master of the situation; in negotiating with him we were not negotiating with a principal. Yet he was the only authority with whom we could negotiate at all.[44]

What utter nonsense! There is not a shred of evidence that Bethmann-Hollweg was not in control of the Wilhelmstrasse at all times. In fact, when German Generals Moltke and Falkenhayn challenged Bethmann and demanded that he order general mobilization in response to extensive Russian measures, Bethmann's flat refusal proved to the Generals and to Grey and the Foreign Office who ruled in Berlin.

Edward Grey even resorts to irrelevant historical precedent:

> The precedent of 1870 was ominous; we all knew how Prussian militarism had availed itself of this time and season of the year at which to strike. The same time and season were now approaching.[45]

Sir Edward was apparently still oblivious that this opinion [about the Franco-Prussian War] was directly contradicted by French leaders themselves, or that it was France – not Prussia – who decided the time to strike.

Edward Grey never mentioned the highly inconvenient truth that it was England herself who had secretly instituted some of the most extensive mobilization measures of all.

> At 10 a.m. on Tuesday morning 28 July, Churchill, Battenberg and the Chief of the Staff together decided that the First Fleet, now concentrated, should be ordered north to its war stations. "I feared to bring this matter before the Cabinet," Churchill explained brazenly in his memoirs, "lest it should mistakenly be considered a provocative action likely to damage the chances of peace."[46] Secret orders were sent at 5 p.m. on the Tuesday evening for the rapid movement of the First Fleet to Scapa Flow, beginning under cover of darkness and passing through the Strait of Dover early next morning without lights. Only officers were to be told the destination. In addition, the Second Fleet was to assemble at Portland.[47] Accordingly, very early on Wednesday morning 29 July, the First Fleet steamed out at speed from Portland. The warships passed through the Channel and then turned north, toward the fleet's war stations.[48] The decision to move the ships to their war stations was made at the Admiralty on the morning of Tuesday 28 July and the orders were issued at 5 p.m. This was before news reached London, at 7.20 p.m., of the Austrian declaration of war against Serbia. Similarly, it came before news confirming that Grey's Ambassadors' Conference was dead, which arrived ... on the Wednesday morning. Therefore, Britain's mighty navy was almost wholly mobilised and the fleet ordered to war stations before it was clear that war would explode, even in the Balkans, and before diplomacy to avoid it was exhausted.[49] Moreover, by Churchill's own admission the two preparatory naval moves pre-empted Cabinet decisions. Churchill acted between Cabinets. Both decisions had the effect of accelerating the "march of events," a phrase Churchill was fond of employing as if events were pushed forward by some quite preternatural power. The truth is that Churchill succumbed to a temptation to frog march events.[50]

Not only the Navy but the British Expeditionary Force and the Territorial Force were mobilized before the Belgian issue was raised in Cabinet deliberations. Lord Haldane tells us:

> At eleven o'clock on Monday morning, August 3, 1914, we mobilized without a hitch the whole of the Expeditionary Force, amounting to six divisions and nearly two cavalry divisions, and began its transport over the Channel when war was declared thirty-six hours later. We also at the same time successfully mobilized the Territorial Force and other units amounting to over half a million men. The Navy was already in its war stations, and there was no delay at all in

> putting what we had prepared into operation. I speak of this with direct knowledge, for the Prime Minister, who was holding temporarily the seals of the War Secretary, was overwhelmed with business, he asked me, tho [*sic*] I had then become Lord Chancellor, to go to the War Office and give directions for the mobilization of the machinery with which I was so familiar, and I did so on the morning of Monday, August 3, and a day later handed it over, in working order, to Lord Kitchener.[51]

Thus the Royal Navy – the core of Britain's military power – was fully mobilized on July 28 and ready for action, while the B.E.F. and the Territorial Force were mobilized on the morning of August 3d – four hours before Grey's speech to the House. Upon returning to Paris from their Russian adventure on July 29, Poincaré and Viviani were greeted by enormous crowds with cries of *"Vive Poincaré!"* and *"Vive l'armée!"* There was little doubt about the purpose of Poincaré's visit to St. Petersburg, and *Le Matin* declared enthusiastically: *"Never, perhaps, has a chief magistrate heard an ovation so vibrant, so unanimous!"*[52]

From the beginning, Sir Edward had always felt that the best solution would be found in "direct conversations" between Austria and Russia. Accordingly, he wired his Ambassador in St. Petersburg:

> It would be very desirable that Austria and Russia should discuss things together if they become difficult. You can speak in this sense if occasion seems to require it.[53]

And in two later telegrams on the 28th, Grey stated:

> As long as there is a prospect of direct exchange of views between Austria and Russia, I would suspend every other suggestion, as I entirely agree that this is the most preferable method of all.... It is most satisfactory that there is a prospect of a direct exchange of views between the Russian and Austrian Governments.[54]

No doubt, this was an excellent suggestion from Grey but it was met *"by instant and emphatic condemnation from President Poincaré when Buchanan proposed it to him during the visit to St. Petersburg."*[55] Buchanan reported:

> His Excellency [President Poincaré] expressed opinion that a conversation à deux between Austria and Russia would be very dangerous at the present moment, and seemed favorable to moderating counsels by France and England at Vienna.[56]

This astonishing refusal by Poincaré of what Grey considered to be the "best" proposal is not given a single mention by Grey in his memoirs, but historians have expressed their utter amazement:

> "Very dangerous" to have Austria and Russia converse with a view to coming to a friendly and peaceful solution of the Austro-Serbian conflict? One rubs one's eyes to see if one has read aright. Very dangerous to what? Certainly not to the peace of Europe. But perhaps to M. Poincaré's policy of having the Triple Entente stand as a solid block in opposition to Germany and Austria, refusing conciliatory arrangements with either of them, and preparing to force them to accept diplomatic defeat or fight against superior forces ... M. Poincaré's contemporary telegrams and his later memoirs continually reiterate the desire to have the Triple Entente always concert together their line of action before any one of them approached Germany or Austria. So now, quite in keeping with his whole policy since he became Minister of Foreign Affairs in January, 1912, he thought "a conversation à deux between Austria and Russia would be very dangerous."[57]

Thus Grey spent most of a chapter on his proposal for a Conference of Ambassadors and disingenuously trying to explain how its rejection prevented him from moderating Russia, but never mentioned Poincaré's abrupt, unconditional veto of his "best method of all" or that it was later implemented by the German Ambassador, Pourtales, which resulted in a promising exchange [July 26-28] between Sasonov and Austrian Ambassador Szapáry. Already on the 27th, when Count Benckendorff, in a conversation with Grey, expressed Russian fears that England would "stand aside in any event," Grey helpfully pointed out that Churchill's order,

> ...to First Fleet, which happens to be concentrated at Portland, not to disperse for manoevre leave ought to dispel this impression.[58]

Not surprisingly, this served to dispel any remaining doubts that England would intervene and a day later, Russia made plans to announce general mobilization at midnight, July 29. Sir Edward was of course fully cognizant of what would happen as a consequence of Russian general mobilization. He wrote:

> The latest news was that Russia had ordered a complete mobilization of her fleet and army. This, it seemed to me, would precipitate a crisis, and would make it appear that German mobilization was being forced by Russia.[59]

Fay notes that these revealing words from Grey:

> ...were suppressed from the British Blue Book of 1914 (No. 119). They show that Grey realized the truth, but allowed it to be sup-

> pressed in order to support the Franco-Russian effort to minimize the importance of Russia's step.[60]

On the morning of July 30, Sasonov met with the Russian Chief of Staff (Ianushkevitch) and the Minister of War (Sukhomlinov), both of whom insisted that Sasonov return to Peterhof at once and get the Czar to change his mind a second time and agree to change from partial to general mobilization. Sasonov was in full agreement. Ianushkevitch pressed him to call as soon as he was successful in persuading the Czar. *"After this,"* added the Chief of Staff, *"I will retire from sight, smash my telephone, and generally take all measures so that I cannot be found to give any contrary orders for a new postponement of general mobilization."*[61] The General then telephoned Dobrorolski: *"There is hope for an improvement of the situation. Be ready to come to me with all the documents immediately upon my telephone call in the afternoon."*[62]

Just before noon, July 30, the German Ambassador, Pourtales, begged Sasonov for a proposal which would satisfy Russia and have at least a chance of resolving the crisis. Sasonov then wrote out the following "formula":

> If Austria, recognizing that the Austro-Serbian question has assumed the character of a question of European interest, declares herself ready to eliminate from her ultimatum points which violate the sovereign rights of Serbia, Russia engages to stop her military preparations.[63]

Sasonov then spoke with Buchanan and Paléologue and told them of the "formula" he had written for Pourtales minutes earlier and said:

> If Austria rejects this proposal, preparations for a general mobilization will be proceeded with, and European war will be inevitable. For strategical reasons Russia can hardly postpone converting partial into general mobilization, now that she knows Germany is preparing, and excitement in the country has reached such a pitch that she cannot hold back if Austria refuses to make concessions.[64]

But without waiting for "concessions" from Austria (for which Bethmann was waiting at that very moment) or any reaction at all, Sasonov proceeded to Peterhof to get the Czar's authorization for the fatal order. Fay has well noted that,

> [British Ambassador] Buchanan evidently made no effort to deter Sasonov from his purpose of converting partial into general mobilization; his failure to do so must have been an encouragement to the Russian Minister.[65]

Just hours later after arriving at Peterhof, the following conversation took place between the Czar and his Foreign Minister:

> **Czar**: Think of the responsibility which you are advising me to take. Think of the thousands and thousands of men who will be sent to their death!
>
> **Sasonov**: It only remains to do everything necessary to meet war fully armed and under conditions most favorable for us. Therefore it is better without fear to call forth a war by our preparations for it, and to continue these preparations carefully, rather than out of fear to give an inducement for war and be taken unawares.[66]

In this brief but historic exchange the Czar acknowledged that mobilization means war and Sasonov admitted that it meant *"... to call forth a war ..."* At this very moment Bethmann was pressuring Austria and awaiting a response from Berchtold promised for the 31st, while the Czar had telegraphed the Kaiser just that morning:

> Thank you heartily for your quick answer. Am sending Tatishvhev [the Czar's representative at the Kaiser's court] this evening with instructions. The military measures which have now come into force were decided five days ago for reasons of defence on account of Austria's preparations. I hope from all my heart that these measures won't in any way interfere with your part as mediator which I greatly value. We need your strong pressure on Austria to come to an understanding with us.[67]

Thus with this hopeful note and the prospect of a real diplomatic solution in sight, Russia ordered general mobilization and inaugurated the war before German pressure on Austria could yield the inevitable concessions that would have preserved the peace. The Austro-Hungarian Empire was an ancient one that preceded Germany's by many centuries and was in no wise inclined to take her marching orders from Berlin, but Austria could not fight Russia and Serbia alone. Germany held all the military cards and this sobering fact would have obliged Austria to make concessions.

In his *Conclusion*, Fay writes:

> It was the hasty Russian general mobilization, assented to on July 29 and ordered on July 30, while Germany was still trying to bring Austria to accept mediation proposals, which finally rendered the European War inevitable.

And:

> Russia's responsibility lay also in the secret preparatory military measures which she was making at the same time that she was carrying on diplomatic negotiations. These alarmed Germany and Austria. But it was primarily Russia's general mobilization, made when Germany was trying to bring Austria to a settlement, which precipitated the final catastrophe, causing Germany to mobilize and declare war.

But this – negotiating while secretly mobilizing – was no more than Russian policy:

> Mobilization does not necessarily mean the immediate beginning of hostilities because it may be of advantage to complete the marshalling of our troops without beginning hostilities, in order that our opponent may not be entirely deprived of the hope that war may still be avoided. Our military measures will then have to be masked by clever, *pretended diplomatic negotiations* in order to lull the fears of the enemy as completely as possible. If by such measures we can gain a few days, they absolutely must be taken![68]

General Palitsyn, the Russian Chief of Staff in 1915, would later boast about the success of this Russian Protocol in deceiving Germany and Austria:

> Just think what would have occurred if the Austrians had thrown their troops solidly against us. Our march to the frontier would not have succeeded, and the Austrians would have inflicted partial defeats on us. But for a long time they did not believe we would declare war. They devoted all their attention to Serbia in the full conviction that we would not stir. Our mobilization struck them like a thunderbolt. It was then too late for them. They had become involved with Serbia. The Germans too permitted the first days to elapse without action. Altogether we gained twelve days. Our enemies committed a huge blunder [by regarding Russian diplomatic efforts as sincere] and conceded to us at the same time an incalculable advantage.[69]

The British Government was meanwhile doing its best to soothe Germany and Austria with false promises of neutrality and was successful. On July 25, Bethmann telegraphed the Kaiser that *"for the present, at least, Sir E. Grey is not considering direct participation by England in a possible European war."*[70] German confidence in British neutrality was greatly strengthened when the Kaiser's brother, Prince Henry, on a visit to England, had been assured by King George V on July 26: *"We shall try all we can to keep out of this, and shall remain neutral."* This was duly reported back to Berlin: *"King of Great Britain said to Prince Henry of Prussia that England would maintain neutrality in case war should break out between Continental Powers."*[71]

On the evening of July 30, the King of England sent the following telegram to Prince Henry of Prussia:

> So pleased to hear of William's efforts to concert with Nicky to maintain peace … My Government is doing its utmost suggesting to Russia and France to suspend further military preparations, if Austria will consent to be satisfied with occupation of Belgrade and neighboring Serbian territory as a hostage for satisfactory settlement of her demands, other countries meanwhile suspending their war preparations. Trust William will use his great influence to induce Austria to accept this proposal, thus proving that Germany and England are working together to prevent what would be an international catastrophe. Pray William that I am doing and shall continue to do all that lies in my power to preserve the peace of Europe.[72]

This was sent three hours after the Russian order for general mobilization had been sent out over the wires, but the conniving King actually had a very different opinion:

> On August 2, the King informed Sir Edward it was "absolutely essential" Britain go to war in order to prevent Germany from achieving "complete domination of this country."
>
> When Sir Edward said the Cabinet had yet to find a justifiable reason to enter the conflict, the King replied: "You have got to find a reason, Grey."
>
> The King told Grey "that, if we didn't go to war, Germany would mop up France and having dealt with the European situation would proceed to obtain complete domination of this country.
>
> For that reason he felt that it was absolutely essential that whatever happened we had got to find a reason for entering the War at once … "[73]

Thus we see that in the case of King George V, the eldest surviving son of Edward VII, the apple did not fall far from the tree.

On the afternoon of Monday, August 3d, Sir Edward Grey delivered his famous address to the House of Commons. With regard to British obligations he stated:

> I come first, now, to the question of British obligations. I have assured the House – and the Prime Minister has assured the House more than once – that if any crisis such as this arose, we should come before the House of Commons and be able to say to the House that it was free to decide what the British attitude should be, that we would have no secret engagement which we should spring upon the House, and tell the House that, because we had entered into that engagement, there was an obligation of honour upon the country.

No "obligation of honour?" Minutes later in this same speech, Grey intoned solemnly:

> If, in a crisis like this, we run away from those obligations of honour and interest as regards the Belgian Treaty, I doubt whether, whatever material force we might have at the end, it would be of very much value in face of the respect that we should have lost.

Thus by invoking Belgium, Grey refutes his own egregious lie about France. The list of British diplomats who have refuted this flagrant falsehood is too long to be included here, but a few examples will suffice.

> The mere fact of the War Office plan having been worked out in detail with the French General Staff… has certainly committed us to fight, whether the Cabinet likes it or not, and that the combined plan of the two General Staffs [French and British] holds the field.[74]

Churchill joined Gooch, Beazley, Dickinson, Esher, Chamberlain, when he expressed the opinion of virtually everyone except Grey:

> It is true to say that our Entente with France, and the military and naval conversations that had taken place since 1906, had led us into a position where we had the obligations of an alliance without its advantages.… We were morally bound to come to the aid of France.[75]

But as Fay notes, Grey had made his decision three days earlier:

> Already, however, on this same Friday (July 31st], before hearing of the dubious German reply in regard to Belgium, Sir Edward Grey determined in his own mind, in agreement with Nicolson and Crowe, that England's obligation of honor to France and her own material interests made it imperative for her to intervene on the Franco-Russian side.[76]

Grey devoted most of his speech to explaining that obligations of honor to France did not exist, but that obligations of honor to Belgium did. He reported the German demands made of Belgium the previous evening but failed to disclose that Anglo-Belgian military planning had forfeited Belgian neutrality. Grey did not know on August 3d that the relevant Belgian diplomatic documents would fall into German hands in a few weeks. The speed of the German advance through Belgium in 1914 was not anticipated and the Belgian Government in Brussels escaped to Antwerp barely ahead of the quick-moving feld-grau columns, leaving behind many incriminating documents relating to Anglo-Belgian military conversations. After a detailed study, Dr. Alexander Fuehr quotes these documents in support of his final conclusion:

> Of such intimacy was Belgium's co-operation with England and France before the outbreak of the war! 'Neutral' Belgium had in reality become an active member of the coalition concluded against Germany.[77]

Thus the Treaty of 1839 was indeed a "scrap of paper" to which it had been reduced by Anglo-Belgian planning and the shame was on Great Britain for invoking it as a cause of war.

Grey knew and had always known the policy that would have prevented the war. On July 30, he expressed it in a telegram to Sir Edward Goschen, the British Ambassador in Berlin:

> And I will say this: If the peace of Europe can be preserved, and the present crisis safely passed, my own endeavour will be to promote some arrangement to which Germany could be a party, by which she could be assured that no aggressive or hostile policy would be pursued against her or her Allies by France, Russia, and ourselves, jointly or separately.[78]

Here is another statement from Edward Grey intended for the galleries and to be later cited as exculpatory evidence before the bar of history. In fact, since 1906 Grey had followed the precise opposite policy and vigorously and repeatedly opposed any manner of "arrangement" with Germany or any policy which he now recommended to Goschen for fear of alienating France. Even now, at this late hour, there was still time for Grey to make a "representation" at St. Petersburg, as general mobilization would not be ordered for another six hours. But Grey had from the beginning made no attempt to moderate either France or Russia and was not about to start. Belgium had long ago been assigned the important task of transforming overwhelming public opposition to the war into its opposite. The Treaty of 1839 was Grey's backdoor to war and it would swing wide open the moment it was violated by Germany – as was fully expected by Grey.

A particularly odious and vocal British warmonger was one Leopold "Leo" James Maxse (1864-1932), editor of the *National Review*. On the night of August 1st, he organized a meeting of the "war hawks" among Conservatives and formulated the following letter sent to Asquith and Grey on the afternoon of August 2nd: [79]

> "Lord Lansdowne and I feel it our duty to inform you that in our opinion, as well as that of all the colleagues whom we have been able

> to consult, it would be fatal to the honour and security of the United Kingdom to hesitate in supporting France and Russia at the present juncture and we offer our unhesitating [support] to the Government in any measure they may consider necessary for that object."

As Lord Loreburn comments:

> Not a word in it, observe, about Belgium. To support France and Russia: that was the thing to be done.[80]

Obligations of honour to France and Russia could not begin to command British public opinion. This was the important task reserved for Belgium. Grey had already taken great care to unlock the Belgian back door by telegraphing the British Minister in Brussels:

> You should say that I assume that the Belgian Government will maintain to the utmost of her power her neutrality, which I desire and expect other Powers to uphold and observe. You should inform the Belgian Government that an early reply is desired.[81]

The Belgian Government replied at once:

> Belgium expects that other Powers will observe and uphold her neutrality, which she intends to maintain to the utmost of her power.[82]

To further bait the trap, Grey addressed a request to the French and German Governments the same day asking each for an assurance that it would respect the neutrality of Belgium so long as no other Power violated it. Through extensive British military planning with France and Belgium, Grey had arranged that France would not be the first to violate Belgium and would therefore reply in the affirmative. From the same source, he knew as well that the Schlieffen Plan called for an advance through Belgium and that the German reply would therefore be non-committal. With the Belgian trap thus set and fortified by Bonar Law's promise of support from a number of the most important Unionist leaders, Sir Edward Grey was ready. He did not have long to wait. Already on August 2, he had given the very first concrete promise of military support to France:

> If the German fleet comes into the Channel or through the North Sea to undertake hostile operations against the French coast or shipping, the British fleet will give all the protection in its power.[83]

This was a de-facto declaration of war and was so regarded by Cambon, who wrote in his memoirs:

> I was satisfied that the game had been won. A Great Power does not go to war with half measures. The moment it decides on carrying on war at sea it has no choice left but to prosecute it on land as well.[84]

The next day, August 3rd, Grey admitted the truth of Cambon's interpretation and convicted himself with his own words. After informing the House that Britain could not look on with arms folded while the undefended coasts of France were being attacked and reading the assurance given to Cambon the previous day, he stated that Britain could only stand aside if she immediately issued a proclamation of neutrality. This is where Grey, despite himself, lets the cat out of the bag:

> There is but one way in which the Government could make certain at the present moment of keeping outside this war, and that would be that it should immediately issue a proclamation of unconditional neutrality. We cannot do that. We have made the commitment to France that I have read to the House which prevents us from doing that.[85]

With these words, Grey admits that British commitments to France did indeed preclude neutrality, even after having denied the existence of any such commitments just minutes earlier.

After the speech and a Cabinet meeting in the evening, Grey confided to Cambon that the Cabinet had decided to send an ultimatum to Berlin demanding the withdrawal of the German ultimatum. *"If they refuse,"* so said Sir Edward, *"there will be war."*[86]

After receiving the British ultimatum, a final stormy confrontation between British Ambassador, Goschen, and German Chancellor, Bethmann-Hollweg, took place:

> I [Goschen] said that in the same way as he and Herr von Jagow wished me to understand that for strategical reasons it was a matter of life and death for Germany to advance through Belgium and violate her neutrality, so I would wish him to understand that it was, so to speak, a matter of 'life and death' for the honor of Great Britain that she should keep her engagement to do her utmost to defend Belgium's neutrality if attacked. That solemn compact simply had to be kept, or what confidence could anyone have in engagements given by Great Britain in the future?[87]

The surprise and agitation of Bethmann and Berchtold in response to the British ultimatum is eloquent testimony to the success of Grey's policy of "deliberate ambiguity." On August 5, the British Foreign Office issued the following official statement:

> Owing to the summary rejection by the German Government of the request made by his Majesty's Government for assurances that the neutrality of Belgium will be respected, his Majesty's Ambassador to Berlin has received his passports, and his Majesty's Government declared to the German Government that a state of war exists between Great Britain and Germany as from 11 p.m. on August 4, 1914.

It should again be emphasized that Belgian "neutrality" had long ago been forfeited by 1. the political actions of King Leopold II and his dealings and atrocities in the Congo, and 2. Anglo-Belgian military planning conducted during the reign of Albert I (see Fuehr above). It should also be noted – again – that a virtual legion of British statesmen – Palmerston, Lord Derby, Gladstone, Salisbury – have all affirmed that the Treaty of 1839 did not bind England to defend Belgian neutrality. Lord Loreburn stated the case:

> All that we did in 1839 was to sign, together with Austria, France, Russia, and Holland, an agreement that Belgium should be a perpetually neutral State. We bound ourselves, as did the others, not to violate that neutrality, but did not bind ourselves to defend it against encroachment of any other Power. That is the plain effect of the document.

In the third volume of his distinguished Cambridge History of British Foreign Policy, G.P. Gooch agreed with Loreburn:

> The Guarantee of 1839, as Palmerston pointed out, gave a right, but did not impose an obligation to defend Belgian neutrality. Gladstone's Treaties with France and Prussia in 1870 were only necessary because that of 1839 did not automatically invoke action.

Grey believed Germany to be *"a European aggressor as bad as Napoleon"*[88] and it is ludicrous to suppose that he would not have acted to protect his country from the danger as he saw it by employing the Triple Entente so carefully crafted by himself and King Edward. Thus on July 30, when Austria had promised to reply to Bethmann's pressure the next day and the prospects for peace had never looked better, the Triple Entente had to act fast.

– Forgotten was the decision of the Russian Ministerial Council of July 24 *"to advise Serbia not to offer armed resistance if Austria should invade her territory but to announce that she was yielding to force and entrusting her fate to the judgment of the Great Powers."*[89]

–Forgotten was Sasonov's advice that *"if the helpless situation of Serbia is indeed such as to leave no doubt as to the outcome of an armed conflict with Austria,"* it would be better not to make armed resistance, but retreating, let Austria occupy territory without a fight and appeal to the Powers to intervene.[90]

–Forgotten was Sasonov's July 27 statement to Pourtales that *"a way must be found of administering a deserved lesson to Serbia, while respecting her rights of sovereignty."*[91]

–Forgotten was Grey's opinion that *"even if the Austrian demands on Serbia went beyond, what facts, as known hitherto, justified, it was better that Serbia should give way than that European peace should be broken."*[92]

–Forgotten, finally, was that Grey himself had endorsed the Kaiser's "Halt in Belgrade" proposal.

What was suddenly remembered like a thunderbolt was that Berchtold was scheduled to reply to Bethmann's urgent demands the very next day, July 31, and that this could result in concessions which might lead to a resolution of the crisis and the preservation of peace. This would mean the loss of a decade of military planning and preparation. Already, Germany had twice prevented a European war. The Bosnian crisis of 1908 had been successfully resolved by a German initiative, and in 1913 during the 2nd Balkan War, Germany stopped Austria from intervening thus again preserving the peace of Europe. Now, in the crisis of 1914, Germany threatened to preserve the peace yet again by her pressure on Austria. Serbia had lately hinted that she might accept points 5 & 6 of the Austrian Note, and Berchtold had promised a reply to Bethmann the next day. There was no time to lose! The nations of the Triple Entente were at the peak of their power and a golden opportunity such as this might never come again. It was now or never! Hours later at precisely 6:00 P.M., Russia, with Anglo-French backing, rolled the dice ...

As noted above, criticism of Grey that he was unqualified such as that levelled by Lloyd George is false. Like his mentor, King Edward VII, Grey worked for the military defeat of Germany because he genuinely believed, however mistakenly, that it was necessary and he did so with skill, foresight, and planning. We can only speculate about Sir Edward's inner thoughts as he trimmed his roses and listened to bird calls during, say, the Battle of the Somme, but did he ever have any real regrets? A telegram sent to Sasonov on April 6, 1915, by Benckendorff included this:

> Grey is filled with a constant feeling, not without some justification, that it was he above all who, at a moment when public opinion in

> Britain and all Ministers were undecided, brought Britain into the war.[93]

During May, 1914, President Wilson's personal representative, Colonel House, toured Europe and reported his impression of "militarism run stark mad" and "too much hatred, too many jealousies." In a marvel of brevity, he summed up a complex political situation in a single brief, succinct sentence:

> Whenever England consents, France and Russia will close in on Germany and Austria.[94]

This comports perfectly with the final conclusion of Hermann Lutz in his biography of Edward Grey:

> This [Grey] was the man who in the last resort held in his hand during the crisis of July 1914 the decision between peace and war.[95]

***

Endnotes

1. Nicolson, *Lord Carnock*, 390.
2. Dickinson, *The International Anarchy*, 477.
3. "Austria Declares War on Serbia", *Daily Citizen*, 27 July 1914.
4. Bethmann to Pourtales, July 26, 1:35 P.M., K.D., 198.
5. Paléologue, *An Ambassador's Memoirs*, I, 2f.
6. Lutz, *Lord Grey and the World War*, 300.
7. Geiss, Imanuel, *July 1914, The Outbreak of the First World War*, 288-90 .
8. Newton, Douglas The Darkest Days, Kindle Location 323.
9. Gooch, *Revelations*, 31.
10. Lutz, *Lord Grey and the World War*, 267.
11. K.D., 271.
12. William II to Jagow, July 28, 10:00 A.M.
13. Bethmann to Tschirschky, July 28, 10:15 P.M., K.D., 323.
14. Bethmann to Pourtales and the other German Ambassadors abroad, July 28, 9 P.M., K.D., 315.
15. Goschen to Grey, July 28, midnight, B.D., 249.
16. Bethmann to Tschirschky, July 29, 8:00 P.M., K.D., 361.
17. Tschirschky to Bethmann, July 29, 11:50 P.M., received July 30, 1:30 A.M., K.D., 388.
18. Bethmann to Tschirschky, July 30, 3 A.M.; K.D., 396.
19. Lichnowsky to Bethmann, July 29, 2:08 P.M.: K.D., 337.
20. Bethmann to Tschirschky, July 30, 12:30 A.M.; K.D., 384.
21. Tschirschky to Bethmann, July 31, 1:35 A.M., K.D., 465.
22. Minute, July 28, on B.D., 185.
23. Sasonov's tg. No. 1521 to Isvolsky in Paris and Benckendorff in London, July 27.

24. Isvolsky to Sasonov, tg. No. 198, July 28.
25. Grey, II, 26, cited in Lutz, *Lord Grey and the World War*, 271.
26. Isvolsky to Sasonov, tg. No. 210, July 30; M.F.R., 521; L.N., II,290.
27. Isvolsky to Sasonov, July 31, 1:00 A.M.; M.F.R., 522; L.N., 294.
28. Paléologue, *Revue Deux Mondes*, January 15, 1921.
29. Fabre-Luce, Alfred, *La Victoire.*
30. Fay, *The Origins of the World War*, II, 291-3.
31. Paléologue, *An Ambassador's Memoirs*, I, 27.
32. Dobrorolski, 103 (German trans., 21 f.).
33. Fay, II, 379.
34. B.D., 10.
35. Grey, *Twenty-Five Years,* I, 320, 1.
36. Bilinski's remark in the Ministerial Council of July 31, 1914; A.R.B., III, 79.
37. Fay, II, 474.
38. Grey, I, 306.
39. Ibid., 311.
40. Ibid., 320.
41. Fay, II, 321.
42. Grey, I, 321.
43. McMeekin, Sean, *July 1914 - Countdown to War*, 397.
44. Grey, I, 312.
45. Ibid., 313.
46. Churchill, *The World Crisis*, I, 171.
47. Admiralty to C. in C. Home Fleets, 28 July 1914.
48. Churchill, *World Crisis*, I, 171.
49. Bunsen to Grey, B.D., vol. XI, Doc. 226.
50. Newton, Douglas, *The Darkest Days,* Kindle Locations 1261-1272.
51. Haldane, *Before the War*, 45-6.
52. *Le Matin*, July 30, 1914.
53. Grey, II, 365.
54. B.D., Nos. 203, 218.
55. Fay, II, 366.
56. Buchanan to Grey, July 22; B.D., 76 (omitted from B.B.B.).
57. Fay, II, 366.
58. Grey to Buchanan, B.D., 177.
59. Grey to Bertie, July 31, B.D., 367.
60. Fay, II, 535.
61. *Schilling's Diary*, 64.
62. Dobrorolski, 108 (German ed. 27).
63. Pourtales to Bethmann, July 30, 1:01 P.M.; K.D., 421.
64. Buchanan to Grey, July 30, 1:15 P.M., received at 3:15 P.M.; B.D., 302.
65. Fay, II, 470-1.
66. Schilling's Diary, 63; and Paléologue, I. 39.
67. Czar to Kaiser, July 30, 1:20 A.M., received 1:45 A.M.; K.D. 390.
68. Protocol of the Special Military Commission of Nov. 8, 1912.

69. Fedor Fedorovich Palitsyn *Memoirs,* 1924, 22, cited in *Current History,* March 1927, 855-6.
70. K.D., 182, 221.
71. German Naval Attaché in London to German Naval Office, July 26; K.D., 207.
72. George V to Prince Henry, July 30, 8:54 P.M., received 11:08 P.M., K.D., 452.
73. Appendix 2 (this volume).
74. Fraser, Peter, *Lord Esher: A Political Biography* (Kindle Locations 4868-4869).
75. *Peace Conference Hints,* 205.
76. Fay, II, 537.
77. Fuehr, Alexander, *Breakdown of Belgian Neutrality,* Ch. IV.
78. Grey, I, 318.
79. Loreburn, *How the War Came,* 210; L.J. Maxse in *The National Review,* Aug. 1918.
80. Ibid., 209.
81. B.D., No. 351.
82. Ibid., No. 128.
83. Grey to Bertie, Aug. 2, 4:45 P.M., B.D., 487.
84. *Revue de France,* July 1, 1921; *Carnets de Georges Louis,* II, 150.
85. Grey's August 3 speech to the House is given in Grey, II, Appendix D.
86. Cambon to Viviani, Aug. 4, 12:17 A.M.
87. Goschen to Grey, Aug 6; B.D., 671; see also 666, 667.
88. Morley, Lord, *Memorandum on Resignation,* 11.
89. Fay, II, 297.
90. Sasonov to the Russian Chargé d'Affaires in Belgrade, July 24.
91. D.D., 282.
92. Grey, I, 300.
93. *Die Kriegschuldfrage,* September, 1923, 52.
94. *Intimate Papers of Colonel House,* Vol. 1, 249.
95. Lutz, Hermann, *Lord Grey and the World War,* 194.

Epilogue

Henry Woodd Nevinson was a well-known crusading British war correspondent during the 2nd Boer War and the First World War. He published the following article in the *Saturday Review of Literature* for November 20, 1926:

> "Shameful and disastrous as was the whole Treaty of Versailles, there was one clause in it that surpassed all others in shame. It was *Article 231,* and it ran:
>
> "The Allied and associated Governments affirm, and Germany accepts, the responsibility of herself and her allies for causing all the loss and damage to which the Allied and Associated Governments and their nationals have been subjected as a consequence of the war imposed upon them by the aggression of Germany and her allies.
>
> "Other Articles in the Treaty are shameless in their bullying treatment of a gallant and vanquished enemy and in their acquisitive greed that is sure to engender future wars, but that Article expresses a lie of such grossness that I wonder the hand which first wrote it did not wither. I do not wonder that the German representatives to whom it was first shown refused to sign such an atrocious perversion of the truth. Ultimately a German did consent to sign, and his consent is the most terrible evidence of the abject misery to which war, disease, and the starvation of women and children owing to the British blockade for seven months after the Armistice had reduced the German people. Whether M. Clemenceau or Mr. Lloyd George concocted the lie, I cannot be sure, but amid all the orgy of iniquity that prevailed in Versailles in 1919, that Article stands out conspicuous, and no historian will ever dare repeat it except with indignant scorn. This is quite certain, no matter what view of the war's origin history may take."

The sheer absurdity of *Article 231* soon caused it to collapse of its own weight, but the larger *Kriegschuldvrage* was not addressed until the late twenties when the American revisionists, Profs. Barnes and Fay, published their books based on the documents released by Germany, Austria, Great Britain, France, and Russia. Historical revisionism, temporarily eclipsed by World War II, took another form in the sixties when German historian, Fritz Fischer, decided to address the vexing issue of the German motive for starting the Great War which was becoming increasingly conspicuous by its absence. Emerging from years of Herculean labor in the archives, Mr. Fischer published in 1961 *Griff Nach der Weltmacht* (translated as *Germany's Aims in the First World War).* Put briefly, Fischer's thesis was that Germany started the War to establish hegemony, first in Europe, then the world, and presented Bethmann's 1914 September Programme as proof. The response within Germany to Fischer's book was one of outrage and triggered a heated debate in Germany's historical community led by Gerhard Ritter. In 1965 Fischer published *Weltmacht Oder Niedergang* (World Power or Decline) to answer his growing legion of critics. Few historians today take Fischer seriously and perhaps the only reason his book got any traction at all was that some in Germany wished to accept blame for the 1st World War by way of atonement for their Nazi past; perhaps they felt it was the least they could do. But as one Oxford historian has noted:

> The unescapable fact is that no evidence has ever been found by Fischer and his pupils that these objectives [Bethmann's September Programme] existed before Britain's entry into the war.... All that Fischer can produce are the pre-war pipe dreams of a few Pan-Germans and businessmen, none of which had any official status, as well as the occasional bellicose utterances of the Kaiser, an individual whose influence over policy was neither consistent nor as great as he himself believed.[1]

What Fischer finally ended up proving, despite himself, was that in 1914, Germany had no motive other than self-defense. Others in Germany and elsewhere found comfort in *"the military myth that wars are caused by stupid, evil, aggressive nations on the other side of the world who refuse to get along with the intelligent, good, peaceful people on this side."*[2]

With few exceptions[3] German leaders of 1914 shared a remarkable degree of unanimity on the causes of the Great War. Slowly but surely, the historical verdict increasingly confirms the judgment of the unfortunate German Kaiser as he expressed it in the following letter sent from his exile in Doorn, Holland, to the American journalist, George Sylvester Viereck:

> Grey knew the land-grabbing hunger of Russia directed against Germany and Austria-Hungary; he knew the burning desire of France to re-conquer the 'lost provinces', the old German territory of Elsass-Lothringen; he knew the envy in British industrial and capitalistic circles against Germany's successful competition. Hence, he 'engineered' the necessary events and complications that presented the Russian hate, the French lust for revenge, and British commercial envy with the wished-for opportunity to satisfy their criminal intentions at the expense of an unsuspecting Germany.

> Result: A junction of pirates surprising a tranquil land and a tranquil people profoundly at peace with themselves and the world. Sir Edward Grey played the rôle of interested observer who shrugs his shoulders, when appealed to, exclaiming, "Not my fault. Can't help it! Those Germans are exasperating." Realizing the heinousness of their offense, those responsible for the conspiracy, knowing that in time truth, like murder, will out, created a scapegoat to turn away the wrath of the world from themselves. They chose for their victim the monarch of the nation they feloniously attacked and saddled him with their crime by inventing the War-Guilt Lie. International capital and the press placed itself at the disposal of the pirates and by propaganda (Northcliffe) they disseminated the War-Guilt Lie all over the world until even their victims, the Germans, began to believe it.
>
> Ever yours, Wilhelm, I,R

On the eve of war, the Kaiser expressed the same view and even praised Edward VII:

> If mobilization can no longer be retracted—which is not true—why then, did the Czar appeal to my mediation three days afterward without mention of the issuance of the mobilization order?
>
> Either we are shamefully to betray our Allies, sacrifice them to Russia – thereby breaking up the Triple Alliance, or we are to be attacked in common by the Triple Entente for our fidelity to our Allies and punished, whereby they will satisfy their jealousy by joining in totally ruining us. That is the real situation in nuce, which, slowly and cleverly set going, certainly by Edward VII, has been carried on and systematically built up by disowned conferences between England and Paris and St. Petersburg; finally brought to a conclusion by George V and set to work. And thereby the stupidity and ineptitude of our ally is turned into a snare for us. So the famous encirclement of Germany has finally become a complete fact, despite every effort of our politicians and diplomats to prevent it. The net has been suddenly thrown over our head, and England sneeringly reaps the most brilliant success of her persistently prosecuted purely anti-German world policy, against which we have proven ourselves helpless, while she twists the noose of our political and economic destruction out of our fidelity to Austria, as we squirm isolated in the net. A great achievement which arouses the admiration even of him who is to be destroyed as its result! Edward VII is stronger after his death than am I who am still alive! And there have been people who believed that England could be won over or pacified by this or that puny measure! Unremittingly, relentlessly she has pursued her object with notes, holiday proposals, scares, Haldane, etc., until this point was reached. And we walked into the net and even went into the one-ship-program in construction with the ardent hope of thus pacifying England! All my warnings, all my pleas were voiced for nothing.

With the benefit of hindsight, study, and reflection, the Kaiser produced this more cogent analysis of the cause of the War from Doorn,

> "The general situation of the German Empire in the period before the war had become continually more brilliant, and for that very reason continually more difficult from the point of view of foreign politics. Unprecedented progress in industry, commerce, and world traffic had made Germany prosperous. The curve of our development tended steadily upward. The concomitant of this peaceful penetration of a considerable part of the world's markets, to which German diligence and our achievements justly entitled us, was bound to be disagreeable to older nations of the world, particularly to England. This is quite a natural phenomenon, having nothing remarkable about it. Nobody is pleased when a competitor suddenly appears and obliges one to look on while the old customers desert him. For this reason I cannot reproach the British Empire because of English ill humor at Germany's progress in the world's markets. Had England been able, by introducing better commercial methods, to overcome or restrict German competition, she would have been quite within her rights in doing so and no objections could have been made. It simply would have been a case of the better man winning. In the life of nations nobody can find it objectionable if two nations contend against each other peacefully by the same methods – i.e., peaceful methods – yet with all their energy, daring, and organizing ability, each striving to benefit itself. On the other hand, it is quite another matter if one of these nations sees its assets on the world's balance sheet threatened by the industry, achievements, and super business methods of the other, and hence, not being able to apply ability like that of its young competitor, resorts to force – i.e., to methods that are not those of peace, but of war – in order to call a halt upon the other nation in its peaceful campaign of competition, or to annihilate it.
>
> Our situation became more serious since we were obliged to build a navy for the protection of our welfare, which, in the last analysis, was not based on the nineteen billions yearly to which German exports and imports amounted. The supposition that we built this navy for the purpose of attacking and destroying the far stronger English fleet is absurd, since it would have been impossible for us to win a victory on the water, because of the discrepancy between the two navies. Moreover, we were striding forward in the world market in accordance with our desires and had no cause for complaint. Why, then, should we wish to jeopardize the results of our peaceful labors? In France the idea of revenge had been sedulously cultivated ever since 1870-71; it was fostered, with every possible variation, in literary, political, and military writings, in the officer corps, in schools, associations, political circles. I can well understand this spirit. Looked at from the healthy national standpoint, it is, after all, more honorable for a nation to desire revenge for a blow received

than to endure it without complaint. But Alsace-Lorraine had been German soil for many centuries; it was stolen by France and taken back by us in 1871 as our property. Hence, a war of revenge which had as its aim the conquest of thoroughly German territory was unjust and immoral. For us to have yielded on this point would have been a slap in the face to our sentiments of nationality and justice. Since Germany could never voluntarily return Alsace-Lorraine to France, the French dream could be realized only by means of a victorious war which should push forward the French boundary posts to the left bank of the Rhine. Germany, on the contrary, had no reason for staking what she had won in 1870-71, so the course for her to pursue was to maintain peace with France, all the more so because of the fact that the combination of the powers against the German-Austrian Dual Alliance was continually becoming more apparent.

As to Russia, the mighty empire of the Tsars was clamoring for an outlet on the sea to the southward. This was a natural ambition and not to be harshly judged. In addition, there was the Russian-Austrian conflict of influence, especially in Serbia, which also concerned Germany in so far as Germany and Austria-Hungary were allies. The Russia of the Tsars, moreover, was in a state of continual internal ferment and every Tsarist Government had to keep the possibility for a foreign conflict ever in readiness, in order always to be able to deflect attention from inner troubles to foreign difficulties; to have a safety valve as an outlet for the passions that might lead to trouble at home ...

Thus England, France, and Russia had, though for different reasons, an aim in common – viz., to overthrow Germany. England wished to do so for commercial-political reasons, France on account of her policy of revenge, Russia because she was a satellite of France and also for reasons of internal politics and because she wished to reach the southern sea. These three great nations, therefore, were bound to act together. The union of these ambitions in a common course of action, duly planned, is what we call the 'policy of encirclement ...' the aims of the Entente could be attained only through a war, those of Germany only without a war."[4]

The Kaiser had always considered the 1904 Entente Cordiale as the beginning of Germany's encirclement. Thus when German troops overran France in 1940, the Kaiser wrote to the Duchess of Brunswick: *"Thus is the pernicious Entente Cordiale of Uncle Edward VII brought to naught."*[5]

In September, 1914, a month after the outbreak of war, the German Chancellor, Theobald von Bethmann-Hollweg, presented the German case to the Reichstag in a more lawyerly fashion:

Where the responsibility in this greatest of all wars lies is quite evident to us.

Outwardly responsible are the men in Russia who planned and carried into effect the general mobilization of the Russian army.

But in reality and truth the British Government is responsible.

The London Cabinet could have made war impossible if they had unequivocally told Petersburg that England was not willing to let a continental war of the Great Powers result from the Austro-Hungarian conflict with Serbia.

Such words would have compelled France to use all her energy to keep Russia away from every warlike measure.

Then our good offices and mediation between Vienna and Petersburg would have been successful, and there would have been no war!

But England has chosen to act otherwise. She knew that the clique of powerful and partly irresponsible men surrounding the Czar were spoiling for war and intriguing to bring it about.

England saw that the wheel was set a-rolling, but she did not think of stopping it. While openly professing sentiments of peace, London secretly gave St. Petersburg to understand that England stood by France and therefore by Russia too.

This has been clearly and irrefutably shown by the official publications which in the meantime have come out, more particularly by the Blue Book edited by the British Government.

Then St. Petersburg could no longer be restrained. In proof of this we possess the testimony of the Belgian Charge d'Affaires at St. Petersburg, a witness who is surely beyond every suspicion.

He reported (you know his words, but I will repeat them now), he reported to his Government on July 30th that:

England commenced by making it understood that she would not let herself be drawn into a conflict. Sir George Buchanan said this openly. To-day, however, everybody in St. Petersburg is quite convinced – one has actually received the assurance – that England will stand by France.

This support is of enormous weight and has contributed largely toward giving the war-party the upper hand.

Up to this summer English statesmen have assured their Parliament that no treaty or agreement existed influencing England's independence of action, should a war break out, England was free to decide whether she would participate in a European war or not.

Hence, there was no treaty obligation, no compulsion, no menace of the homeland which induced the English statesmen to originate the war and then at once to take part in it.

The only conclusion left is that the London Cabinet allowed this European war, this monstrous world war, because they thought it was an opportune moment with the aid of England's political confederates, to destroy the vital nerve of her greatest European competitors in the markets of the world.

Therefore, England, together with Russia (I have spoken about Russia on the 4th of August), is answerable before God and man for this catastrophe which has come over Europe and over mankind.

The Belgian neutrality which England pretended she was bound to shield, is but a mask.

On the 2nd of August, 7 p.m., we informed Brussels that France's plan of campaign was known to us and that it compelled us, for reasons of self-preservation, to march through Belgium, but as early as the afternoon of the same day, August 2nd, that is to say, before anything was known and could be known of this step, the British Government promised unconditional aid to France in case the German navy attacked the French coastline.

Not a word was said of Belgian neutrality. This fact is established by the declaration made by Sir Edward Grey in the House of Commons on the 3rd of August.

The declaration was communicated to me on August 4th, but not in full, because of the difficulties experienced at that time in the transmission of telegrams. Besides, the very Blue Book issued by the British Government confirms that fact.

How, then, can England allege that she drew the sword because we violated Belgian neutrality? How could British statesmen, who accurately knew the past, talk at all of Belgian neutrality?

When on the 4th of August I referred to the wrong which we were doing in marching through Belgium, it was not yet known for certain whether the Brussels Government in the hour of need would not decide after all to spare the country and to retire to Antwerp under protest.

You remember that, after the occupation of Liege, at the request of our army leaders, I repeated the offer to the Belgian Government.

For military reasons it was absolutely imperative that at the time, about the 4th of August, the possibility for such a development was being kept open. Even then the guilt of the Belgian Government was apparent from many a sign, although I had not yet any positive documentary proofs at my disposal.

But the English statesmen were perfectly familiar with these proofs. The documents which in the meantime have been found in Brussels, and which have been given publicity by me, prove and establish in what way and to what degree Belgium has surrendered her neutrality to England.

The whole world is now acquainted with two outstanding facts:

(1) In the night from the 3rd to the 4th of August, when our troops entered Belgian territory, they were not on neutral soil, but on the soil of a state that had long abandoned its neutrality.

(2) England has declared war on us, not for the sake of Belgian neutrality, which she herself had helped to undermine, but because she believed that she could overcome and master us with the help of two great military powers on the Continent.

Ever since the 2nd of August when England promised to back up the French in this war, she was no longer neutral, but actually in a state of war with us. On the 4th of August she declared war, the alleged reason being our violation of Belgian neutrality.

But that was only a sham motive and a spectacular scene intended to conceal the true war motive and thus to mislead both the English people and foreign neutral countries.

The military plans which England and Belgium had worked out to the minutest details now being unveiled, the policy of English statesmen is branded for all times of history to come. But English diplomacy still added to this. At its call, Japan snatched from us Kiautschau, so bravely defended, and thus violated Chinese neutrality.

Has England interfered with that breach of neutrality? Has she shown in this instance her scrupulous anxiety about the neutral states?

When, in 1910, I became Chancellor, the Triple Alliance had to reckon with a solid counter-combination of Powers. England had created the Triple Entente and knitted it firmly for the purpose of maintaining the "balance of power."

For centuries it had been a fundamental tenet of British policy to turn against that Continental Power which was strongest, and this principle was to find its most efficient instrument in the Triple Entente.

Thus, whilst the Triple Alliance was of a strictly defensive character, the nature of the Triple Entente was offensive from the beginning. In this lay all the elements of a terrific explosion.

A nation as great and efficient as the Germans are does not allow its free and pacific development to be thwarted. In the face of this aggressive combination the course of German policy was clear. We had to try to come to a separate understanding with each member of the Triple Entente in order to dispel the clouds of war, and at the same time we had to increase our armaments so as to be ready if war actually broke out.

Gentlemen, you know that we have done both. In France we encountered, again and again, sentiments of revenge. These sentiments being fed and fostered by ambitious politicians proved stronger than the wish, undoubtedly cherished by a part of the French people, to live with us, as neighbours should, on friendly terms.

We made, indeed, some specific agreements with Russia, but her close alliance with France, her opposition to our Austro-Hungarian ally and an anti-German feeling, born and bred of the Pan-Slav craving for power, made agreements impossible which would have averted all dangers of war in the case of a political crisis.

Freer than France and Russia was England. I have already reminded you how British statesmen in parliament, again and again, proudly affirmed Great Britain's absolutely unrestricted right to steer her own course. The attempt to come to an understanding, which would have safeguarded the peace of the world, was easiest to make with England.

On these lines I had to act and I did act. I well knew that it was a narrow road, not easy to tread. In the course of centuries, the English insular way of thinking had evolved the political maxim that England had a right to an "arbitrium mundi," which she could only uphold by an unrivalled supremacy on sea and by the maintenance of the balance of power on the Continent. I never had any hopes that my persuasion could break that old English maxim.

What I did hope and thought possible was that the growth of German power and the increase of the risks of a war might open England's eyes to the fact that her old-fashioned maxim had become untenable and impracticable, and that an amicable settlement with Germany was preferable.

But that old doctrine of hers more than once stood in the way of a peaceful understanding. The crisis of 1911 gave a new impetus to the negotiations. The English people suddenly realized that they had stood at the brink of a European war.

Popular sentiment forced the British Government to a rapprochement with Germany. After long and arduous negotiations we finally arrived at an understanding on various disputed questions of an economic character, regarding Africa and Asia Minor. This understanding was to lessen every possible political friction. The world is wide. There is room enough for both nations to measure their strength in peaceful rivalry as long as our national strength is allowed free scope for development.

German policy always stood up for that principle. But during the negotiations England was indefatigable in her endeavours to enter into ever closer relations with France and Russia. The decisive point was that beyond the political sphere of action one military agreement after the other was made in view of a possible continental war.

England kept these negotiations as secret as possible. When something about them would percolate, it was declared, both in the press and in Parliament, to be perfectly harmless. But things could not be concealed, as you know from the official papers that were published by me.

The general situation was this: England was indeed ready to come to an understanding on single items, but the first and foremost principle of her policy was the "balance of power" as a means of checking German strength in its free development.

This forms the border-line of England's amicable relations with Germany; and the purpose was the utmost strengthening of the Triple Entente. When the Allies demanded military assurances in return, England was at once ready to give them. The circle was closed. The English were sure of the following of France and hence of Russia.

But they, too, had to abandon their free-will. As the jingoes of France and Russia found their strongest support in the military accommodation promised by her, England, as soon as either of the two Allies began the war, was morally bound to support them.

And all this was done to what purpose? Because Germany was to be kept down. We have not been remiss in warning the British

> Government. As late as the beginning of last July I gave them to understand that their secret negotiations with Russia about a naval agreement were well known to me. I called their attention to the grave danger which such policy implied for the peace of the world. As soon as a fortnight afterward my predictions came true.
>
> We have taken the consequences of the general situation. In quick succession I have laid before you the hugest war bill which history ever recorded, and you, gentlemen, fully recognizing the country's danger, have gladly made the sacrifice and have granted what was necessary for our national self-defence.
>
> And when war broke out, England dropped the mask of hypocrisy. Loudly and openly she declares her determination to fight until Germany is laid prostrate both in an economic and military sense. Anti-German Pan Slavism joins its jubilant notes, France with the full strength of an old warlike nation hopes to redeem the humiliation inflicted on her in 1870.
>
> Our only answer to our enemies is Germany does not allow herself to be crushed![6]

The documents show that German leaders in 1914 – Wilhelm II, Bethmann-Hollweg, Jagow – were essentially correct in their assessment of responsibility for the War. Recent books tend increasingly to reflect their views. On the overall cause, there is *The Pity of War* by Niall Ferguson (1999, Basic Books), *The Sleepwalkers* by Christopher Clark (2014, Harper Perennial), *The Russian Origins of the First World War* by Sean McMeekin (2011, Harvard University Press). With specific regard to Britain's role there is *The Darkest Days* by Douglas Newton (2014, Verso), Fatal *Fortnight* by Duncan Marlor (2014, Frontline Books). Perhaps the best of these is *How the First World War Began: The Triple Entente and the Coming of the Great War of 1914-1918*, by Edward E. McCullough (1999, Black Rose Books). In his *Conclusion*, Professor McCullough writes:

> "The currently popular history of Europe between 1870 and 1914 is pure mythology. The picture of Germany as an aggressive, expansionist disturber of the peace is completely unrelated to the actual events of the period. Until after the turn of the twentieth century it was almost universally recognized that the German Empire was a conservative, stabilizing force whose policy upheld the status quo. It was equally apparent that the restless, aggressive Powers on the continent were France and Russia, whose policies frequently led them into near collision with the British Empire ... The Anglo-French Entente was the crucial event which determined the history of the twentieth century. England's decision to ally herself with France involved her in France's aggressive designs and inevitably brought her into conflict with Germany. The immediate result was the beginning

of a period of strife, initiated by the French foreign minister Théophile Delcassé. He had the conviction that with British support he could challenge Germany by ignoring her interests in Morocco and proceeding with the conquest of that country …

The spectacular growth of German industry and trade had made Germany a world power in a single generation. It was the desire to block this German rise to power that provided the mainspring of Anglo-German antagonism.

It becomes quite clear as we follow the imaginary history written by entente myth writers that Germany was a usurper who had no right to be treated as an equal amongst the European Powers. She had no right to follow all the other Powers in building a modern navy, no right to acquire bases or coaling stations, no right to have an army to defend herself against the larger armies of her neighbors, and no right to compete for the trade of the world. In fact, Germany had no right to exist as a Great Power, but should have been content to remain disunited, a permanent parade ground for French armies.

At the same time, Germany is described as the deux ex machina which determined the whole course of events after 1900. She not only encircled herself by creating the Triple Entente but supposedly initiated all the events which threatened the peace of Europe in the succeeding years. No reader of this mythical history could guess that France was the country which undertook the military conquest of Morocco in 1900 and carried it forward continuously until its completion in 1912, or that every German move was a reaction to this French campaign."

Professor McCullough might have mentioned the two occasions when Germany actually saved Europe from the perilous diplomacy of the two Edwards. The first occurred when King Edward's bumbling Russian protégé, Isvolsky, created the 1908 Bosnian Crisis. Much to the relief of all Europe, this was resolved in 1909 by an initiative introduced by German Chancellor von Bülow. The second came in 1913 when the Balkan League, created by Russia, pushed Europe to the brink. Germany used her influence and prevailed upon her Austrian ally to not intervene in the 2nd Balkan War.

About the July Crisis McCullough writes:

A statement by German leaders that they will fight to preserve the existence of Austria-Hungary demonstrates the warlike tendencies of Germany while repeated declarations by British statesmen that they will fight to prevent the defeat of France shows the strictly defensive attitude of England.

The implied answer of entente historians is that Austria had no right to go to war with Serbia to maintain her existence, but that Russia was entitled to start a European war to sustain Serbia's ability to threaten that existence and to bolster her own prestige in the Balkans.

> Germany has been criticized for failing to influence Austria in the direction of compromise soon enough to have any effect: Germany was the only Power which made any attempt at any time to suggest that an ally should make concessions in the interest of peace.[7]

Quite apart from the nostrum that the victors in war write history, the question of how a false narrative of the cause of the War which indicts Germany and absolves England has managed to maintain traction for over a hundred years is explained in good part by the fact that England has engaged in a massive, systematic cover-up of her diplomatic documents since before World War 1. This was reported by *The Guardian* in 2013, and may be seen in Appendix 1 or by clicking on (or pasting) the following link:

> http://www.theguardian.com/politics/2013/oct/18/foreign-office-historic-files-secret-archive

This comes on top of the fact that King Edward's will had directed that all his private and personal correspondence was to be destroyed. The task was unfortunately carried out with great thoroughness by Lord Esher and Lord Knollys and a vast number of documents were burned and lost forever. Lord Grey left similar instructions in his will which were carried out with the same thoroughness as those of the King.

Of the defenders of Lord Grey we may ask what can possibly be said of a British Foreign Minister who writes:

> "Our own relations with France and Russia made it certain that they would not enter upon an aggressive or dangerous policy."[8] In fact, precisely the opposite was true. British relations with France and Russia had resulted directly in both Moroccan crises as well as the Bosnian crisis!
>
> "Before 1914 France had given up the idea of going to war to recover them [Alsace-Lorraine], but, once war was forced upon her, she was determined to fight on to win them."[9] It is inconceivable that Grey, who was intimately acquainted with Delcassé, Cambon, Poincaré, Clemenceau, and King Edward VII, could have believed such a thing.
>
> "The immense growth and strength of Germany had smothered all French intention to attempt a revanche. The idea of recovering the lost provinces of Alsace and Lorraine had tacitly been dropped, though the French Government might not have dared to say in public that it had been forever abandoned. The Franco-Russian Alliance did not contemplate or cover a French revanche."[10] It is difficult to respond to something as absurd as this as the truth was precisely the opposite.
>
> "No one can doubt that his [the Czar's] suggestion to the German Emperor for a settlement by use of the machinery of the Hague Tribunal was genuine, nor can the Russian mobilization be fairly

construed as evidence of a desire for war."[11] Did Grey not understand that the Astro-Serb dispute was far beyond the scope of the Hague Tribunal and was therefore utterly ignored by everyone including Sasonov? Did he not understand that mobilization meant war and was very specifically defined as such by the men who ordered and executed the fatal order on July 30?

Grey redeems himself somewhat by his observation that "I believe that neither the Emperor nor Bethmann-Hollweg nor Jagow planned or desired war"[12] though he states the exact opposite elsewhere.

One of Grey's biographers wrote:[13]

> In the prelude to his activities as Foreign Secretary we became acquainted with the political predilections and prejudices which so extraordinarily clouded his vision. During his tenure of office these gained such a hold over him that as early as 1908 he believed in the inevitability of war with Germany, and in 1910 he was convinced of the absolute desire for peace of all the Great Powers except Germany, who in his view was aiming at the hegemony of Europe. He was continually in the grip of this bogey. It led him to load fetter after fetter on the Central Powers, to hem in Germany's economic development, to arrange for plans for joint operations in the event of a general war to be worked out by the British General and Naval Staffs with France and Russia, and to come more and more closely into association with these Powers. He was so unable to see clearly that to this day he is outraged at the annexation of Bosnia and is blind to the worse violations of treaties of his own group so that he gives the impression of a complete hypocrite. From fear of Germany he follows Russia's trail, and yet clings to the tenuous fiction of being a free agent. And around him and behind him are other forces which without his knowledge influence and warp his course.

In England, the first four days of August, 1914, saw an overwhelming majority of neutralists being outmaneuvered by a tiny clique of interventionists led by Grey who urged England to stand by "our friends," France and Russia, but Grey was obliged to continue his policy of "deliberate ambiguity" until he could unleash his Belgian imposture. Playing his cards with skill and panache, Grey waited until the German ultimatum to Belgium and the actual crossing of the Belgian frontier by German troops finally allowed him to pull the Belgian ace from his sleeve and circumvent public opposition to the war. From here on out France and Russia were no longer mentioned. From this point forward it was all Belgium all the time. Atrocity propaganda[14] so vast that it may never be possible to separate fact from fiction served very well to arouse and inflame hatred and war fever.

Churchill said that *"The measured, silent drawing together of gigantic forces, the uncertainty of their movements and positions, the number of unknown and unknowable facts made the first collision a drama never surpassed."*[15] Churchill might well have concluded the same about the post-1918 consequences. The titanic clash of Europe's armies in 1914 was and remains the seminal event of modern times.

***

Endnotes

1. Ferguson, Niall, *The Pity of War*, 169-70.
2. McCullough, Edward E., *How the First World War Began*, back cover.
3. Lichnowsky, Prince, *My Mission to London, 1912-1914.*
4. Wilhelm II, *The Kaiser's Memoirs: A Firsthand Account of the German Empire and the First World War by Wilhelm II, Emperor of Germany 1888-1918* (Kindle Locations 3448-3503).
5. Palmer, Alan, *The Kaiser*, 4.
6. *Source Records of the Great War, Vol. I,* ed. Charles F. Horne, *National Alumni 1923.*
7. McCullough, Edward E. *How The First World War Began*, 330.
8. Grey, I, 292.
9. Ibid., II, 128.
10. Ibid., 22.
11. Ibid., 23.
12. Ibid., 26.
13. Lutz, *Lord Grey and the World War*, 192.
14. Ponsonby, Arthur, *Falsehood in Wartime: Propaganda Lies of the First World War.*
15. Hastings, Max, *Catastrophe 1914: Europe Goes To War*, 2.

Bibliography

Primary Sources and abbreviations

A.R.B. Austrian Red Book, 1919 (Diplomatische Aktenstucke zur Vorgeschichte des Krieges, 1914, 3 vols.
B.D. British Documents on the Origins of the War
B.D.D. Belgian Diplomatic Documents
D.S.I. Der Diplomatische Schrifwechsel Iswolskyis
Dugdale, E.T.S., German Diplomatic Documents
F.O. Foreign Office
F.Y.B. French Yellow Book
G.P. Die Grosse Politik der Europaischen Kabinette 1871-1914
H.C.D. House of Commons. Debates.
H.L.D. House of Lords. Debates
J.O. Journal Officiel de la République Francaise
K.D. Kautsky Documents (Die Deutschen Dokumente Zum Kriegsausbruch)
L.N. Un Livre Noir
M.F.R. Materials for the History of Franco-Russian Relations
R.A.V. Royal Archives, Queen Victoria's Diary
R.A.W. Royal Archives, Prince of Wales's Diary
R.O.B. Russian Orange Book
S.B.B. Serbian Blue Book

Secondary Sources

Aflalo, *The Truth About Morocco*
Albertini, Luigi, *The Origins of the War of 1914*, 3 Vols.
Anderson, E.N., *The First Moroccan Crisis*
Andrew, Christopher, *Théophile Delcassé and the Making of the Entente Cordiale*
Aronson, Theo, *The King in Love*
Asquith, H.H., *Memories and Reflections*
Barlow, I.C., *The Agadir Crisis*
Barnes, Harry Elmer, *The Genesis of the World War*
Benson, E. F., *King Edward VII*
Berghahn, V.R., *Germany and the Approach of War in 1914*
Bernhardi, Friedrich von, *Germany and the Next War*
Bethmann-Hollweg, Theobald von, *Reflections on the World War*
Bierman, John, *Napoleon III and his Carnival Empire*
Bismarck, Otto von, *Reflections and Memories*
Blunt, Wilfrid, Scawen, *My Diaries*
Bogitschevitch, *Causes of the War*
Brook-Shepherd, Gordon, *Uncle of Europe*

Buchanan, George, My Mission to Russia, 2 Vols.
Bülow, Bernhard, *Deutsche Politik*
Bülow, Bernhard, *Imperial Germany*
Bury, J.P.T., *Gambetta and the National Defense*
Callwell, C. E., *Field Marshal Sir Henry Wilson*
Cassels, Lavender, *The Archduke and the Assassin*
Churchill, Winston, *Great Contemporaries*
Churchill, Winston, *The World Crisis* (six volumes)
Clark, Christopher, *The Sleepwalkers*
Cochran, M. H., *Germany Not Guilty in 1914*
Combarieu, A., Seven years at the Elysee with President Loubet.
Cowles, Virginia, *The Kaiser*
Crankshaw, Edward, *Bismarck*
Crankshaw, Edward, *The Fall of the House of Hapsburg*
Dangerfield, G. *Victoria's Heir*
De Siebert, B., *Entente Diplomacy and the World*
Dedijer, Vladimir, *The Road to Sarajevo*
Dickinson, Lowes, *The International Anarchy*
Dillon, Emile, *The Eclipse of Russia*
Docherty & MacGregor, *Hidden History*
Doyle, Arthur Conan, *Great Britain and the Next War*
Dunlop, Ian, *Edward VII and the Entente Cordiale*
Dunn, Ross, E., *Resistance in the Desert*
Dupin, *M. Poincaré et la Guerre de 1914*
Durham, M.E., *Twenty Years of Balkan Tangle*
Eckhardstein, Hermann Freiherr, *Ten Years at the Court of St. James*
Esher, Viscount, *The Influence of King Edward*
Farrar, James Anson, *England under Edward VII*
Fay, Sidney Bradshaw, *The Origins of the First World War*
Ferguson, Niall, *The Pity of War*
Fischer, Fritz, *Germany's Aims in the First World War*
Florinsky, Michael T., The End of the Russian Empire
Fraser, Peter, *Lord Esher, A Political Biography*
Fromkin, David, *Europe's Last Summer*
Fromkin, David, *The King and the Cowboy*
Gardner, Hall, *The Failure to Prevent World War 1*
Geiss, Imanuel, German Foreign Policy, 1871-1914
Geiss, Imanuel, *July 1914: The Outbreak of the First World War*
George, David Lloyd, War Memoirs
George, Kennan, F., *The Decline of Bismarck's European Order*
George, Kennan, F., *The Fateful Alliance*
Gilbert, Martin, *The First World War*
Gooch, G. P., *History of Modern Europe: 1878-1919*
Gooch, G.P., *Before the War*
Grey, Edward, Viscount of Fallodon, *Twenty-Five Years* (two vols.)
Guillen, Pierre, L'Allemagne et le *Maroc* de 1870 à 1905
Gwynne/Lucius, *The Life of Sir Charles W. Dilke*
Haldane, Richard, *Before the War*
Hale, O,J., *Germany and the Diplomatic Revolution.*
Haller, Johannes, *Philip Eulenburg: The Kaiser's Friend*
Hamilton, *Great Britain and France*
Harrison, Frederick, *The German Peril*

Hibbert, Christopher, *Edward VII: The Last Victorian King*
Holstein, Friedrich von, *The Holstein Papers* (Edited by Norman Rich & M.H. Fisher)
Howard, Michael, *The Franco-Prussian War*
Huddleston, Sysley, *Poincaré.*
Isvolsky, Alexander, *The Memoirs of Alexander Iswolsky*
Jarausch, K.H. *The Enigmatic Chancellor*
Jelavich, Barbara, *History of the Balkans*
Joll, James, *The Origins of the First World War*
Judet, Ernest, *Georges Louis*
Jullian, Philippe, *Edward VII*
Keiger, J.F.V., *Raymond Poincaré*
Kennedy, Paul M., *The Rise of the Anglo-German Antagonism, 1860-1914*
Kiste, John van der, *Kaiser Wilhelm II: Germany's Last Emperor*
Langer, William l., *European Alliances and Alignments*
Lee, Sidney, *King Edward VII* (two vols.)
Legge, Edward, *King Edward, the Kaiser and the King*
Legge, *More About King Edward*
Lichnowsky, Karl Max, *My Mission to London 1912-1914*
Loreburn, Robert, *How The War Came*
Lutz, Hermann, *Lord Grey and the World War*
MacKenzie, David, *Apis: The Congenial Conspirator*
Magnus, Philip, *King Edward the Seventh*
Mahan, A. T., *The Influence of Sea Power upon History*
Mansergh, N., *The Coming of the First World War*
Margutti, *The Emperor Franz Joseph and his Times*
Massie, *Nicholas and Alexandra*
Massie, Robert, *Dreadnought*
Matthew, Henry Colin, *The Liberal Imperialists*
McCullough, Edward, *How the First World War Began*
McMeekin, Sean, *July 1914: Countdown to War*
McMeekin, Sean, *The Russian Origins of the First World War*
Middlemas, Keith, *The Life and Times of Edward VII*
Miranda, Carter, *George, Nicholas, and Wilhelm*
Mombauer, Annika, *Helmuth von Moltke and the Origins of the First World War*
Monger, G. *The End of Isolation, British foreign Policy 1900-1907*
Montgelas, Max, *The Case for the Central Powers*
Morel, E. D., *Morocco in Diplomacy*
Morel, E. D., *The Years of Secret Diplomacy*
Morley, John, *Memorandum on Resignation*
Neilson, Francis, *How Diplomats Make War*
Nekliudov, *Diplomatic Reminiscences Before and During the World War, 1911-1917*
Newton, Douglas, *The Darkest Days*
Nicolson, Sir Arthur, *Portrait of a Diplomatist*
Nicolson, Sir Harold, *Sir Arthur Nicolson: A Study in the Old Diplomacy*
Nish, Ian, *The Anglo-Japanese Alliance*
Novak, Karl Friedrich, *Kaiser and Chancellor*
Paléologue, Maurice, ***An Ambassador's Memoirs*, 3 Vols.**
Palmer, Alan, *The Kaiser*
Passos, John Dos, *Mr. Wilson's War*
Poincaré, Raymond, *Origines de la Guerre*
Ponsonby, Arthur (M.P.), *Falsehood in Wartime*
Ponsonby, Arthur, *Fatal Fortnight*

Porch, Douglas, *The Conquest of Morocco*
Quigley, Carroll, *The Anglo-American Establishment*
Quigley, Carroll, *Tragedy and Hope*
Redesdale, Lord, *Memories*
Reinach, Joseph, *Depeche's, Circulairs, Decrets, Proclamations et Discours de Léon Gambetta.*
Repington, *The First World War*
Reventlow, Ernst, *The Vampire of the Continent*
Rohl, *Young Wilhelm*
Sazonov, Serge, *Fateful Years – 1909-1916*
Schiemann, Theodor, *Deutschland und die Grosse Politik*
Schmitt, Bernadotte, E., *England and Germany*
Seymour, Charles, *Intimate Papers of Colonel House*
Spender, J.A., *Fifty Years of Europe*
Stavrianos, L. S., *The Balkans Since 1453*
Stieve, Friedrich, *Isvolsky and the World War*
Tardieu, *France and the Alliances*
Tomaszewski, F., *A Great Russia: Russia and the Triple Entente*
Trevelyan, G. M., *Grey of Fallodon*
Tuchman, Barbara, *The Guns of August*
Tuchman, Barbara, *The Proud Tower*
Viereck, George Sylvester, *The Kaiser on Trial*
Viereck, George Sylvester, *The Strangest Friendship in History*
Waldersee, Count von, *A Field Marshal's Memoirs*
Walton, C.W., *Kiderlen-Wechter and the Anglo-German Problem, 1910-1912*
Waterhouse, Michael, *Edwardian Requiem: A Life of Sir Edward Grey*
Wilhelm II, Kaiser, *The Kaiser's Memoirs*
Wilhelm II, *My Early Life*
Wilkinson, Spenser, *Britain at Bay*
Williams, Joyce Grigsby, Colonel House and Sir Edward Grey
Williamson, S.R., *The Politics of Grand Strategy*
Williamson, Samuel, R., *Austria-Hungary and the Origins of the First World War*
Wilson, K.M., *Policy of the Entente*
Witte, Count, *The Memoirs of Count Witte*
Woodward, E.L., *Great Britain and the German Navy*
Wright, Gordon, *Raymond Poincaré and the French Presidency*
Wright, Peter E., *At the Supreme War Council*

Newspapers and Periodicals

Berliner Neweste Nachrichten
Berliner Tageblatt
Daily News
Daily Telegraph
Die Zukunft
John Bull
Journal des Débats
Kölnische Zeitung
La Petite République
Lokal Anzeiger
Manchester Guardian
Morning Post

National Review
Neue Freie Presse
Neuste Nachrichten
Novoye Vremya
Reichsbote
Rheinisch Westflischezeitung
Slavonic Review
Temps
The English Historical Review
The Fortnightly Review
The New York Times
The Times
Vanity Fair
Voschisse Zeitung
Westminster Gazette
Whitby Gazette

Appendix 1

Foreign Office hoarding 1m historic files in secret archive

The Foreign Office has unlawfully hoarded more than a million files of historic documents that should have been declassified and handed over to the National Archives, the Guardian has discovered.

The files are being kept at a secret archive at a high-security government communications centre in Buckinghamshire, north of London, where they occupy mile after mile of shelving.

Most of the papers are many decades old – some were created in the 19th century – and document in fine detail British foreign relations throughout two world wars, the cold war, withdrawal from empire and entry into the common market.

They have been kept from public view in breach of the Public Records Acts, which requires that all government documents become public once they are 30 years old – a term about to be reduced to 20 years – unless the department has received permission from the lord chancellor to hold them for longer. The secret archive is also beyond the reach of the Freedom of Information Act.

The Foreign Office is not the only government department that has been unlawfully hoarding files. This month the Guardian disclosed that the Ministry of Defence was unlawfully holding more than 66,000 historic files at a warehouse in Derbyshire, including thousands of files from the army's Northern Ireland headquarters.

However, the Foreign Office's secret archive, which is estimated to hold around 1.2m files and occupies around 15 miles of floor-to-ceiling shelving, is believed to be far larger than the combined undisclosed archives of every other government department. One of Britain's leading historians describes its size as "staggering".

A basic inventory of the hidden archive gives a clue to its enormousness: batches of files are catalogued according to the length of shelf space they occupy, with six metres and two centimetres dedicated to files about Rhodesia, for example, and four metres and 57 centimetres holding files about Guy Burgess and Donald Maclean, the KGB spies who operated inside the Foreign Office and MI6. There are 50 metres of files on Hong

Kong, 100.81 metres about the United States and 97.84 metres of "private office papers".

No length is given in the inventory for other categories such as Colonial Office files or records from the permanent under-secretary's department, the point of liaison between the Foreign Office and MI6.

The inventory says there is one bag of records from the Foreign Office's now notorious cold war propaganda unit, the Information Research Department. And buried away within the archive, wedged between files from the British military government in post-war Germany and lists of consular officials, are papers about the treaty of Paris, which concluded the Crimean war in 1856.

The Foreign Office's realisation that it would eventually need to admit to the existence of such a vast repository appears to have come at a time when its lawyers were waging a court battle with a group of elderly Kenyans. It was a battle that it eventually lost, with the result that it was obliged to issue an unprecedented apology and pay millions of pounds in compensation to thousands of men and women who suffered severe mistreatment during the 1950s Mau Mau insurgency.

denied the existence of a much smaller secret archive of 8,800 colonial-era documents, known as the migrated archive. It was eventually obliged to admit that this did exist, and that its contents corroborated the Kenyans' allegations about widespread acts of murder and torture by the colonial authorities.

As a first step, the Foreign Office gave its colossal secret a name, the Special Collections. Then last November the justice secretary, Chris Grayling, was asked to sign a blanket authorisation that is said to have placed the retention of the files on a legal footing for 12 months. No announcement was made.

Finally, a written statement about "public records" by the Foreign Office minister David Lidington was quietly issued in the Commons on a Friday afternoon. The statement included two sentences that referred to a "large accumulation" of documents.

As a result of the manner in which the matter was handled, the existence of the archive has remained all but unknown, even among historians. Anthony Badger, the Cambridge history professor who has been overseeing the declassification of the migrated archive, has written that he believes "it is difficult to overestimate the legacy of suspicion among historians, lawyers and journalists" that resulted from the concealment of those 8,800 files.

The discovery that the colonial-era documents are just a very small part of a hidden archive of more than a million files is certain to cause enormous damage to the Foreign Office's reputation among historians and others. A Foreign Office spokesperson said the archive had accumulated over time and that "resources have not been available to review and prepare" them for release.

The handful of historians who have become aware of the archive are deeply skeptical about this claim, however. Richard Drayton, Rhodes professor of imperial history at King's College London, said the size of the hidden archive was staggering, and it was "scandalous" that papers of such significance could be concealed for such a long time. "It's a working archive, for a department which believes it has a long-term, historic interest in many parts of the world," he said.

It was unclear whether there is any "truly explosive" material within the files, Drayton said, or whether officials were attempting to manage the country's historic reputation. "It may be that from the perspective of the state, 50 years is a short time. But the idea that the British state today has an obligation to protect the reputation of the British state of 50 years ago seems to me wholly inappropriate. It would be a manipulation of history, which we associate with iron curtain regimes during the cold war, regimes that managed and controlled the past."

Mandy Banton, senior research fellow at the Institute of Commonwealth Studies, said it was "extremely likely" that the archive had been culled to remove material that would most damage the reputation of the UK and the Foreign Office. Banton, a Colonial Office records expert who worked at National Archives at Kew, south-west London, for 25 years, said she had been "very angry" when she discovered that the migrated archives had been withheld. "I would have been incandescent had I learned while still working there. In lying to me, the Foreign Office forced me to mislead my readers."

Freedom of information campaigners believe that the hoarding of such a huge amount of papers is symptomatic of a culture of secrecy and retention at the Foreign Office and across many other UK government departments. Maurice Frankel, director of the Campaign for Freedom of Information, an NGO that works to ensure the Freedom of Information Act is properly implemented, said: "The FoI system depends on people knowing what they hold and being transparent about what they hold."

The archive is kept at Hanslope Park, a sprawling Foreign Office and MI6 outstation in the heart of the Buckinghamshire countryside. Sometimes referred to by Foreign Office staff as "Up North" – although it is only 60 miles north of London – Hanslope Park is also home to Her Majesty's Government Communications Centre, a facility where hundreds of government scientists and technicians develop sophisticated counter-espionage measures.

They include measures intended to protect the UK government and its allies from the sort of surveillance that Edward Snowden's leaks have shown to have been perfected by the National Security Agency and Britain's GCHQ.

Two wire fences, one 10ft high and topped with razor wire, encircle the cluster of buildings at Hanslope Park. Between them is a no man's land with intruder alarms. CCTV cameras are positioned every few yards and the entire perimeter is covered by floodlights. Inside, posters on the walls carry the half-joking warning: "Careless talk costs jobs."

Curiously, many of the offices are said to house row after row of typewriters rather than computers, with incinerators at the end of each room for the disposal of typewriter ribbons – a measure to reduce electromagnetic emissions, which can travel for hundreds of yards and be deciphered by foreign governments.

Hanslope Park is not only a highly secure facility, it is also a place that appears to be accustomed to handling – and destroying – large amounts of paperwork. This, possibly, explains why the special collections have been held there.

The blanket authorisation signed by Grayling put the secret archive on a legal footing for 12 months, during which time the Foreign Office is expected to devise a plan for its declassification and transfer to Kew. A spokesperson said a plan would be presented next month to a committee that advises the National Archives and the Ministry of Justice.

It will be quite a task. Declassification of the migrated archive has taken two and a half years, with the final tranche of documents due to arrive at Kew next month. At that rate, clearing up the special collections would take around 340 years.

Appendix 2

Revealed: how King George V demanded Britain enter the First World War

Record of previously unknown meeting between George V and his Foreign Secretary reveals that the King told him to "find a reason" to go to war with Germany

The letter documents a previously unrecorded meeting between George V (left) and Sir Edward Grey (right) Photo: Alamy/Jay Williams

By Anita Singh, Arts and Entertainment Editor
7:00AM BST 26 Jul 2014

It is a letter that throws fresh light on one of the darkest periods in Britain's history.

A note which has remained in private hands for a century details a previously undocumented meeting between George V and his Foreign Secretary, Sir Edward Grey, on the eve of the First World War.

The King, mindful of his position as a constitutional monarch, made no public declarations about the situation in Europe in the lead-up to the conflict.

But in the newly-disclosed meeting, the King informed Sir Edward it was "absolutely essential" Britain go to war in order to prevent Germany from achieving "complete domination of this country".

When Sir Edward said the Cabinet had yet to find a justifiable reason to enter the conflict, the King replied: "You have got to find a reason, Grey."

Historians have no record of the meeting which took place at Buckingham Palace on August 2 1914, two days before Britain went to war.

It was revealed in a letter written by Sir Cecil Graves, Sir Edward's nephew, who met with the King a month after his uncle's death in 1933.

George V had summoned Sir Cecil – a future director-general of the BBC - to the Palace, where he offered his condolences before recalling the events of 1914.

The King "told me of the interview he had with Uncle Edward two days before the outbreak of war. It lasted for one and a half hours," Sir Cecil wrote.

"He told me that Uncle Edward had said that he could not possibly see what justifiable reason we could find for going to war.

"HM said in reply, 'You have got to find a reason, Grey.'"

The King told Grey "that, if we didn't go to war, Germany would mop up France and having dealt with the European situation would proceed to obtain complete domination of this country.

"For that reason," Sir Ceci wrote, "he felt that it was absolutely essential that whatever happened we had got to find a reason for entering the War at once...

"The next day he had a private letter from Poincaré [the French President] urging our participation in the War, and almost at the same time a telegram arrived from King Albert [of Belgium] about the violation of Belgium.

"He sent this straight across to Uncle Edward with a note to the effect that here was the reason and there was no need for him to try and think of anything."

On August 3, shortly after receiving the King's note, Sir Edward gave a speech to Parliament in which he said "it is clear that the peace of Europe cannot be preserved".

He returned to his room in the Foreign Office and made the now famous remark as he watched the lamps being lit outside: "The lamps are going out all over Europe; we shall not see them lit again in our lifetime."

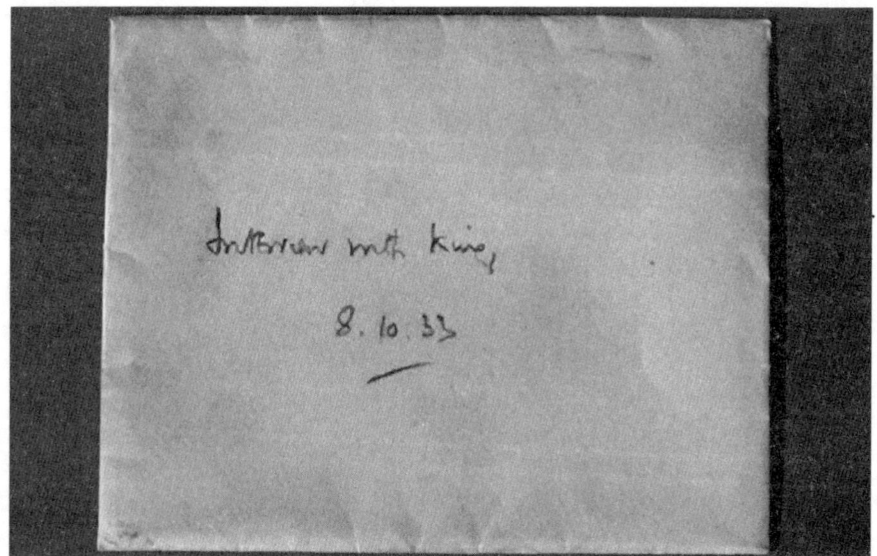

The envelope that Adrian Graves discovered among his grandfather's records

Mr Graves said: "I hold it and think: was my great-great-uncle feeling the hands as they approached 11pm and realising that war was almost upon us?"

The pocket watch belonging to Sir Edward Grey, Foreign Secretary during the First World War

At the time of the meeting with George V, Britain's Cabinet remained divided over whether Britain should go to war.

Prof Hew Strachan, military historian and author of the recent The First World War: A New History, said: "It is clear that the King took a more active role in thinking about the country's foreign policy than most conventional accounts allow for.

"If Grey said these things, it was in order to make clear to the King that the Government was not yet in a position to support France. Belgium provided everybody with the way in.

"The letter stresses the thrust of Grey's policy: the need to be firm with Germany while not encouraging the French and Russians to rush into war. Grey wants a diplomatic deal."

Prof David Reynolds of Cambridge University, author of The Long Shadow: The Great War and the 20th Century, said: "What we are hearing here, if this is a true rendition of events nearly 20 years before, is a weary Grey airing his worries in private on August 2.

"The document also reminds us that George V, although always conscious of his place as a constitutional monarch, was a king who privately offered strong views to his ministers and that those views were taken seriously.

"From this document, we do learn something about Grey but we learn rather more about George V."

Index

A

B

C

N

O

P

Q

R

S